# Conversations with Children

# Conversations with Children

By

## Edith F. Hunter

*Beacon Press   Boston*

# Acknowledgments

This book began in a questionnaire. It has gone through several metamorphoses since then and may be unrecognizable to those who gave me the benefit of their thinking in the early stages.

Mrs. Jean Hueston, Mrs. Grace Martin, Mrs. Eileen Day and Mrs. Mary Grooms wrote me in some detail, sharing their experiences and philosophies.

The members of the Curriculum Committee of the Council of Liberal Churches reacted to some of the material in its earlier forms, and Dr. Lucile Lindberg and Dr. Sophia Fahs have gone over much of it in later stages. Dr. Dorothy Spoerl has worked closely with me in the final stages of the book.

No one except myself however, is responsible for the form that the material has finally taken, although a great deal of helpful criticism has been given along the way and gratefully accepted.

Mrs. Ruth Clark, Miss Betty Whitman, Mrs. Eileen Day, Mrs. Margaret Barr and Mrs. Mildred Lester used a few of the conversations experimentally in the church schools of which they are the directors. Some of their teachers gave most helpful reactions. I am particularly grateful to Mr. Richard Tarble, Mrs. M. Whittier Day and Mrs. Martha Schroeder.

Mrs. Mary Jane Neuendorffer gave several of the conversations a trial run in *Junior Fellowship News,* of which she is the editor. Mrs. Neuendorffer also wrote two of the conversations herself. Mr. Raymond Breakstone, editor of *Growing Up,* ran two of the conversations in his publication.

Mrs. Jean Thompson and Kristin reacted to several of the conversations and made some original contributions. I am especially indebted to Mrs. Mary Jane Dunwiddie and Peter, Tom, Jean and Alice for experimenting with many of the conversations, criticizing them and contributing material of their own. Mrs. Phyllis Buddenberg gave me permission to use two of her stories and experimented with some material with her family. Mrs. Patricia Shuttee, Mrs. Dorothy Brandt, Miss Ardanelle Dishon and Mrs. Beth Scherer allowed me to adapt and use a story by each of them.

Dr. Charles Carlston was kind enough to read the conversations in the area of geology to check them for accuracy.

Many people submitted material, often at my request, that

in the end I did not use. I am nonetheless indebted to them also. I should like to thank the library staff at the Wadleigh Memorial Library in Milford, New Hampshire, for the help they have frequently given me. As always, my husband and my children have helped in a thousand ways.

I also wish to thank the following sources for permission to reprint selected material:

The Christian Science Monitor for "I Would Be a River" by Helen Harrington (June 27, 1960). Longmans, Green and Company, Inc., for the selection from Waterless Mountain by Laura Adams Armer, copyright 1931, 1959. Child Life Magazine for "Mud" by Polly Chase Boyden, copyright 1930 by Rand McNally & Company. G. P. Putnam's Sons for the selection "A Dreadful Sight" from All Together by Dorothy Aldis, copyright © 1952 by Dorothy Aldis. Julian Messner, Inc. for the selection from "Louis Braille, Windows for the Blind by J. Alvin Kugelmass. J. P. Lippincott Company for the selection from High, Wide and Lonesome by Hal Borland. National Geographic Magazine for the selection from "How Old Is It?" by Lyman J. Briggs and Kenneth F. Weaver. The Society of Authors, as the literary representatives of the estate of the late Miss Rose Fyleman, for the selection from "The Sky" by Rose Fyleman. The John Day Company, Inc., for selections from Child and Universe by Bertha Stevens. Simon and Schuster, Inc., for the selection from The Enduring Pattern by Hal Borland, copyright © 1959 by Hal Borland. Harper & Brothers for the selection from By the Shores of Silver Lake by Laura Ingalls Wilder, copyright 1953. The Book House for Children for the selections from Little Pictures of Japan. Alfred A. Knopf, Inc., for the selection from The Singing Wilderness by Sigurd Olson. The World Publishing Co. for the selection from People and Places by Margaret Mead. Doubleday & Company, Inc., for the selections from The Story of My Life by Helen Keller, copyright 1902, 1903, 1905 by Helen Keller; and for permission to adapt the illustrations for "Vocabulary," "A Woodland Tragedy," "The Skunk and the Unwise Bobcat" from Animal Tracks and Hunter Signs by Ernest Thompson Seton. Appleton-Century-Crofts, Inc., for the selection from Education and the Democratic Faith by Ephraim Vern Sayers and Ward Madden, copyright © 1959, Appleton-Century-Crofts, Inc. The Viking Press, Inc., for the selections from The Grapes of Wrath by John Steinbeck and Four Ways of Being Human by Gene Lisitzky, copyright © 1956 by Gene Lisitzky. Houghton Mifflin Company for selections from The Wilderness World of John Muir edited by Edwin Way Teale; A Cup of Sky by Donald Culross Peattie and Noel Peattie; and A Field Guide to Animal Tracks by Claus J. Murie. Harvard University Press for the selection from Philosophy in a New Key by Suzanne K. Langer. Young People's Records for the selection from "The Little Gray Ponies." Perkins School for the Blind, Watertown, Mass., for permission to adapt the illustration of the Braille alphabet and "six dots." W. W. Norton & Company, Inc., for the selection from Little Britches by Ralph Moody, copyright 1950 by Ralph Moody. Little, Brown and Company for the selection from Complete Poems of Emily Dickinson, 1960. Victor Records for the selection "Horace the Horse." Columbia Records for the selection from "Now We Know." Beacon Press for the selections from Martin and Judy Songs and From Long Ago and Many Lands by Sophia L. Fahs. Random House, Inc., for selections from Leaves of Grass (Modern Library edition) by Walt Whitman and All About Prehistoric Cave Men by Sam and Beryl Epstein, copyright © 1959. Harcourt, Brace and Company, Inc., for selections from Windy

*Morning,* copyright 1953 by Harry Behn; and from *Good Morning, America* and *The People, Yes* by Carl Sandburg. The Macmillan Company for selections from *Science and the Modern World* by Alfred North Whitehead; *The Changing Face of New England* by Betty Flanders Thomson, copyright © 1959; and "The Falling Star" from *Stars Tonight* by Sara Teasdale.

# Contents

# Chapter IV. Some Suggestions for Using the Conversations

# Introduction

"Do you know what I used to think?" asked William.

"No," I said. "What did you used to think?"

"I used to think that 'law' was a place."

"What do you mean 'law'?" I asked.

"Well, you know, someone says they have a sister in Boston and a brother-in-law. I used to think 'law' was where their brother was, like Boston was where their sister was."

"Hey Mum," said Graham.

"What?" I asked.

"Guess what?" he said.

"What?" I said.

"I was thinking. What if everybody had the same face? You wouldn't be able to tell people apart just by looking at them then, would you?"

"No, I guess you wouldn't," I said.

"But they'd still be different people underneath their faces, wouldn't they? And if they were different under their faces, wouldn't it make their faces look different?"

"You know what I wonder about sometimes?" said Elizabeth.

"What do you wonder about?" I asked.

"I wonder why some people are smarter than other people. Everybody would like to be smart, but how do you get to be smart? Are you born smart? It doesn't seem to me to be fair if some people are born smart and other people aren't."

Once we are past the preliminary "Hey Mum's," "Guess what's," and "I wonder's," there is nothing quite so rewarding to people who enjoy children as good conversation with them.

What a miracle it is to be able to convey our thoughts, our feelings, our wonderings to other persons in conversation. To be able to share our joys and our worries, to be able to divulge past misconceptions and confusions, to be able to take an idea and turn it around and over and upside down with them, to be able to wonder together about aspects of human experience that have perplexed other thoughtful growing persons — all these are miracles too easily taken for granted.

Teaching religion through the give-and-take of conversation has been a method used by some of the greatest religious figures of the past. Buddha, Socrates and Jesus, to mention only three, used the method of conversation extensively. In dialogue, unforgettable to those who knew them, they helped simple people grow in religious understanding. This way of teaching is based on the conviction that we learn primarily through our own experience. The teacher's most important role is that of midwife to thought rather than imparter of wisdom.

Over one hundred years ago that great, if impractical, teacher, Bronson Alcott, shocked a generation of Bostonians by teaching religion to the children in his experimental school through the method of conversation.[1]

Alcott said: "Education, when rightly understood, will be found to lie in the art of asking apt and fit questions, and in thus leading the mind, by its own light to the perception of truth."[2]

Although we may feel that teacher Alcott's questions were rather loaded, and that he often managed to extract from the minds and mouths of his pupils ideas and words that they probably never intended, he was still far in advance of many of his educational contemporaries, and many of ours.

His premise was the still unpopular one, that human nature is potentially good. Why does this good human nature so often fail to come to flower? He laid the blame, in part, on "our low estimate of human nature and consequent want of reverence and regard for it."[3]

Although, like the majority in his day, he believed that divinity could be seen perfectly revealed in the distant figure of Jesus, he was impatient that so many of his contemporaries were blind to the perfect and recurring revelation of divinity in every child that is born. "We seek the Divine Image alone in Jesus in its fullness: yet sigh to behold it with our corporeal senses. And this privilege God ever vouchsafes to the pure and undefiled in heart: for he ever sends it upon the earth in the form of the Child."[4]

His purpose in teaching religion through conversation, therefore, was not to make children good, but to encourage the goodness in every child to come to its natural flowering and fruition.

The purpose of this book is similar. It has been written with children between the ages of six and ten, primarily, in mind. But it

---

[1] The record of this short-lived experiment may be found in Bronson Alcott's *Record of Conversations on the Gospels* (2 vols.; Boston: James Munroe, 1836).

[2] *Ibid.*, II, 266.

[3] *Ibid.*, p. xliii.

[4] *Ibid.*, p. 1.

has been my experience that children and grownups, in their learning, do not proceed from the unknown to the known in one direct step. Rather, we move in a spiral motion, learning something from an experience or story or discussion, going on to the next experience, coming around again to an area where we have some knowledge, but on this trip finding new meanings, new relationships, deeper truths.

For this reason, a good deal of this material may be suitable for first-graders, on one level of complexity, and for fifth-graders on another level. It should therefore be useful with groups of mixed ages and in families. I have tried to keep the basic language and concepts within the range of first-graders, but may not always have succeeded.

The fifty conversations contained in Chapter III are not verbatim records of conversations with children, as were those of Bronson Alcott. Instead, they are brief essays, often written in conversational style and sometimes as stories, which invite participation at frequent intervals. They are in areas that I have found are important to children. The hope is that teachers, in both day school and church school, ministers, club leaders and parents may find them useful.

The ideas for these conversations have come from several sources. My own four children, ranging in ages from two to fifteen, are my best and most constant source. Even two-year-old Charles makes his contribution. He and I went out to get the mail the other day. We were too early and it had not yet come.

"No mail," I said.

Charlie, thinking of the many times I have gone to the cupboard and said "no peanut butter" or to the refrigerator and said "no milk," nodded his little head knowingly and said, "Buy some."

"Mail, Charles," I said out loud, to myself, "is something that money cannot buy. I have a conversation on that. I'll add 'mail' to the list of things that 'money cannot'."

In addition to gaining ideas from my own children, I am also in debt to many other children. I have also profited from written reports from schools, church schools and families, from reading, and from listening to tapes and discussions.

As indicated, a few of the conversations actually have been written by others, but scattered throughout the rest are ideas and examples garnered over the years from the minds and hearts of many unnamed parents, teachers and children.

How much we miss when we fail to keep the channels of communication open between ourselves and growing children! I know of nothing more beautiful than a child's thought, earnestly and freshly stated.

William and I were riding along in the car. We had passed several statues relating to the Revolutionary War, and he had asked many questions. In spite of the fact that he was not yet six, I had made a not very successful — but, I felt, necessary — attempt to clarify the power situation that existed about 1775.

Nothing had been said for some time. Then with a big sigh out it came: "You know, even us, way down now, if it hadn't been for those men who didn't want to be for kings, we wouldn't have our freedom now."

According to Bronson Alcott: "We greatly underrate the genius of children. We do not apprehend the inward power that but awaits the genial touch to be quickened into life. The art of tempting this forth we have scarce attained. We have outlived our own simple consciousness, and have thus lost our power of apprehending them."[5]

Perhaps some ideas in this book will help those who "have outlived [their] own simple consciousness" once again to make contact with the world of children. When we do succeed in "quickening into life the inward power in children," we make the happy discovery that we ourselves are quickened into life.

[5] *Ibid.,* pp. xvi–xvii.

# Conversations with Children

*I believe every child has hidden away somewhere in his being noble capacities which may be quickened and developed if we go about it in the right way; but we shall never properly develop the higher nature of our little ones while we continue to fill their minds with the so-called rudiments. Mathematics will never make them loving, nor will the accurate knowledge of the size and shape of the world help them to appreciate its beauties. Let us lead them during the first years to find their greatest pleasure in Nature. Let them run in the fields, learn about animals and observe real things. Children will educate themselves under right conditions. They require guidance and sympathy far more than instruction.* — HELEN KELLER, The Story of My Life\**

## I. Religious Experience Through Conversation with Children

We cannot talk with children if we do not listen to them. Many of us never do listen to them, really. Our minds are preoccupied with supper menus, problems at the office or how dirty the speaker's face happens to be.

Both we and the children are the poorer for our not listening. If we do not listen, the children know it. They are then increasingly less likely to try to talk with us. This means that they gradually cut themselves off from any emotional support that closeness with us might give them. They will also be less open to any information and insight we may want to share with them.

We are the poorer because we lose the warmth of young friends. We also lose the stimulation of fresh ideas and fresh feelings that close association with children gives to any sensitive adult.

Long before children talk with words, real communication between them and those habitually with them is possible. And even after language is established, a person attuned to children "listens" to the light in their eyes, the rhythm of their movements, as well as to the words of their mouths.

This book, however, is concerned largely with communication through spoken words, and it is concerned with it on the level of

\* (New York: Doubleday, 1954), p. 318; quoting Anne Sullivan.

the religious. By "religious," I mean having to do with those aspects of our experience that are basic and universal.

Conversation with children can move on this level far more often than many of us realize. By "conversation" I mean a give-and-take of ideas, either between a few individuals or between a leader and a group. In the latter case the give-and-take may be limited to a few moments at the beginning and end or to an occasional comment "from the floor." There may even be no actual back-and-forth conversation, but simply a sense of rapport, a sense of having the children with us.

A group of children once walked into a room where a meeting was to take place. It was an early spring morning and an enormous vase of lilacs had been placed on a table at the front of the room. The children entered, it was apparent, with eyes that did not see the lilacs and with noses that did not smell them.

The adult in charge, noticing this, said: "Did you realize that the lilacs opened this week? Have you stopped and really looked at them? Have you taken a deep, deep smell of them?" She walked over and inhaled their fragrance deeply.

"Did you ever stop to think that you can only see the lilacs open about seventy-five times in your whole life? You have only one chance a year. I've already used up quite a few of my chances."

The effect of these few remarks on the group was startling. Many of the children spontaneously came forward to see and smell the lilacs. They acted as though they truly felt that here was something that they had better not miss.[1]

In that moment of really noticing the lilacs and of being made vividly aware of the briefness of the seventy-five years ahead of them, the adult and probably many of the children had a religious experience. There were many possible facets to the experience, some shared by all, some experienced by only a few of the children and some that only an adult could experience.

As they looked at the lilacs together, they were having a religious experience on the most primary level: direct contact with a natural phenomenon. On another level, the level of ideas, it was a religious experience for some of the children as they became conscious that the miracle of spring occurs only approximately seventy-five times in a person's life.

The adult brought to the situation a longer time perspective and a richer acquaintance with her cultural heritage. There may, therefore, have been a religious quality to the experience for her as she felt the age difference between the children and herself vanish

[1] Reported by Mary Grooms, Rochester, New York.

before the immensity of time in which lilacs have been opening. She knew they had opened long before anyone in the room was born and that they would continue to open long after any of them would be alive.

> We have thus far exhausted trillions of winters and summers,
> There are trillions ahead, and trillions ahead of them.[2]

As she saw the children caught up in the experience, she may have been aware of the poets, painters and musicians who have celebrated the opening of lilacs. She may have seen these children joining the ranks of all human beings who have delighted in spring lilacs. In this awareness she may have felt herself and the children part of something larger and more enduring than their isolated selves, members of the family of man. This feeling has often been associated with a deep religious experience.

All of the possible facets of this brief incident would not be lighted up for any one individual. But if one fresh experience has been felt, one new insight gained, something important and worthwhile has happened.

Why do we want this kind of experience for our children and ourselves? We want it because we know that such experiences enrich the quality of our living. Through such experiences we increase our sensitivity and develop sounder values.

Children and adults are an ideal combination for the occurrence of such experiences. Children bring to the occasion fresh eyes, fresh ears, fresh ways of using language, tremendous curiosity and a wonderful frankness and openness. Although, in the situation with the lilacs just described, it was the children who were not noticing, it is usually the other way around. Many young mothers will testify to the way a first child has opened their eyes to such common wonders as ants, dandelions and shadows. This awareness is one gift children can bring to adults.

Adults can bring to children a longer time perspective (but not too long), relevant factual information (but not too much), some acquaintance with other cultural points of view, and related ideas and questions that may excite the already curious children to further wondering and imagining.

In talking with children on a level of real depth, we are aided by two things: the natural curiosity of children and the nature of

---

[2] Walt Whitman, "Song of Myself," *Leaves of Grass and Selected Prose*, ed. John Kouwenhoven (Modern Library ed.; New York: Random House, 1950), p. 67.

the world. Anyone living intimately with children realizes how
eager they are to savor life deeply. It is only adult ineptness that
succeeds all too soon in causing the "shades of the prison house . . .
to close."[3] In many children of nine or ten, natural curiosity and
spontaneous interest are already crushed and deadened. This can
be the result of such widely different causes as adult indifference to
all questioning, or satiation from too many answers and too much
information. But to begin with, in all healthy children, curiosity is
"given."

The second great "given" is the nature of the world itself. We
do not have to make reality outside of children interesting or in-
tellectually challenging; it comes that way. The natural world, other
people and themselves are all fascinating to them.

And so it is that as every generation of children is born and
begins to have experiences, they very naturally try to understand and
evaluate what is happening in them and around them. They question and experiment and begin to establish what are for them satis-
fying ways of reacting, acting and thinking.

All over the world and from time immemorial, the same great
themes have demanded attention: ourselves and the process of
birth, growth, sickness and death; our human feelings and ways of
living together; the natural world outside of us; the forces that are
felt in the world and that seem to control it; questions and wonderings about how this great drama began, how it will end and what, if
anything, it means.

From culture to culture and from age to age, the perspective
from which men have looked upon this drama and the concepts in
which they have expressed their understanding and feelings about
it, have differed and have changed. But the broad outlines of the
realities that have goaded people on to wonder, and the human
nature that impels us to want to express our ideas and feelings, are
universal and relatively changeless.

Wherever and whenever, for example, human beings have sat
out under the sky for any length of time, they have found themselves
wondering: Are there patterns in the movements of the stars? Why
does the moon wax and wane? What determines the daily course of
the sun? And everywhere, men, women and children have reacted
to the sheer beauty and majesty of the skies.

Whether men watched as shepherds in Babylonia, or as Indian
shepherds on our own American plains, they saw similar phenomena
and wondered. The configurations in which different peoples

[3] William Wordsworth, "Ode: Intimations of Immortality . . . ," *Anthology of Romanticism,* ed. Ernest Bernbaum (3rd ed.; New York: Ronald, 1948), p. 232.

grouped the same stars were amazingly alike from culture to culture, but the myths with which they clothed these constellations were the product of their individual cultures.

Our children and we ourselves can look up at this same sky. What we see will most probably be interpreted by us in terms derived from modern science. But whether we interpret with ancient myths or with modern scientific concepts, our interpretations are not what give the experiences their religious quality. What are sacred, with a sacredness that binds us all together, rather than dividing us, are the common sky above us and our universal human nature with its curiosity and instinctive reverence.

Oddly enough, although we may believe that our modern scientific explanations are closer approximations to the truth than were any ancient myths, the average modern man and child have far less firsthand experience of many of the great phenomena of nature than did those who developed and accepted the ancient myths. We know more about nature, perhaps, but they knew the realities better than we.

A danger that confronts modern children, therefore, is that in the midst of increasingly accurate scientific knowledge and acquaintance with the mythologies of many peoples, they may have almost no firsthand experiences of natural phenomena. We live in an increasingly man-made environment. Unless we make the effort, our children may never do such things as get out under the stars. But they should. They need the experiences that made men ask questions before they are given the myths and explanations that have been worked out in answer to these questions.

Almost without exception our religious education of children proceeds backwards. We begin with theologies and answers instead of with experiences and questions. It is a presupposition of all the conversations in Chapter III that the children and the adults are having a variety of firsthand experiences with both the natural world and with many kinds of people. Without such experiences, there can be no deepening of awareness through conversation. The two must go hand in hand.

Children need experiences so that they may be building up meanings for the words with which we flood them. We adults need firsthand experience as a constant check on our own wordiness.

As these sentences were being written, the telephone rang. A neighbor reported that the northern lights (aurora borealis) were visible. We hurried outside to see them, and as we watched them shoot up, ripple, gather in a great whirling arrangement overhead, we felt the sky like a great bowl over us. Suddenly seven-year-old

William said, "Now I know what that song at school is talking about." "What song?" I asked. And he repeated the now meaningful words:

> The sky by night is high and round,
> The edges rest upon the ground.
> The sky by day goes stretching on,
> Without a thing to rest upon.

Children should have such experiences often.

Children should also have opportunities to plant seeds, to water the soil and to wait and wait, until the first sprout appears. They should observe the forming leaf, the first bud, the flower, the swelling seed, and the new seed drop into the soil. It takes many years and many experiences for children really to observe this and to observe it with understanding.

And they should see death too. It is everywhere. The withered flower, the smashed wasp, the mouse in the mousetrap, the pet kitten in the road, the beloved Grandmother gone or the playmate killed by a car — all these are death brought home to a child. Unless we allow them to know death, they cannot appreciate the wonder of life.

Children should have frequent opportunities to walk in the wind and rain. What understanding can they have of the ideas of the gods of thunder and storm, if they have never felt the forces that gave rise to these ideas? They should have a chance to see rivers full to flooding, and the same rivers reduced to a trickle. Only with such real experiences will they be able to appreciate the mystery and wonder of the water cycle that keeps our world bathed in the same water, over and over again. Unless we make the effort to give our children such experiences, they may know only of water that comes in never varying supply from household faucets.

Children should have experiences with many different kinds of people, so they may realize that their own particular skin color is not the norm, their own way of talking not necessarily the "right" one. They should hear ideas expressed quite different from the ideas of their own family. They need to develop a tolerance of difference and a capacity to accept change.

Curiosity, insight and understanding grow in the soil of wide experiencing. With such a background we can engage in rewarding conversation with children.

Conversation is an ideal method in religious education because the response from the children, whether it is in actual words or simply in the rapport we feel, serves as a constant check on whether we are still "with them." There is nothing quite so obvious as having "lost our audience" when we talk with children, whether we are talking with fifty or with five.

The method of conversation also has the advantage of being, potentially, a creative experience. The ideas and fresh sensitivity contributed by the children may make the whole process one of joint discovery, with the adult involved gaining as much as the children.

These conversations, I hope, can be used as a place to "stand" as we dip into our past experience with children and together reflect on, highlight, discover religious values in that experience. Our aim is to provide a setting in which mutual stimulation of religious awareness can occur between children and adults.

There is a religious quality to the sheer enjoyment we feel when we achieve real communication with children. Beyond this, many of us feel a religious quality in conversation when we succeed in sharpening children's awareness, broadening their sympathies, easing some of their tensions, helping them to increased self-understanding, sharing information on a frontier of their learning, discovering with them some of the clues to the kind of world this is, or standing with them on the threshold of uncharted areas that no child or adult has yet explored.

Conversation with children may be a religious experience as we wash dishes together, as we talk together before bed, as we meet with a class at church school or public school, or as we lead a large assembly. The religious quality of the experience is a by-product of the communication we achieve and of the basic and universal values with which we are dealing. It does not depend on any particular setting.

But, to achieve the kind of communication that makes such an experience possible, we must know the children with whom we want to talk. What are children between six and ten like? What are they interested in, and what ideas have meaning and importance for them? How are basic and universal realities, religious realities, experienced by children?

*The child's world is limited to a small range of experiences nearly all of which are charged with great personal feeling involving himself and people close to him. In contrast, the funded experience of the human race is extended infinitely in time and space and is relatively impersonal. The child's experiences are fluid and non-compartmentalized; whatever is in the child's mind at the moment constitutes for him the whole of reality. In contrast, the organized experience of the race has been classified and logically arranged, in ways that reflect themselves in the divisions and orderly arrangements of the curriculum. The child's life is practical and concrete. In contrast, the experience of the race is expressed by means of abstract propositions which embody whole realms of meaning in a single statement, but meanings that are lost to the child because he does not know, has not himself experienced that to which the abstraction refers and from which it was torn.* — EPHRAIM VERN SAYERS and WARD MADDEN, Education and the Democratic Faith\*


## II. A Glimpse of "Every Child"


"Today I have been thinking about eyes," said William. "How do you see?  Oh, I know you look at things, but I mean what *is* seeing?"

"But what if you don't want to be a soldier and be in a war?" he asks another day. "Do you *have* to?"

"Are stones still being made?"

"Was I really as small as Charles when I was a baby?"

"Is this the same rain that fell on the dinosaurs?"

"Do they really put people in jail?"

> Tell me, tell me everything!
> What makes it Winter
> And then Spring?[1]


What are children between six and ten interested in?  They are interested in everything that impinges upon them, unless, as

\* (New York: Appleton-Century-Crofts; copyright © 1959), p. 374.
[1] Harry Behn, "Curiosity," in *Windy Morning*. By permission, Harcourt, Brace, New York.

suggested earlier, their curiosity has been seriously underfed or overfed.

These children have been described as "simple, direct and eager; with freshness and expectancy they approach a world sighted but unexplored."[2] They are indeed standing on the threshold of the world.

Fortunately for the children, they bring to this enterprise enormous energy. For many adults this energy is a problem. The young explorers are often unaware of the fact that trying to absorb "everything" can be tiring for both themselves and the adults around them. The result is familiar to us all.

> My little Son, who look'd from thoughtful eyes
> And moved and spoke in quiet grown-up wise,
> Having my law the seventh time disobey'd
> I struck him, and dismiss'd
> With hard words and unkiss'd,
> His Mother, who was patient, being dead.
> Then, fearing lest his grief should hinder sleep,
> I visited his bed,
> But found him slumbering deep,
> With darken'd eyelids, and their lashes yet
> From his late sobbing wet.
> And I, with moan,
> Kissing away his tears, left others of my own
> For, on a table drawn beside his head,
> He had put, within his reach,
> A box of counters, and a red-vein'd stone,
> A piece of glass abraded by the beach,
> And six or seven shells,
> A bottle of bluebells,
> And two French copper coins, ranged there with careful art,
> To comfort his sad heart. . . .[3]

In spite of such head-on collisions, we really do want to communicate with such children, and we want them to know that we too love the "red-vein'd stone," the sea-washed glass and pretty shells. But how can we establish rapport? It will help a great deal to know some of the characteristics that children in this stage of development may have in common.

[2] Bertha Stevens, *Child and Universe.* By permission, The John Day Co., Inc., New York, p. 6.
[3] Coventry Patmore, "The Toys," in *The Oxford Book of English Verse* (New York: Oxford, 1927), p. 911.

Familiarity with such books as *These Are Your Children*,[4] *The Child from Five to Ten*,[5] *Childhood and Adolescence*[6] or even the old standby *Baby and Child Care*,[7] can be useful. We should remind ourselves that these descriptions are most relevant to middle-class white Americans, and that no two of these children are exactly alike. But, if we read the material imaginatively, we should gain a rather vivid picture of many of the common characteristics, needs and interests of these children.

For one thing we find that children at six still have a very rudimentary sense of space and time. By the age of ten this has developed a good deal more. But even though the six-year-olds may be vague about the exact historical order of George Washington and Abraham Lincoln, they are nonetheless very much interested in the past, especially way, way back in the long ago.

They may, likewise, be unsure about the exact location of Siam or Palestine, but they are very curious about people on the other side of the world — how they look and their different ways of eating, dressing and carrying on life in general. By nine or ten they will have a much more accurate sense of time and place, and we can enrich our materials accordingly.

Another gradual development that is of importance to us is their limited ability to grasp causal relations and to generalize and abstract. We can not hurry the development of these understandings, but we can stimulate children with a rich diet of experience in which these abilities are used.

In books that give general age characteristics we find agreement that the "everything" that interests these children radiates out from a center which is themselves. This is not a new development in our times. The recorder of Bronson Alcott's conversations observed: "To a child, all questions touching the Soul are deeply interesting. He loves his own consciousness. It is a charmed world to him."[8]

Children in these years are very much interested in their own feelings, their own abilities, their own problems and their own ideas. This interest in themselves includes not only the self that they are now, but all of their past, right back to their own beginnings. Baby books, picture albums, family movies, tapes and diaries are a delight to them. They love to hear about their own first words, their early mispronunciations, their funny misconceptions and their

---

[4] Gladys Gardner Jenkins, *et al.* (Chicago: Scott, Foresman, 1953).
[5] Arnold Gesell and Frances L. Ilg (New York: Harper's, 1946).
[6] L. Joseph Stone and Joseph Church (New York: Random House, 1947).
[7] Benjamin Spock (New York: Pocket Books, 1957).
[8] Bronson Alcott, *Record of Conversations on the Gospels*, p. xvii.

early questions. Their parents' childhood intrigues them too.

This ability to take on the past and their eagerness to dwell on it seems to be a way of consolidating what has gone before. It is important that we take time to do it with them. It is a vital part of their growth as whole persons.

These children are proud of their past accomplishments and they are equally proud of the new skills and achievements that come thick and fast in their first years of school. They feel very good about it as they become increasingly adept at writing, reading and handling numbers. When school is out they revel in riding two-wheel bikes, mastering stilts, roller skates and even skis. To recall these achievements with them in conversation makes them glow. The process of thinking about them together can be a real religious experience.

With these accomplishments in mind they find it interesting to think about the common miracle, the human body. Given a fresh perspective, they may really become more aware and appreciative of our wonderful senses and brain, through which the world is taken in and interpreted. Actually, almost any part of the human body can be the subject for a religious discussion with these children, if it is in the vivid terms of their own lives and in concepts meaningful to them.

Just as they are able to look back at their own beginnings and development because of their emerging time senses, so they are able and eager to look ahead a bit into their own futures. They may think about "what they are going to be" when they are grown up. There begins to be some reality for them in the idea that someday they will be mothers and fathers, even grandmothers and grand-fathers.

They have some awareness that someday they will die. They should be allowed to think about this, as they can and want to. Facing the reality of death is essential in the development of one's perspective on life and in the building of one's sense of values.

Clearly these children are naturally and profoundly concerned with some of the great themes of all religions: birth, growth and death. Although at six their interest may be primarily in their own birth, their own growth and their own death, if we respond with warmth and sincerity, if we have respect for the limits that the stages of development set on their understanding, by ten they will have widened the base of their interest well beyond themselves.

Another area that concerns them is the wide range of human feelings. They are aware of how easy it is, in themselves, to go from a mood of happy serenity to wild fury, from a whisper to a shout, from smiles to tears. The years from six to eight, especially, have been characterized as not unlike two other "difficult" periods in the growing-up process in our culture: two-and-a-half and adolescence. It is, for many of these children, a period of breakup in old behavior patterns and a rather chaotic thrusting out toward new ones.

Again and again the children are described as egoistic, bossy toward their friends, saucy to their parents and, if given a chance, rude to their teachers. They are social experimenters, telling tall tales that are sometimes indistinguishable from lies, indulging in borrowing that often looks like stealing, forming clubs whose sole purpose seems to be to exclude. They often talk with bravado that masks a coward's heart. They want to be first, best and never lose.

Indeed it seems that many first-graders are very nearly an embodiment of all the "vices" that traditional religious education material was produced to combat. The stories, sermons, lessons and songs used sought, through a head-on attack, to win children away from egocentricity to selflessness, away from "bossiness" to submissiveness, from freshness toward their parents to obedience, from exclusiveness, socially, to inclusiveness, from fighting and assertiveness to friendliness and cooperation, from an attitude of experimentation to one of unquestioning conformity.

Of course we all want the children to behave "nicely" and to make our lives with them pleasant. But the relevant questions are: how "nice" is best for them, and how do we achieve it? There are ways of incorporating the positive values in selfishness, such as the liking of one's self, into the beginnings of the more mature attitude of sharing. Bossiness can grow into the ability to plan cooperatively, with independent thinkers pooling their insights. The drive toward independence, often so unpleasant in the fresh first-grader, needs tolerance, channeling and guidance. To curb it completely is to invite trouble.

The children themselves feel some ambivalence about the behavior that so often gets them into difficulties with their families, their teachers and their friends. They too are disturbed by their own feelings that, at times, seem to take over and force them to "seven times disobey" and go unkissed to bed.

There are patterns in our culture that accentuate some of the rather chaotic new developments of these children. The first-graders leave home each day, some of them for the first time, and enter what, to them, is the wide, wide world.

They find here two new symbols of "all wisdom" and authority: their teachers and their friends. They discover many kinds of differences in ways of talking, thinking and behaving. They discover that their new authorities — the teachers and friends — often conflict with their old authorities, mother, father and big brother, and that their new authorities conflict with each other. All this does not contribute to the peace of mind of people only six or seven years old, especially when so many of their authorities claim all truth for themselves.

In their school world they are anxious to work out ways of relating themselves to the other children. On Monday they may be best friends with Joe and Tony, but positively hate Carl and Mike. On Tuesday Carl and Tony are completely acceptable, but Joe and Mike deplorable. It is quite irrelevant to demand that they like Joe, Tony, Carl and Mike equally well every day.

At home they could not choose their parents or their brothers and sisters. At school they need and rejoice in the opportunity to select and reject friends. Their clubs, which may actually never meet but perpetually form and re-form, are arenas of experimentation in human relations. If we recognize them for what they are, we will be less apt to demand that these clubs accept everyone or that they accomplish great ends.

In the schoolroom and on the playground the children may meet the bully, the boss, the shy child, the fat boy. They may meet, for the first time, a blind child, the victim of an accident or of a birth injury. They may have their first encounters with some of the victims of social injustice. They watch others react to these children. They must work out methods of reacting, too.

"Mike's shoes are all torn down the back. They won't even stay on when we play tag. Gosh! Why doesn't he get some better ones?"

"Timmy hits people all the time. No one does anything to him first either. Mrs. Green says he's all mixed up and shouldn't even be in our school. What school should he be in?"

"I *told* Bobby he shouldn't say 'catch a nigger by the toe.' I told him you said Negroes don't like to be called that. I told him you say 'tigger' instead. He says that's crazy! His father says 'nigger' and that's right."

"Jane says God is a Real Man and He sees everything we do. But Toby says God is just make-believe like Santa Claus. His big brother found out this year."

Poverty, mental illness, racial stereotypes and theological controversy all in one school yard, and the student for whom it is an object lesson often just six years old!

It is small wonder that the children frequently return home from their daily foray into the world in a state of psychic turmoil, physical exhaustion and mental perplexity. They have discovered many things on which they must reflect. Much that has happened they must get out of their systems, somehow.

With the youngest of these children, a great deal of reflecting is done in other ways than sitting and talking about what has gone on. They are said to learn and incorporate ideas by a "whole body" reaction. For many first-graders it is almost a compulsion to play school the minute that they get home from real school. In this way they are thinking about their day at school. The most releasing role is that of the teacher, and the second most popular part is that of class villain. If a group of children is not available, their reflecting may be done through dolls, puppets, blocks or even with paint and clay.

Mother is a foil who can be useful in many ways. Perhaps the teacher, feeling the strain of too large a class, has shouted a good deal. On returning home, the children can get this out of their systems by shouting at mother when she asks them to change into play clothes. Mother may also have a more positive role as willing listener to all the triumphs or injustices of the day.

Most of the children feel that they must let their families know about the different ways of doing things and thinking about things that they have discovered. They also want their parents' opinions on some of these matters, but not by directly asking them. Instead, they *do* many of the things and, very often, parents do not appreciate either what they are being "told" or the way they are being told. Children try out this knowledge at home because it is a relatively safe place to experiment. Some children are brave enough to experiment in the church school they attend.

If being fresh to mother when school lets out is a safety valve, and perhaps a way of "being" the shouting teacher, if tripping up little sister is a way the first-grader can live with the third-grader who trips him, and a way of trying the trick himself, we had better think twice before insisting that the only proper attitude toward mother is honor, and toward little sister, kindness.

This doesn't mean that parents just have to "take it." But we should realize that the pressures that are on children produce a real need to experiment, to release tension, somehow to get adult opinion, and to evaluate new knowledge for themselves. Parents can try to provide acceptable after-school safety valves: opportunity for free play; a chance to use releasing art materials; or time to dawdle over a glass of milk and a peanut butter sandwich, with friendly, relatively uncritical adult ears nearby.

Stories about other children with problems like their own are good to use, since such stories enable the children to gain some objectivity about themselves. Stories of how their parents or teacher met the world when they were six years old are fascinating and therapeutic, too. The church, the home and even the public school, which recognizes the existential situation of children and tries to meet some of their needs, is each performing an important religious role.

Besides meeting the emotional needs of these children, we have an important and complex job as we try to meet the intellectual and ethical perplexities that result from their first adventuring into the larger culture beyond the home.

"Why can't Mike have shoes that don't fall off?"

"Mike's father is out of work."

"Why is Mike's father out of work?"

"We are having a slight recession."

"What is that?"

What parent or teacher has not gingerly launched into a discussion of economic depression, racial discrimination, the causes of war or any of our other social problems, and very shortly found himself floundering in water right up around his neck and well over the head of his fellow conversationalist? To deal with such issues with children calls for great skill and sensitivity as to what is meaningful for them.

A child in these years begins to ask about our social institutions also: Why does his family go to this church and not to Tommy's? What are churches anyway? Why does he *have* to go to school? We can have interesting conversations with children on such topics, provided we stay close to their immediate experience and use the specific terms that are understandable to them.

Beyond themselves, their own feelings, their friends, the larger society as it touches their lives, these children have an omnivorous curiosity about the natural world. A glimpse at the contents of one seven-year-old's trouser pockets prior to their descent into the washing machine gives a key to these interests.

In one pocket there are stones, freshly cracked open to show them unweathered. There are the remains of the shell of a robin's egg. A small blue jay's feather and a sunflower seed are wrapped neatly in the notice for last night's P.T.A. meeting.

All these items, except the last, must be carefully saved for the young collector. And collector he is! The other pocket also reflects his passion for collecting, this time from the world of men rather than of nature. Here we find: a penny (dated with his birth year and very important), a bottle top, a foreign stamp, a match box, one of his school papers and a baseball card. To the children these things may be just as valuable as the contents of the other pocket.

Why are children such collectors? In an interesting analysis, Stone and Church suggest: "His collections can be seen as the world reduced to a scale where he can possess and manage and order it."[9] Parents, with eyes for neat rooms, may question the "ordering" that goes on, but some of these avid collectors do seem to be well on the way to possessing the world within the confines of their four walls.

Their interest in the natural world extends beyond those things that fit handily into pants pockets. It extends all the way from puppies and kittens (all animal babies in fact) to such far-flung phenomena as volcanoes, glaciers and such long-ago curiosities as dinosaurs and cave men.

In these days especially, they are very curious about celestial things: the moon, the sun, the stars and the planets. They are beginning to be able to think of the earth itself as a ball in space. "Is there life on any of the other 'space balls'?" "What keeps these balls from falling?" "What keeps them moving?" "What started them moving?" Such questions as these come readily to their minds.

Just as they were curious about their own beginnings, they are curious about all beginnings. "Who was the first man?" "Where did he come from?" "How did anything get to be alive?" "How did the world get made?" "What did it all look like when there wasn't anything?" They themselves discover that we hardly know how to word the questions that pop into our minds when we really catch a glimpse of some of the mysteries of our existence. They find that for some of our questions there are no answers and that for others there are only contradictory ones.

And so even at the ages of six, seven and eight they begin to discover the different philosophies and theologies that divide us. They discover the conflict between science and religion.

Traditionally, the tremendous curiosity of children has been met, as far as religious educators were concerned, with final, clear-cut answers. This has fed the dogmatism that is a common feature of this age group with more dogmatism. The attempt is made in these conversations to meet their curiosity with a more informed curiosity. In this way, instead of closing any doors, many doors should be left open, to be entered over a lifetime.

How can we leave doors open, rather than close them, in religious education? One way of doing this is to dwell on the things themselves that interest the children, rather than to use their interests for our adult ends.

[9] Stone and Church, *op. cit.*, p. 213.

For example, young children are attracted to the way the light strikes the shiny face of a piece of feldspar, the lovely blue of the robin's eggshell, the iridescence and texture of the blue jay feather, the smooth softness of the sunflower seed and its regular black-and-white markings, the enormous size of the dinosaurs. These things they enjoy at first simply for being what they are.

We should let them spend time enjoying them. We should spend time enjoying them too. We should encourage their often spontaneous expression of enjoyment in poetry, dance, music, art, story-making and collecting.

They will also ask questions. For, being human, children do not just enjoy their experiences; they also question, analyze and, within bounds set by their own development, theorize. When they need factual information, we can supply it, or, better still, very often we can help them dig it out. There are now so many excellent books written for children that there is no excuse for ignorance on the part either of children or adults. Many of the books make adequate introductory reading material for adults. Such material may help us to be better learning companions for children than an exhaustive college course taken many years earlier.

But the facts that will serve their needs can not go too far beyond their experience. The children must literally have cracked open pounds and pounds of rock to ask, "Why does feldspar always break open with the same flat, smooth cleavage? Why can I keep peeling off layer after layer of mica?" Only when they have actually experienced the regularity of crystal structure can they appreciate the wonders in the theory of crystallography and beyond that, the higher abstractions about natural law, and beyond that, whatever metaphysic or theology we think are indicated by these phenomena.

But it has been a general practice in religious education to use the very genuine interests and enthusiasms of children first to capture their attention and then to demonstrate with them the validity of some of our adult theories. This seems to me illegitimate and ultimately self-defeating.

Charles and I were driving up a country road. All around us in the distance were great mountain peaks.

"What a view!" I said. "Look at the mountains, Charles."

But instantly I knew that, at the age of eighteen months, he couldn't possibly look at the mountains and there was absolutely nothing I could do to make him see them. The only mountain within his range of vision is the slight rise in the path going out to the swing. This "mountain" is just as exciting to him as mine are to me. The infinitesimal piece of mica that lies on his "mountain" and catches the sun, and the tiny ant that is tugging a crumb of his cooky away — these hold him spellbound. These are the proper objects of his curiosity now.

He'll get to my mountains, in time, and with the same zest and wonder that he now shows, if I don't rush him. Actually, it is impossible to impose our adult mountains on two-year-olds, but not so with children six to ten. They can see the mountains we point out. They can also use the theological words that we put into their mouths.

Therefore we tend to teach them, as soon as they can say the words, that "the Heavens declare the glory of God, and the firmament showeth his handiwork." For us, they well may. But for children there should be years of sky-watching and years of earth-studying before they are ready to assert the meaning of all they are discovering.

It is unfortunate that so much material prepared for the religious nurture of children is sentimental and trivial or expressed in theological concepts beyond their real understanding. We do not have to stoop to the trivial and transient to get children interested in religion. Children are naturally curious about the really profound mysteries and deeply appreciative of universal and enduring values. But we should have the patience not to talk over their heads or beyond their experience. If we had a higher regard for human nature and a greater trust in reality we would not be in such a hurry.

Often, it seems that we adults are afraid to let the children probe the perplexing aspects of experience. We are afraid of the honesty and frankness of children, which, when allowed free expression, so often exposes the incompleteness of our knowledge and the parochialism of so many of our values. Their simple logic and clear young vision is apt to reveal our careless thinking and the yawning gaps between our ideals and social reality. We feel as exposed as the emperor in his new clothes.

Conversation with children should challenge us to grow in curiosity and insight with them.

> Where does the wind
> When it goes away go?
> Tell me! or don't even grownups know?[10]

---

[10] Harry Behn, "Curiosity," *op. cit.*

# III. Fifty Conversations

NOTE. Each conversation has above it a quotation. These quotations are intended to provide stimulation for the adult and are not to be read by the children.

## Section A. Curiosity

*"What color is think?" was one of the restful questions she asked, as we swung to and fro in the hammock.* — HELEN KELLER, The Story of My Life*

### 1. Questions

"Questions are a favorite game of kids the world around. . . ." That is the first line of a song I heard the other day. I think it is only partly true. I don't really think that asking questions is just a game, and children aren't the only ones who ask them. Almost all of us feel that we just *have* to ask questions to understand what is going on around us.

Even a tiny baby asks questions, not with words, at first, but he asks them just the same. First he asks them mostly with his eyes, and then he reaches out with his hands and asks them with his fingers. And then whatever his fingers light on he puts in his mouth, and what a wonderful time he has asking questions with his mouth! Not with words, yet, but with his lips and his tongue and his teeth. How does this taste? Is it hard? Can I eat it? . . . and on and on. At last he begins to talk and then he asks questions with words, and he goes on asking them for the rest of his life, I hope.

I certainly think that the song is right when it says that asking questions happens the world around. I would really like to see what a country would be like made up of people who didn't ask any questions!

I have been collecting other people's questions for several years. I'm going to read some of them to you. As you hear them, ask yourselves three other questions: (1) About how old do you think the person was who asked this question? (2) Do *you* know an answer? (3) How would you answer it for that person? Here are a couple of hints, too. If the question seems silly or terribly easy, the person asking it might be younger than you. If you can't

* (New York: Doubleday, 1954), p. 276.

understand what the question means, probably the person who asked it was a lot older than you are.

Here is the list of questions:

(1) Is this tomorrow?

(2) How does friction cause heat?

(3) If everyone has to die, who will live in all the houses?

(4) Is this the same rain that fell on the dinosaurs?

(5) How do you go to sleep?

Look at the first question: "Is this tomorrow?" How old do you think the person was who asked this question? Three years old. There isn't any day named tomorrow, of course. In a way you never get to it. It is always today and never tomorrow. Does that mean it's a question that you can't answer? No, of course not!

Let's imagine that it is your little sister who asked this question. Your mother told her that she could go to her friend's house tomorrow. Now she has come to you and asked you if this is tomorrow. You might say no, but that after she goes to bed, and the sky has gotten all dark, and she has slept and slept, and finally the sun has come up again, then it will be tomorrow. You would have told her when tomorrow is. Of course the next morning she might come running into your room and ask, "Is this tomorrow?" What would you say then? You *could* tell her that TODAY IS YESTERDAY'S TOMORROW. But she probably wouldn't understand that; it even mixes me up.

Probably you thought that was a pretty silly question when you first heard it. Perhaps you thought it was going to be awfully easy to answer. Whether it is easy or difficult depends on who it is you are talking to. In another year your little sister won't even ask that question. She'll have had enough experience to know what the word tomorrow means. There are many questions like that. They may be awfully difficult to answer now, but, when the person asking them has had more experience and has lived a little longer, they are easy to answer.

"How does friction cause heat?" Perhaps you didn't even understand that second question. Take your two hands and rub them together just as hard and fast as you can. Are they getting hot? The heat is caused by the rubbing and we call that friction. But why does it cause heat? This was one of the favorite questions of a famous scientist, the late Charles F. Kettering. He first asked the question when he was quite a young man, but he still didn't know the answer when he died. It's the kind of question people probably will know the answer to some day, however. Scientists are finding out more about friction all the time.

How about that third question, "If everyone has to die some-time, who will live in all the houses?" That's a funny one, isn't it? A little girl, I think she was three or four, asked her mother that one. She and her mother had been talking about death, and her mother said that everyone has to die. The little girl thought her mother meant that everyone was going to die at the same time. It's very much like a question a little boy asked me once when he was about the same age. He asked me if all the "grave mens" die. I asked him what "grave mens" were. He said they were the men who dig the graves and bury people. I said that, yes, they die, too. "Well," he said, "then who will bury the grave mens?"

Of course, those questions don't seem difficult to answer either. You can just tell a child that the children of the people alive *now* will live in all the houses, and some of these children will grow up and be "grave mens" and bury the others. But, you see, children of three or four can't really understand that some day they are going to grow up and be fathers and mothers and have more babies. The question is difficult to answer only because these children haven't lived long enough yet.

"Is this the same rain that fell on the dinosaurs?" That ques-tion was asked by a boy six years old. He and his mother had been talking about rain. They had been thinking about how moisture gathers in clouds and comes down in rain. And then the moisture on the ground or the plants evaporates, goes up into the air again and forms clouds. So that, in a way, we have the same rain over and over again. How would you answer him then? Is it the same rain that fell on the dinosaurs?

And what about that last question, "How do you go to sleep?" Perhaps you think that's an easy one. And it *was* someone only five years old who asked it. But that is a really hard question. Scientists are very much interested in trying to find the answer to it. How *do* you fall asleep? Do you just close your eyes? Try it. Are you asleep? No. It's more than that. Do you shut off your mind somehow? There are people who just can't go to sleep without taking pills. It would help them a lot if we could find the answer to that question. I think some day we'll know, but we don't yet.

What are some of the questions you find yourself asking? Why not have your father or mother or teacher write down five or six of them. Keep a copy of your list. Look at it again a long time from now, even as long as five years or ten years. I wonder whether some of your questions will have been answered. Do you think that all the questions we can ask will be answered some day?

## OTHER IDEAS

1. Charles Kettering had six questions that he asked over and over again. Many of these questions scientists are working on now.
   (a) Why is the grass green?
   (b) How does friction cause heat?
   (c) How can we transmit power by radio waves?
   (d) Why does a magnet work?
   (e) How can we harness the sun's limitless energy?
   (f) How can we mine the resources of the sea?
2. Children respond warmly to these two questions, when they grasp what is implied:
   (a) How old are you, or when did you really begin?
   (b) Where are you right now and are you really sitting still? (In this room, in this house, in this town, etc. The earth is moving; the solar system is moving; our galaxy is moving, etc.)
3. Ask the children if, by some kind of magic, they could have the answer to three questions, what would their three questions be? Ask them to think carefully before they answer.
4. Three stories in *From Long Ago and Many Lands,* by Sophia L. Fahs (Boston: Beacon Press, 1950), might be used in relation to this conversation: "The Questions of King Milinda," "Gautama Finds Out for Himself," and "A Musician and His Trumpet." The guide for teachers and parents, by Florence Klaber, gives many suggestions for the use of these stories.


## SUGGESTIONS

1. A large blackboard, or tag board and magic marker would be useful to list questions from the group.
2. Many of the poems in the section *"Wondering,"* in the anthology *Poems to Grow On,* by Jean M. Thompson (Boston: Beacon Press, 1957), might be used with this conversation and others in Section I.
3. A song such as "Wonderings," No. 32 in *We Sing of Life,* edited by Vincent E. Silliman (Boston: Beacon Press, 1955), might also be used with many of the conversations in this book.


*Religion will not regain its old power until it can face change in the same spirit as does science. Its principles may be eternal but the expression of those principles requires continual development. This evolution of religion is in the main a disengagement of its own proper ideas from the adventitious notions which have crept into it by reason of the expression of its own ideas in terms of the imaginative picture of the world entertained in previous ages. Such a release of religion from the bonds of imperfect science is all to the good.* — ALFRED NORTH WHITEHEAD, Science and the Modern World*

* (New York: Macmillan, 1937), p. 270.

## 2. *The "Used-to-Thinks"*

Did you ever think something when you were younger and then, when you got to be a little older, find out it wasn't that way at all?

For example, when I was in the first grade, I used to think that children in the third grade were practically grownups! But then when *I* got to be in the third grade, I didn't feel grown-up at all. But *then* I thought the sixth-graders were *really* old!

I wonder whether any of you read *Jack and Jill* magazine? They always have a few pages of material that the readers send in. In almost every issue they have several letters that tell about something one of the readers "used to think." For some reason it's fun to tell other people about your "used-to-thinks."

I've been collecting "used-to-thinks" for quite a few years now. Some of them I found in *Jack and Jill,* some of them were my own, some of them my children told me and some of them other children told me.

Here are some of the "used-to-thinks" I have collected. I wonder whether you used to think any of these things?

I used to think that we lived on the *inside* of the world-ball, not on the outside.

I used to think that when you shut off the TV the program would stop, and then, when you turned it on again, it would begin right where it was when you stopped it.

I used to think you grew bigger on your birthday.

I used to think that when you ordered something out of a catalogue no one else could order *that* thing.

I used to think that when people said that Christmas was just around the corner the people around the corner were having Christmas.

I used to think that when there were double lines down the middle of the highway motorcycles were supposed to go in the space between them.

I used to think that ladies who wore high heels had heels on their feet that went down inside their shoes.

I used to think that when children talked about having homework it meant the teacher gave them work to do at home, like dusting and sweeping.

I used to think that after you've gotten as old as you are going to get you begin to get younger again. When someone told me how old they were, I wondered whether they were on their way to older or younger.


Children are not the only ones who have "used-to-thinks." Almost every day, now that I have grown up, I find out something that makes something that I thought I knew into a "used-to-think." Here are some of my grown-up "used-to-thinks":

I used to think that pickles were a kind of vegetable that grew in the garden. I didn't know they were really cucumbers.

Until we started raising butterflies in our family, I used to think that butterflies were born as small butterflies and grew to be bigger and bigger butterflies.

I used to think that *all* moths eat clothes.

I used to think that the white things you sometimes find on tomato worms were eggs. (Do you know what they really are? See if you can find out.)


But it isn't just grownups and children who have "used-to-thinks." All the people who are alive together at one time think certain things that people living after them find out aren't true at all.

The people who lived in Greece several thousand years ago used to think that it was the trees shaking that made the wind blow.

Many people alive at the time of Columbus used to think that, if sailors rode out into the ocean off Spain, after a while their boats would fall off the edge of the world and monsters would eat them up.

People used to think that tomatoes were poisonous.

The people who lived when my grandmother did used to think that it was positively dangerous to go fifteen miles an hour. They used to think that there never could be a flying machine — it would fall out of the air.

People used to think that man would never, never get to the moon, or to Mars or away from our earth at all. I wonder what is going to happen to *that* "used-to-think" in the next few years?

I guess that as long as there are people in the world there will be "used-to-thinks," because there is always going to be more to find out and there are always going to be new things to find out about what we think we already know. Every time you find yourself with a new "used-to-think" you ought to feel pretty good, because it means you've learned something that you didn't know before.

Now, why don't you try an experiment. First, see if you can remember five of your own "used-to-thinks." Write these down, or ask someone else to. Now ask someone to write down these five questions, and your answers to them:

Do you think dinosaurs ate people?

Do you think rocks are still being made?

Do you think the number *3* and the letter *S* are difficult to write?

Do you think that the rungs on a chair are to put your feet on?

Do you think it is difficult to jump rope?

Next year, at about this time, ask someone to read these questions to you again. See how many of your last year's answers have turned into "used-to-thinks."

There are two things I wonder about. I wonder why our "used-to-thinks" so often seem funny to us and make us laugh? And I wonder what there is that I am thinking today that is going to be a "used-to-think" tomorrow?

### OTHER IDEAS

1. As children become more adept at reading and writing, they discover a kind of "used-to-think" about how words are actually spelled as opposed to how they "used to think" they were spelled. A very amusing discussion can result from this.

### SUGGESTIONS

1. This conversation is most effective with children eight and over (right on up to eighty in fact). The majority of children younger than eight have not yet gained enough perspective to be conscious of their own "used-to-thinks."
2. A rather different meaning of "I used to think," but one that adults might watch for, is mentioned by Bertha Stevens in *Child and Universe*, p. 184: ". . . boys above the age of eight have occasionally, in my experience, allowed a very real sense of beauty and poetic imagination to be invaded with the thought that its expression would be unmanly. When they desire to state something which they feel or think, they may preface it by saying: 'When I was little, I used to think' . . . The truth may be that they are stating a present experience which they are unwilling to acknowledge."
3. The poem "Little Brother's Secret," by Katherine Mansfield, is a delightful example of a "used-to-think." This may be found in *Time for Poetry*, ed. May Hill Arbuthnot (Chicago: Scott, Foresman, 1951).
4. Again a blackboard or large piece of tag board would be useful for listing "used-to-thinks."

### I WOULD BE A RIVER

*If I were a thing, I should like to be a river,*
*testifying to the permanency of sky.*
*the recurrence of clouds,*

*registering sun*
*long into night in warm ripples.*

*Not a tree, however beautiful, untraveled;*
*not a stone, opaque;*
*not the secretive grass*
*or a bush satisfied with itself*
*in bloom. No, and not the ocean*
*limited in largeness*
*but the medium-wide*
*circuitous water*
*that responds to a leaf fallen on it*
*and raindrops*
*and accepts the shadows of factories,*
*birds' wings, overhanging branches,*
*the occasional vaunt of bridges*
*and paddles moving against it.*

*It has the long confidence;*
*secure in source and tributaries, it moves*
*to itself along many banks,*
*spreading sunsets, resting on islands,*
*insistent on the day, significant of night,*
*carrying the kiss of deer come down to it*
*and the bemusement of fishermen.*
                              — HELEN HARRINGTON*

### 3. *If You Could Be . . .*

Are there some things that you especially like to do with your father or mother before you go to sleep at night?

Of course, for one thing, you probably like to have stories read. But sometimes the first-grade boy at our house decides that, instead of stories, he would like to do something a little different.

One of the things we sometimes do is tell each other about "our day." If Dad is putting our boy to bed, first Dad tells what his day was like — what was fun and what wasn't. Then the boy who is in the first grade tells about his day — what happened at school, who his best friend is that day, and things like that.

Another thing he likes to do some nights is this. When something especially interesting has happened, he asks one of us to write

* From *The Christian Science Monitor.* Quoted by permission of *The Christian Science Monitor* and the author.

it down as he tells it to us. We write it in a little notebook that he
keeps just for this. He decided to do this so that he can read this
book to his little boy when he is a Daddy. He likes to have us tell
him stories about when we were little and we can't remember
enough stories to tell.

Some nights, instead of stories, he likes to play games. These
are lying-in-bed games. It is one of these games that I especially
wanted to tell you about.

This is the game of "If you could be something or somebody
different from the person you are, who or what would you like to
be?"

I'm not quite sure why this game is so much fun, but I know
that all of my children have liked to play it, when they were six or
seven years old. Even the older children like to play it with the
first-grade boy now.

I usually say that I would like to be a fern. Some of the things
the children have said they would like to be are: a beautiful stone,
a wild goose, a cloud, and a tree.

I've discovered several things about this game. It's not only
*my* children who like to play it. Many other children play it too.
Do you ever play it?

I've also discovered that it is not only *children* who play it.
I've found several grownups playing it lately. I've found them
playing it in poems they've written.

Here are four poems that I've found that show people playing
"If You Could Be."

This first poem was written down by a grownup as she listened
to a group of children talking.

> I would like to be a digger,
> A digger of dinosaur bones,
> Because I love old things.
> And when I was tired of digging
> I could look at the stars.
>
> I would like to be an old and sturdy tree,
> Or else a young one, just born.
> I would like to be a rainbow,
> Because of the colors.
> I would like to be a flower, or flowers,
> Or a big cloud, soft and fluffy.
>
> I would like to be cool water on a hot day,
> Or the glistening on water, all sparkly.

I would like to be water,
With someone swimming in me.
I would like to be my father,
Because he does so many good things.

Would I like to be my grandfather,
Who is a planter of seeds?
I would like to make things grow,
And to grow myself.

. . . . . . .

I would like to be the whole world
And everything in it.[1]


The second poem was written by a Japanese poet, so I guess
that people all over the world like to play this game, too.

### A WISH

O moon, if born again, I'd be
A pine tree on a mountain's peak,
That when you rise I might be first to see.[2]


The next poem was written by a famous woman poet who died
many years ago, so I guess people have liked to play this game for
a long, long time.  Here are two verses of the poem:

### THE GRASS

The grass so little has to do, —
    A sphere of simple green,
With only butterflies to brood,
    And bees to entertain.

. . . . . . . . . . . . .

And then to dwell in sovereign barns,
    And dream the days away, —
The grass so little has to do,
    I wish I were a hay![3]


---

[1] This poem by Mrs. Grace Martin was inspired by the remarks of a group
of children. Quoted by permission.

[2] A Japanese *hokku* from *Little Pictures of Japan*, ed. Olive Beaupré Miller
(Chicago: Book House for Children, 1925), p. 102.

[3] Emily Dickinson, "The Grass," *Complete Poems of Emily Dickinson*
(Boston: Little, Brown, 1960).

And this last poem I found just the other day in the newspaper, so I know that there are other people playing it all the time. The poem was written for grownups, so some of the lines are difficult to understand. I'll just read you a few ideas from it. This poet knows just what she wants to be and just why she *doesn't* want to be certain other things.

### I Would Be a River

If I were a thing, I should like to be a river,

. . . . . .

Not a tree, however beautiful, untraveled;
not a stone, opaque; [explain]
not the secretive grass
or a bush satisfied with itself
in bloom. No, and not the ocean . . .[4]

The first-grade boy at our house likes to play this game in a little different way than the other children did. He likes to lean back on his pillow, with his hands behind his head, study the ceiling for a few minutes, and then say:

"Which would you rather be — a kite that would fly and never be torn, or a tree that would grow bigger and bigger but never die?"

"Which would you rather be — a very fluffy cloud or a sparkly lake?"

"Which would you rather be — a peacock feather or a sea gull feather?"

Have you ever wondered what you would like to be if you could be something different than what you are? I wonder why we like to play this game?

#### SUGGESTIONS

1. There are many lovely ideas in the poem, "I Would Be a River," to which children respond warmly. The adult might tell about several of the ideas, perhaps closing with the picture of the deer drinking from the river.

2. It would be very effective to have a series of large pictures to use with this conversation: a tall pine tree, a meandering river, an archeologist, or other items mentioned in the poem by the children.

*. . . And one day [Louis Braille] got the notion of dots in variation, that is, of dots that could be interchangeable with what he called*

[4] Helen Harrington, *op. cit.*

*"the alphabet folding back on itself."* — J. ALVIN KUGELMASS,
Louis Braille: Windows for the Blind*


## 4. *Six Dots*[5]

NOTE: For this conversation, it would be a good idea to have on hand a book
printed in Braille. The children could have an opportunity to examine the book and
to feel it. The conversation might then begin like this:

Can you read this book? I can't. But some people can. Do
you know who they are? Yes, blind people. Do you know how
they read it? By feeling of the pages. But I can't read it when *I*
feel of the pages, because I don't know what all the little bumps
mean.

When you started the first grade, you soon learned, with your
eyes and your brain, what the letter A looked like. When a blind
child starts school, he soon learns, with his fingers and his brain,
what the letter A *feels* like. It doesn't feel the way the letter A is
shaped. That is why I can't read this book.

I want to tell you the story of the man who decided what the
letter A should feel like for blind people.


One day about 150 years ago in a small town in France, a
little boy was playing in the sun on the steps of his father's shop.
The little boy was named Louis Braille and he was just three years
old.

His father was a leather worker and made such things as
saddles and boots. He was very busy making some leather reins
for a customer who wanted them by evening. He was proud of his
little son because he already showed signs of great intelligence. He
always enjoyed having him play near his shop, and little Louis
liked to be there because his father let him have the scraps of left-
over leather to play with. On this particular day, Louis had found
a piece that was not quite the shape that he wanted it to be. He
decided to change it.

Children the age of Louis usually watch what grownups are
doing very carefully. He had seen his father shape the leather many
times. He knew just the tool that was needed.

Children as old as Louis are also great ones to want to do
things "all by themselves," even when they are not old enough to do
such things safely. So Louis found the sharp tool that he needed
and started to shape the leather the way he wanted it.

* (New York: Messner, 1951), p. 118.
[5] The information in this story has been taken from J. Alvin Kugelmass,
*op. cit.* Originally titled "Louis Braille" © 1961 by Edith F. Hunter.

Of course, if his busy father had seen what Louis was doing, he would have taken the dangerous tool from him and cut the leather for him.

Suddenly Louis screamed. In trying to cut the leather, the tool had slipped and badly injured his eye. His father rushed to him, wrapped his injured face in a cloth and, with him in his arms, rode his horse to the only doctor in the village, a veterinarian or animal doctor.

After looking at the eye even this doctor could tell that the accident was very serious. Since Louis had great pain in his other eye, too, the doctor was afraid the injury might have damaged it as well. Both eyes were bandaged, and Louis was taken home.

The next day, through an important friend, they were able to take the boy to one of the finest doctors in France. He examined him and then held a bright light before Louis' face. The little boy said he could see nothing. Louis Braille was completely blind and would be blind for the rest of his life.

At the time that Louis Braille was growing up in France there were many who were blind. But people did not realize in those days how much a blind person can learn through his other senses, his ears and his sense of touch in particular. Very few of the blind were given any education, and many of them were cruelly treated. Because they had not been taught how to do anything to earn a living, many of the blind stood on the streets and begged.

Louis Braille was really very fortunate. His father and mother loved him dearly and from the time of his accident they were very careful to put money aside for him. They did this so that he would never have to beg to support himself after they were dead.

But, more important than that, not only for Louis himself but for all of the blind people of the world since then, his parents were able to send him to a special school. At that time there were almost no schools for the blind. Louis was sent to one of the few, and the finest one there was in France.

More than anything else, Louis wanted to learn to read and write. A blind person cannot see the letters that are printed in a book. If he runs his hand over the printed words, he cannot feel the letters, either.

The man who ran the school to which Louis went was experimenting with ways of printing so that the blind students could feel the letters. By the time Louis came to the school, there was a small library of books. These had been printed in a special way so that each letter stood up from the paper. This is called embossing.

But, in order that the children could feel each letter clearly, the letters had to be very large. They were an inch tall. That is as tall as the letters often are in a newspaper headline. This meant that each page of writing could contain only a few lines, and each line only a few words. One book in the library might be a great big volume and weigh as much as twenty pounds, but even then it would include just a small part of the whole book. In addition to this, the whole process of embossing was extremely expensive.

Louis loved to read and soon learned to read these embossed books. But he was not satisfied. To read in this way is very slow, since the shape of each letter must be followed. Moreover, he didn't want to read just little parts of books; he wanted to be able to read the whole book just as seeing people could.

And so, for years and years, these questions were in the back of Louis Braille's mind: how could books be printed for the blind so that they could be read quickly, so that the whole book could be printed, and so that they would not be too expensive? He also hoped to discover a way in which a blind person could write and then be able to read what he had written to himself. In this way, he could correct any mistakes he had made.

One day, when he was twenty years old, a friend was reading the newspaper to him. She read a short story about an army captain who had invented a system of writing that soldiers could read and write in the dark. Why do you suppose it might be useful for someone in the army to be able to read in the dark?

The writing was not done with a pencil, but with a sharp pointed piece of metal. The tool, called a bodkin, made a bump in the paper, but not a hole in it. The person read what was written with his fingers by feeling of the bumps.

Instead of arranging the punches in the shapes of our letters, the army captain had worked out some special symbols. For example, a circle of punches meant "We are surrounded"; a triangle of punches meant "We are being attacked from three directions."

As Louis Braille sat listening in the darkness in which he always sat, he suddenly became terribly excited. Here, as the army captain himself suggested, might be a kind of writing that the blind could both write and read. Louis was so excited at the idea in the story that he asked the woman who was reading to him to take him to talk to the army captain that very day.

For Louis Braille this was only the beginning of the journey toward the great discovery that has made his name a word in our language. Have you ever heard of "Braille"? It is the system of writing for the blind now used all over the world — the one that Louis Braille finally worked out.

He decided to use the army captain's idea of making punches in the paper. But he could not use the symbols, such as circles and dots, for words. He needed to work out a system of arranging the dots that would make it possible to say everything that is in ordinary books. Circles and dots would not do at all.

For the next three years Louis Braille experimented with his metal bodkin and with pieces of paper. Although he was now a famous organist and taught the blind every moment he could, he worked on the problem of how to arrange the dots.

### Braille Alphabet and the Six Dots

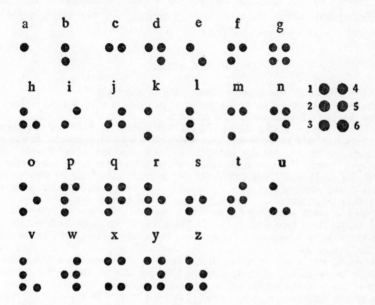

He knew it would not work well to arrange them in the shape of each of our letters. That would be almost the same thing as embossing and it would have to be very large, because each letter would take so many dots. This would be slow to read and write, too. He had also thought of having one dot for the letter *a*, two dots for the *b*, and so on until there would be — how many dots for the letter *z*? No, that would never do!

And then, after trying hundreds of plans, he suddenly hit on a wonderfully simple arrangement, now known as the "Braille cell." This cell or block of dots has six dot positions. It is two dots wide and three dots high.

The letter *a* is one dot, in position *1*. The letter *b* is two dots in positions *1* and *2*. The letter *c* is two dots too, but in positions *1* and *4*. Even the letter *z* is only four dots, in positions *1, 3, 5* and *6*.

No letter can take up more space than two dots wide and three dots high. A page written in Braille is larger, but not much larger, than a normally printed page.

Louis Braille was thrilled when he discovered his system. He worked out a simple method, using his dots for writing numbers and for writing music. He found that if someone read aloud to him he could write down what they said almost as quickly as they read. He could re-read what he had written and find his own mistakes.

With his six dots he had solved all of the problems that had bothered him about the old ways of writing for the blind, all with six dots — six very special dots.

### OTHER IDEAS

The following ideas would be interesting to older children.

1. Braille is now used all over the world. If you gave a blind man in China one of our books in Braille, could he read it?

2. Although Louis Braille discovered his cell system in 1829 and on several occasions was able to demonstrate it before very influential groups, it was not accepted and he was actually forbidden to teach it at the school for the blind where he taught. The reason for this, apparently, was that the older method of embossing books was firmly entrenched and a great deal of money was invested in books and printing equipment. Not until 1854, two years after his death, did his system gain acceptance. He died a heartbroken man of forty-five.

3. People are still searching for ways to make life easier for the blind. It has been known for a long time that many blind people, but some in particular, are able to "sense" the presence of objects in a room. By some means they are able to "see" them and avoid bumping into them. Careful experiments have now been made, and it has been well established that their means of doing this is through "echolocation." Sounds from the blind person's footsteps, voice, clothing, cane or anything else hit the objects and return echoes to the extremely sensitive ears of the blind person. This discovery has led to further experiments, still in process, to develop an effective sound source that a blind person might carry, such as a clicker or cane. The book *Echoes of Bats and Men,* by Donald Griffin, in the Science Study Series (Anchor, 95¢), contains information on this subject that would make interesting discussion material for Junior High and older young people. See especially Chapter 6, "Suppose You Were Blind."

4. The *First Book of Codes and Ciphers,* by Sam and Beryl Epstein (New York: Watts), might be used as a resource for other conversations along these lines.

### SUGGESTIONS

1. It would add greatly to this conversation to have a Braille slate and stylus with which to demonstrate the writing of Braille. The children would be thrilled to have their names written in Braille for them to keep. Slate, stylus and paper can be bought from The Howe Press, Perkins School for the Blind, Watertown 72, Massachusetts, and The American Printing House for the Blind, 1839 Frankfort Avenue, Louisville 6, Kentucky. They are inexpensive.

2. A large blackboard on which the Braille alphabet could be written would be useful.

> *At that time (when she was 8), a dear relative who was also an earnest Christian, tried to tell her about God, but, as this lady did not use words suited to the comprehension of the child, they made little impression upon Helen's mind. When I subsequently talked with her she said: "I have something very funny to tell you. A. says God made me and everyone out of sand; but it must be a joke. I am made of flesh and blood and bone, am I not?" Here she examined her arm with evident satisfaction, laughing heartily to herself. After a moment she went on: "A. says God is everywhere, and that He is all love; but I do not think a person can be made out of love. Love is only something in our hearts. Then A. said another very comical thing. She says He (meaning God) is my dear father. It made me laugh quite hard, for I know my father is Arthur Keller."*
> — HELEN KELLER, The Story of My Life*

## 5. *Thinking About Ideas of God*

Probably every one of us has heard the word *God* many times. But many of us, children and grownups, often feel quite mixed up when we hear the word *God* used.

Why is this? For one thing, different people say such different things about what God is and what God does. They do not seem to agree about it at all.

Listen to some of the things that I have heard people say that God *is*.

God is nature.

God is a great force.

God is life.

God is everything.

God is love.

God is what makes things grow.

God is our father.

Have you heard people say some of these things?

Here are some of the things that I have heard people say that God *does*.

God made the world.

God makes there be something instead of nothing.

God can do anything. He's magic.

* (New York: Doubleday, 1954), p. 311.

God sees everything we do.
God keeps the world from falling.
God takes people when they die.
God is in everything.
Have you heard people say some of these things?

There seem to be many different ideas here, don't there? They don't fit together very well either. I don't think you could believe all of these things at the same time, if you really thought about them.

So it seems to be true to say that people don't all mean the same thing when they use the word *God*.

You may have a different idea of what God is and of what God does from any of the ideas I have listed here, or you may not have any ideas at all about God.

Perhaps your very best friend says that God is one thing and you say that you don't think that at all. This has happened over and over again in the world: people have not agreed about ideas of God. And there just isn't any way to make absolutely certain which idea of God is *the* right one, or even whether any idea of God is the right one. It would be very nice if there were some way of finding this out for sure, but there isn't.

Ideas of what God is and what God does have been so important that some people have even killed other people because they would not agree with their idea about God. And sometimes the person who was going to be killed has said: "Go ahead and kill me, but I won't change what I think."

Because this has happened so often, there is one very wonderful rule or law in our country. That law is that anyone who lives in the United States must always be allowed to decide for himself what he thinks God is and what God does.

There is no *one* way of thinking about God that everyone must agree to in our country. We even are free to have no idea of God. No one church is the American church. We have religious freedom.

The rule about religious freedom is a good rule for our country. It means that every one of us has the right to do our own thinking about these ideas.

(One session might stop here, if much discussion has been aroused.)

Why are there these different ideas of God? Why can't we just show each other exactly what we mean by this word?

The answer to that is that God does not seem to be something that we can show each other. God is not something like a table or a chair that we can point to and say: "There, that is what I mean by God."

God is not something we see or hear or touch. God is something people have figured out because of what we see and hear and touch. For this reason there have been and still are many different ideas of God.

One idea of God that people in many parts of the world have gradually figured out is the idea of God as a Person, a very special kind of Person. When people say that God sees, or God hears or God loves, it usually means that they have this idea of God as a special kind of Person.

People with this idea usually believe that God can not be seen or touched or heard as other people can. They say He does not live in the world of nature as you and I do. They usually believe that He made the world and that He can make things happen in the world. They would say that God is above nature — He is *super*-natural.

There are many people with this idea of God. And there are many other people who do not think that this idea of God is the right one.

But there is no way that a person who believes that this is the right idea of God can show this god person to someone who does not believe that this is the right idea of God.

Another idea of God that many people in the world have worked out is the idea that God is the Life Force in things. They believe that God is the life in a seed, the life in a person, the life in a growing tree. Sometimes people with this idea of God believe that even stones have some of this life in them. They believe that God is somehow in everything.

Do you think that a person who has this idea of God could show God to someone else? No, because although the other person can see that some things are alive, he may not choose to call the life force "God." He may say, "I just think some things are alive."

Another idea of God that many people have worked out is the idea of God as the power that keeps the sun, the planets, the stars, our earth moving in the regular way in which they always move. People with this idea think of God as the power that keeps the tiniest things, like atoms, moving in an orderly way, too.

There are many other ideas of God. Probably there are ideas of God that haven't even been thought of yet.

Ideas of God grow and change very slowly as people live and wonder about this world of ours. People cannot seem to help wondering and trying to understand.

You are just at the beginning of your life. You are just learning how to do all kinds of things: jump rope, ride a two-wheeler, walk on stilts. And you're just learning how to read and write and figure things out.

All through your life you'll find yourself learning new things and thinking. One thing you will think about is different ideas of God. You don't have to decide today which idea I've told you about is true, or whether any of them are. You couldn't really decide that yet: you haven't lived long enough. But it is something you'll find interesting to think about for your whole life. It is something no one else can do for you.

## OTHER IDEAS

1. Two stories in *From Long Ago and Many Lands*, "The Fig Seed" and "The Lump of Salt," could be the focal point of subsequent conversations. Both are concerned with the idea of God.
2. With older children it might be interesting to try to discover what ideas of God are implied in several hymns. Songs 33–38 in *We Sing of Life* might be examined for this purpose.

## SUGGESTIONS

1. This conversation and the two that follow are not included because they are about matters that naturally fascinate children. Children are interested in the realities that have caused men to evolve concepts of God, miracle and natural law. But these evolved concepts are so abstract and generalized that children have a difficult time (as did little Helen Keller) making much out of them. However, because of adult pressures, the concepts are often the subject of heated debates among children, and therefore a discussion may give the children some emotional relief. It might also provide some intellectual preparation for grappling with the concepts in the years ahead. These conversations should be used with discretion and perhaps over several sessions.
2. An adult using this material would find *Religion in the Making*, by Alfred North Whitehead (New York: Meridian), stimulating for background reading.

*Everywhere I am hindered of meeting God in my brother, because he has shut his own temple doors and recites fables merely of his brother's or his brother's brother's God. Every new mind is a new classification.* — RALPH WALDO EMERSON, "Self-Reliance"*

## 6. *Where Do Ideas of God Come From?*

A little boy once asked me this question: "Where did people ever get the idea of God?" No one can touch God. No one can hear God. No one can see God. So where did they get the idea of God?

* *Essays*, First Series, I. (Boston: Houghton Mifflin, 1904), 79.

Do you think that, if no one ever told you his idea of God, you would ever think of an idea of God by yourself?

What is there that might make you think of such an idea, if you hadn't heard the word?

If there *is* anything that would give you this idea, it must be just about everywhere in the world, because ideas of God have grown up in every part of the world. And whatever it is must always have been in the world, because men from earliest times until now have had some idea of God or of gods.

What are some of the things that *are* everywhere now and probably always have been everywhere? What things might the very earliest people have struggled with and wondered about that every single one of us wonders about, too? Can you think of anything?

The sun, the moon, the stars and the planets and our own earth — these are things that have always been here and about which people have always wondered.

How can the sun come up every morning in one place in the sky and go down every night in just about the opposite direction? How does it get back to the first place again? Is there a tunnel under the ground? How can it do it every day and never miss once? What keeps the sun hot all the time? If it is on fire, why doesn't it burn up?

And the moon — is there anything that you wonder about the moon? Does anyone live there? Can man live on it? Long ago people wondered about it for other reasons. They had to travel a great deal of the time to find food. The moon was very important to them as a source of light at night. They needed to know when the moon was going to be full, when it was going to be just a tiny piece of a moon, and when there was going to be no moon at all.

How can it be that, at times, great bites have been taken out of the moon, at other times it is a full round ball, and at other times we don't see it at all? And how can it be that sometimes it is all covered up by a great shadow? What makes the moon shine? Can you tell by looking at it? How do you suppose men found out the answer to that question?

The stars make us wonder too. How many are there? Why do some twinkle? Why are some red, some blue and some yellow?

Why do some stars seem to shoot across the sky and fall? Why don't the other stars fall, and the sun and the moon too? Why do all the stars seem to move together around one star like a great wheel over our heads?

All except a few stars, that is. These few stars don't twinkle. Why? They don't move with the other stars in the great sky-wheel. These few "stars," the planets, wander on paths of their own. *Planet* means "wanderer." Do they really just wander?

Where did sun, moon, stars, planets and our earth all come from? What keeps them all moving in such a beautiful, orderly way?

Such wonderings as these, and many more, have occurred to people all over the world for thousands and thousands of years. Thoughts and feelings about the sun, moon, stars, planets and our earth have been an important part of all people's ideas of God.

What other things are there in the world that are everywhere, always have been everywhere and have made people think and wonder? How about the wind, water and fire? They are everywhere in the world, aren't they?

"What makes the wind *start* blowing?" a little boy asked me once. Your little boy will probably ask you too. We are still finding out the answer to that question.

Why is the wind warm and gentle, sometimes, and cold and wild at other times? Why does it come from the east on one day, and the north, south or west on another? What forms it into a tornado? What gives it the strength of a hurricane?

And the rain, snow and hail: where do they fall from? Will the rain ever be all used up? Why does it fall sometimes and not at other times? Why does it almost never fall over a desert? What shapes the snowflake and the frost crystal? Why do hard balls of ice sometimes come beating down?

What's happening up in the sky to make those rumbling noises, sometimes soft and distant, sometimes so loud and close it makes you cover your ears and duck your head? And those flashes of lightning at times like waves of light, and at other times great jagged streaks that seem to tear the sky apart: where do they come from and what do they mean? How can they sometimes turn a tree into a flaming torch, and sometimes start a whole forest burning?

If we lived out of doors much of the time, as did so many of our ancestors, we would have feared and wondered about many of these things much more than most of us do now. But, whether people think about these things often or just once in a while, what people think about them is also an important part of their idea of God.

Is there anything else that is everywhere and always has been everywhere? There is man himself, and all the things that happen to us.

We are born. Have you ever seen anything be born: a chicken hatch out of an egg, a butterfly pull itself out of a chrysalis, a kitten come out of its mother's body? Have you ever seen a tiny new baby, all pink and folded up like a flower bud? All people everywhere have seen such things and they have wondered.

We die. Why do we die? What makes the breath come regularly out of the living person, and then one day not come out? What is this breath? When a baby is born, for a second or two it does not breathe. Is the breath the life? Or is the blood the life? If a man loses very much blood, he dies. When a man dies, does the life go some place? Did it come from some place?

Have you ever wondered what was the difference between your little pet turtle that could crawl and poke out his head, and your pet turtle that was dead?

What people have thought about birth and death has also been an important part of their ideas about God.

There are many other things that happen to everyone, everywhere, that have made people wonder, think and try to understand. Much of this understanding has been expressed in ideas of God.

Where do ideas of God come from? They come very slowly from our living and thinking.

### OTHER IDEAS

1. The story "Gautama Finds Out for Himself," in *From Long Ago and Many Lands,* might be told in another session as an example of the kind of experiences that forced one man to make his religious pilgrimage. It might be interesting for older children to discuss the religious atheism of Buddha.
2. Men have always wondered whether there was anything that they could do to make the hurricane stop, the rain fall on their dry ground or the lightning avoid them. What men have decided could be done has changed and is still changing. This might lead into a discussion of ideas of prayer.

### SUGGESTIONS

1. The record *"Now We Know"* (Columbia Records, CL–670) has many songs that might be used in combination with this conversation.
2. Some may prefer to dwell on only one area in this conversation, such as the stars, or human beings. By making some of the wonders of one area very vivid, the relation between the experiences and the deduced idea of God might be clearer to children.
3. The book *Beginnings: Earth, Sky, Life, Death,* by Sophia Fahs and Dorothy Spoerl (Boston: Beacon Press, 1958), is a collection of myths from all over the world. They reflect men's early attempts to solve the riddles of existence. The

modern scientist's story is also included. The stories are written for upper elementary children and would make excellent background material for adults.

*Why, who makes much of a miracle?*
*As to me I know of nothing else but miracles,*
*Whether I walk the streets of Manhattan,*
*Or dart my sight over the roofs of houses toward the sky,*
*Or wade with naked feet along the beach just in the edge of the*
*        water,*
*Or stand under trees in the woods,*
*Or talk by day with any one I love, or sleep in the bed at night with*
*        any one I love,*
*Or sit at table at dinner with the rest,*
*Or look at strangers opposite me riding in the car,*
*Or watch honey-bees busy around the hive of a summer forenoon,*
*Or animals feeding in the fields,*
*Or birds, or the wonderfulness of insects in the air,*
*Or the wonderfulness of the sundown, or of stars shining so quiet*
*        and bright,*
*Or the exquisite delicate thin curve of the new moon in spring;*
*These with the rest, one and all, are to me miracles,*
*The whole referring, yet each distinct and in its place.*

*To me every hour of the light and dark is a miracle,*
*Every cubic inch of space is a miracle,*
*Every square yard of the surface of the earth is spread with the*
*        same,*
*Every square foot of the interior swarms with the same.*
*To me the sea is a continual miracle,*
*The fishes that swim — the rocks — the motion of the waves — the*
*        ships with men in them,*
*What stranger miracles are there?* — WALT WHITMAN, "Miracles"*

## 7. What Is a Miracle?[6]

Do you know what a miracle is?

Once some children were asked this question, and these are some of the answers they gave:

A little boy said: "A miracle is something that seemed like it

* *Leaves of Grass and Selected Prose,* ed. John Kouwenhoven (Modern Library ed.; New York: Random House, 1950), p. 306.
[6] This conversation is adapted from material by Mary Jane Dunwiddie.

couldn't happen, but it did, and you can hardly believe it is true."

"Tell me a miracle," I said.

"The grass was all brown and dry and looked dead, and then the rain came and it was all green."

A little girl said: "How a tree can grow from a tiny seed, that's a miracle."

Another little girl said: "You look at an egg. It looks dead; but a hen sits on it and a little chick comes out. That's a miracle."

And another boy said: "A big six foot man grows from something no bigger than a germ. That's a miracle."

Yes, those are just exactly what some people mean when they use the word *miracle.*

A famous poet, Walt Whitman, wrote a whole poem about miracles like these. The poem is about some of the most common things in the world, and yet Walt Whitman believed that if we would really think about these things, we would realize that each one of them is a miracle.

(Read some lines from his poem, "Miracles," quoted at the beginning of this conversation. Dwell on one or two examples a bit so that the children really grasp why Whitman called them miracles.)

The poet asked a question at the end of his poem. "What stranger miracles are there" than these? He asked this because he knew that some people do not use the word *miracle* to describe these common wonders, but they use it to describe some very uncommon things.

Probably you have already heard of some of these "strange" things that some people call miracles. In one of the stories told about the birth of Jesus, a great star appeared in the sky and led the wise men to the place where the new baby lay.

Some people would say that God made the star suddenly appear: He performed a miracle. They would not call the way the grass turns green in the spring a miracle, or the hatching of an egg, or a little boy growing into manhood. They would say all these are just ordinary things. But Walt Whitman, and people who think about the world the way he did, would say, "Oh, but if we really think and pay attention to these ordinary things, we see they are really *extra*ordinary — *outside* of the ordinary — every one of them. Everything that nature or God does is a miracle." When Walt Whitman used the word *God,* he meant the same as *nature.*

He would say that the regular way in which the stars move in the sky, and the way that it is possible for us to know just where every star will be on a certain night ten or one hundred or even a thousand years from now — this, he would say, *is* a miracle. He would say that for him the wonderful orderliness of the stars is far more of a miracle than having a star just suddenly appear in the sky.

Another one of these "strange" miracles of which you may have heard has to do with stories told about Jesus at Easter. Some people say that after Jesus died, at Easter time, his body rose up from being dead and became alive again. People who believe that this really happened say that this was a miracle.

But people who see the world as Walt Whitman did and who use the word *miracle* in the way he did say, "No, when a person's body is buried, his body cannot become alive again." But the miracle that we do celebrate at Easter is the bursting forth of new life in the spring. Is it not a miracle that, somehow, all living things can form an egg or seed through which the spark of life is handed on? "What stranger miracle is there" than this?

You will find these two ways of using the word *miracle* among your friends, both grownups and children. If you listen carefully, perhaps you can figure out which way they are using the word. Do they think a miracle is some "strange" happening, some unusual thing like a great star suddenly appearing in the sky or dead people coming alive again? Or do they think a miracle is some "common" happening, some *extra*ordinarily ordinary thing, like a baby being born or a seed sprouting?

You can not say that one person is using the word *miracle* in the right way, and that the other way is wrong. People all over the world have used the word in both of these ways.

But what you can and must decide, not today but gradually as you are growing up, is: which way of using this word fits in with my ideas about the kind of world this is?

Of course, it isn't people who choose which kind of world this is. The world is the way it is, and all we do is try to discover what it is like. Does it seem to be the kind of place in which dead bodies sometimes come alive again? Do enormous stars sometimes just suddenly appear?

All during the years that you are growing and learning, you will be asking yourself: "What kind of world is this, really? What am I going to think is a miracle?"

### OTHER IDEAS

1. The way a person uses the word *miracle* is related to what he means by *God*, also. If this conversation is used with more mature groups, the relation of this conversation to those on ideas of God might be pointed out and developed.

2. A Jewish group using this material might want to use such examples as the oil at Hanukka or Moses and the Red Sea. These are both "strange" miracles related to the "common" miracles of the winter solstice and spring equinox.
3. Other miracles might well be used, but a few examples were dwelt on here in order to keep this complex subject as simple as possible. It is a subject that confronts even young primary children in the form of heated arguments with friends.

### SUGGESTIONS

1. The poem "Talking In Their Sleep," p. 64 in *Poems to Grow On* (Boston: Beacon Press), might give children a vivid sense of the common miracle of spring.

## Section B. Long Ago

*And somehow, standing in the warm Spring sunlight on the high plains, I comprehended the matter of eons and ages. Without knowing geology, I sensed geologic time. I touched the beat of the big rhythms, the coming and going of oceans and the rise and fall of mountains. And, for a little while I was one not only with the Indians who had been there before me, but with those who were there before the Indians; not only with the grass which had greened with a thousand springs, but with that which was there before the grass. There had been ranchmen before we came, and Indians before ranchmen, and buffalo before the Indians. And long before the buffalo there had been an ocean, and clams. Back, back — how far back? And how far ahead? Time was indeed a strange thing. The time of the ant, the time of the tumble bug, the time of the prairie dog, the time of a boy. The time of a fossil clam.* — HAL BORLAND, High, Wide and Lonesome\**

### 8. *A Long Time Ago*

Have you ever found an Indian arrowhead? I used to look for them when I was little. I found a few, too.

When you hold something old in your hand, it makes you wonder. What was the Indian like who chipped that piece of stone into an arrowhead? And the Indian who shot it, what was he shooting at — a buffalo, another Indian or a pioneer going west?

You can never know the answers to questions like these, but you feel like asking them just the same.

Of course there are things that are a lot older than Indian arrowheads, aren't there? Time goes back long before the Indians.

\* (Philadelphia: Lippincott, 1956), p. 215.

Do you know something you might find that is much older than an arrowhead?

Have you ever found a rock with a print of a shell or a leaf on it? Do you know what you call a rock like that? It is called a fossil.

How did the print get on that stone? The rock is very hard. If you press the shell against it, it doesn't make a mark. You'll probably just break the shell.

And how could a fern leaf leave a print of itself on a rock? But it has! There are even fossil prints of butterflies, bird feathers, waves, raindrops, the comb of a wasp's nest and a spider with some of the thread it was using to make a web!

You probably know the answer to how this could happen. The rock that is now so hard was once soft. It was mud or sand or rock in some other soft form. The print of the plant or shell or other more delicate things was made thousands, even millions of years ago. There are fossils 500 million years old.

The shell that left its print in the rock may have been lying on sand and then gradually been covered over by more sand. The layers of sand pressed down on each other for thousands and thousands and thousands of years. As they pressed down, they hardened and were cemented together. The sand became sandstone.

There are places in our country where you can find sandstone just full of fossils. If you take a rock hammer and crack the sandstone open you'll find hundreds of shell prints inside.

The fossils that show leaf prints may be in stone that was once mud. Have you ever made a leaf print on clay? You find a leaf that has a pretty shape and press it into the soft clay. Then, very carefully, you lift the leaf off the clay. If you let the clay dry, the leaf print will stay right there.

Some fossil prints of leaves were made by nature in much the same way. Of course, no person carefully laid the leaf on the mud. It may have been blown there by the wind or it may have floated to the bottom of a river or drifted onto a mudbank at the side of a river.

However it happened, the leaf was then buried by more mud, and after thousands and thousands of years, this mud turned to rock, perhaps to shale. When that rock is cracked open, the print of the leaf will be found.

Finding fossils is exciting. There are many other kinds of fossils beside prints in stones. Old bones, tracks in stone, wood that has turned to stone ("petrified" wood) and shells that have turned to stone are some of the other kinds of fossils you might find.

There are certain parts of our country where you are more likely to find fossils than in other parts. If you want to go fossil hunting, be sure you go to a place where fossils are apt to be found. (See Suggestion 1.) If there is a science museum near where you live, someone there can give you help on this.

I want to read you a page from a book in which a man tells about something that happened to him when he was a boy. He was living in Colorado and he was out riding on his horse. This is what he wrote:

. . . As I rode down the hollow I came to a fresh cut bank that had washed out in the Spring melt. The grass had caved away leaving a bank of fresh gravelly soil. Such a place was always worth searching for arrowheads. I got off and began poking through the gravel.

It was different from the gravel on our land, coarser and full of lumps of sandstone. The sandstone was grayish yellow. There was a thin ledge of it reaching back under the grass. I sifted a few handfuls through my fingers and stood up, about to leave. Then I scuffed at it with my toe and a smooth, rounded flat piece caught my eye. It wasn't a pebble. It was almost the size of a silver dollar, but smooth and rounded.

Even as I picked it up I sensed that here was something out of time so remote [long ago] that my mind could not quite grasp the distance. It was a fossil clam, and the place I found it was fifteen hundred miles from the nearest ocean.

There it was, a clam turned to stone, a petrified clam with fluting around the edges of the twin shells, with bits of sandstone still clinging to it. Different from the fresh-water clams of the Missouri river, but still a shellfish, something from an ocean that once had been where I stood.[7]

Well! That was quite a find. A shell turned to rock! He had found something a lot older than an Indian arrowhead!

If you look at the map of the United States, you'll see that Colorado is a long way from any ocean now. But it wasn't always that way. Several times in the three or four billion years since our earth has been formed, oceans have covered parts of the world that are now land.

Was there ever an ocean over the part of the country where you live? See if you can find out. If there was, it might make for interesting fossil hunting.

We think of oceans and mountains as things that have always been just the way they are now. That is because we live for such a short time compared to the age of our earth. If we could live for a million years, we could see that our earth is always changing, and always has been changing.

Some mountains are wearing down and getting smaller as the

[7] Hal Borland, *loc. cit.*

rain beats on them and the wind blows on them. Some mountains are getting bigger as the earth trembles and pushes up. Oceans are sinking down and oceans are pushing higher, but to the eyes of human beings like us, mountains and oceans seem to stay the same.

It's fun to find old things like Indian arrowheads and fossil shells. If Indian arrowheads or fossil shells could talk, think of the stories they could tell of Indians and cave men and animals of thousands of years ago.

### SUGGESTIONS

1. *An Illustrated Guide to Fossil Collecting,* by Richard Casanova (San Martin, Calif.: Naturegraph, 1957), is full of material that will enrich this conversation. Pages 72–78 list known collecting localities, state by state.
2. Excellent information and pictures can be found in "Fossils Lift the Veil of Time," by Harry S. Ladd and Roland W. Brown, the *National Geographic,* March 1956. See also: *Rocks and Minerals,* a Golden Nature Guide, by Zim and Shaffer (New York: Simon and Schuster).
3. The leader should have several arrowheads and fossils to show. Many children will have these and will be eager to share them.

*Mike, age five, and I went to the Museum of Natural History. This in itself is a moving experience, but of most interest to him were the dinosaurs.*

*When we went into the huge room with the immense Tyrannosaurus, I noticed that he was very studiously avoiding looking at the big fellow in the middle of the room. He was concentrating on the smaller exhibits on the walls of the room.*

*Finally I said, "Mike, aren't you going to look at the Tyrannosaurus?" (We had recently studied about this particular dinosaur.)*

*"Oh I will, Mama, but I'm saving the very best 'til the last."*
— AN UNKNOWN MOTHER

### 9. *Dinosaur Tracks* — $25

How would you like to buy a dinosaur's footprint? You really can, in Texas, near Dallas. It might cost about $25.

Perhaps you are wondering how you could *buy* a footprint. A footprint has to be *in* something. These are in rock that has been dug out of other rock. But it wasn't rock when the dinosaur made the print. Even though some of these dinosaurs weighed as much as 60,000 pounds, that isn't weight enough to push rock in and make a footprint.

No, when the dinosaur walked on it 150 million years ago it wasn't rock; it was mud. Then the mud dried and dried and was pushed down, and heated by the earth, and finally turned into rock. Now it's a fossil footprint.

What would you do with one of those footprints if you did buy one? You'd need a truck to bring it home, because it would probably weigh several hundred pounds. Some of these footprints are three feet long. Do you know how long that is? They go down very deep in the rock. If you filled one up with water it would hold over fifty quarts of water. Perhaps you could put it out in the garden and use it as a bird bath, or even a wading pool for your baby brother. Some of the dinosaur footprints in Texas were along the side of a river and little children did use them for wading pools.

But maybe instead of buying one you'd rather just see one in a museum. You can see some very special ones in the Natural History Museum in New York City. It's interesting to know how they got there. (See Suggestion 1.)

They were found in Texas by a man named Mr. Roland Bird. He had been interested in dinosaurs for a long time and had been looking for dinosaur bones all summer in Wyoming. As he was driving home through Texas, he saw a sign over a roadside stand: DINOSAUR FOOTPRINTS FOR SALE — $25.

He stopped to look at them. They were big three-toed prints. Mr. Bird's special interest was one kind of dinosaur, the biggest one of all, *Brontosaurus.* One thing scientists didn't know was whether or not a Brontosaurus could actually walk. They thought that perhaps he was so huge and so heavy (seventy feet long, and weighing thirty tons) that his legs couldn't hold him up. Perhaps all he could do was crawl on his stomach or swim. So Mr. Bird thought that if he could find a set of four footprints, then he'd know — what?

He knew that the footprints that were for sale were not those of a Brontosaurus because the ones for sale had only three toes and the Brontosaurus had five toes. The bones of a Brontosaurus had already been found in Wyoming. But Mr. Bird thought that if he went to the place where the three-toed tracks were found, he might find some of the five-toed ones, too.

And that is just what happened. In several places he found both kinds of footprints. In fact, the trail made by the two kinds of dinosaurs was so clear that he could see that one kind of dinosaur was actually chasing the other!

The men at the museum for which Mr. Bird worked thought it would make a wonderful exhibit to have the real dinosaur footprints right underneath the dinosaur skeleton. Mr. Bird hired some helpers and they chiseled, or dug, out a whole section of the trail of dinosaur tracks. They had to take it out in pieces, the tracks were so huge and so heavy. As they were doing it, many of them broke into smaller pieces. Before they started chiseling, they took some pictures of the trail, so that when they got the pieces to New York, they could put them all together again like parts of a puzzle. Each piece was carefully numbered and wrapped as it was cut out. It took five months to make the puzzle when they got to New York.

If you ever see this exhibit of dinosaurs and their tracks, try to imagine that the dinosaur bones have flesh and skin and that the dinosaur is alive. And try to imagine that the tracks in the rock have changed back to mud again. And then try to imagine that you are really standing there watching this dinosaur race. But — do you know what? You just never could have been there! Not you, or your grandfather, or your grandfather's grandfather. Because when the dinosaurs lived, no *people* were yet alive. Dinosaurs lived 200 million to 60 million years ago. But the first man probably lived only 2 million years ago, or maybe only 500,000 years ago. People and dinosaurs were never alive at the same time!

### OTHER IDEAS

1. Those tracks had been right there in Texas for years and years and years. But until Mr. Bird found them, no one had really *seen* them. Children used to wade in them, fish used to be caught in them, but until Mr. Bird, who knew about different kinds of dinosaurs, studied them, no one knew about the dinosaur chase in Texas. What we see depends partly on what we know.
2. A workman, who was helping Mr. Bird dig out the footprints, asked a question one day. The trail of footprints disappeared under some rocks. Mr. Bird asked the workman to dig away the rocks. "Why?" asked the workman. "That great huge dinosaur couldn't have squeezed under those rocks." Mr. Bird laughed. Why did he?
3. When people heard what Mr. Bird and the workmen were doing, ten thousand sightseers came to watch and ask questions. Why were so many people interested? Why is the dinosaur room in any museum one of the most popular? Why did a librarian say that she thought she would never have enough dinosaur books for her library? Why do they sell model dinosaurs for boys and girls to make now? Why do people enjoy looking at and thinking about dinosaurs so much? A boy six years old said: "Because dinosaurs are so big." A boy seven years old said: "I don't know, but I just like to think back and back and back. I even like to think about *before* dinosaurs." A girl, thirteen, said: "I like to think that when those dinosaurs were there, Texas wasn't a bit like it is now. There were giant fern trees and swamps, and it was much hotter. But — the sun was just the same, I guess, and probably the stars and the moon. And probably the mud felt nice to the dinosaur, too, just like it does to us — but there weren't any of us to play in that mud."

### SUGGESTIONS

1. This is based on an article in the May 1954 issue of *National Geographic* magazine (vol. CV, No. 5), "We Captured a Live Brontosaur," by Roland T.

Bird. The pictures in this article are excellent and would add a great deal to the account, if the children could see them.

2. Dinosaur tracks can be bought in other parts of the country also. If you buy one from the Connecticut Valley you can carry it easily: the dinosaurs who made these were much smaller.

3. Large pictures of several of the dinosaurs, especially the Brontosaurus, should be posted. Of course, if anyone has dinosaur tracks they would be a great addition. A model dinosaur might also be brought in.

*It has been pointed out that for a penguin in Antarctica the Ice Age is here and now.* — BETTY FLANDERS THOMSON, The Changing Face of New England*

## 10. *A Fossil Forest*

I want to tell you about a very strange kind of forest — a fossil forest.

You know what a fossil is, don't you? Perhaps you have a stone with the print of a shell in it. Or perhaps you have a piece of petrified wood, wood that has been changed into stone. These are both fossils.

The fossil forest in Two Creeks, Wisconsin, is not a print of a whole forest in stone. And it isn't a forest that has turned to stone, either. There are such forests, petrified forests. There is one in Arizona that you may have visited.

This fossil forest is really a buried forest. I have some small pieces of wood from it. At first when you look at them, they just look like regular wood: little pieces of bark and small twigs.

But if you look more carefully, you can see that the twigs are actually rather flat. That is because they were pressed down by something very heavy, for thousands of years.

How do you suppose a whole forest could be flattened down and buried?

Perhaps you have seen men getting ready to build a new highway. They bring in enormous bulldozers, and if there are forests or hills in the way, they knock them down and move them away.

It wasn't a man-made bulldozer that flattened the fossil forest. It was one of Nature's bulldozers. Nature has several kinds of bulldozers it can use. I wonder whether you could guess what some of them are? Some work very quickly and some work very slowly.

Nature has high winds and rain, especially hurricanes and tornadoes. Have you ever seen a forest after a hurricane or a tornado? Giant trees are often pulled right up by their roots.

* (New York: Macmillan, 1959), p. 17.

Sometimes they are carried long distances and then thrown down. But it wasn't a hurricane or a tornado that flattened the fossil forest.

Nature also has earthquakes and volcanoes and landslides that can do the work of giant bulldozers. But it wasn't any of these. Nature has tidal waves and floods that can sweep away forests and whole towns. But none of these buried this fossil forest.

No. There is still another kind of bulldozer that Nature has, near the North and South Poles and in some of the highest mountains. Nature hasn't really used this bulldozer in the United States for about ten thousand years.

This bulldozer is a glacier. Do you know what a glacier is? A glacier is a great sheet of ice, hundreds of feet thick. Sometimes it is even a mile or two thick. It was a glacier that flattened the fossil forest, ten thousand years ago!

Three or four times in the last million years something happened to the weather in the far northern part of our world. Each winter snow fell as usual; and in summer it melted, but not quite all of it. Then when the first snow fell in the autumn, it covered some snow left from the winter before.

Scientists aren't sure, yet, why this happened. It may have been that our earth was tipped in a little different way. Anyhow, the snow began to pile up year by year, hundred years after hundred years. The snow packed down and turned to ice. When it grew thick enough it began to spread, the way a pile of wet sand spreads out at the bottom if you keep piling more sand on top of it. And so sheets of ice began to push down over large parts of the world, including northern Wisconsin.

Do you know what scientists call the time that this was happening? They call it the Ice Age, and it lasted about a million years. There are still large glaciers in Greenland and Antarctica, and smaller ones in such places as Canada, Alaska and Switzerland. But they are not as huge as those of the Ice Age and they are gradually melting.

During the Ice Age, a glacier would start growing in the north and slowly spread over a large area. You just can not imagine how *slowly* this "slowly" is. If you went away for a year and came back it might not seem to have moved much. Sometimes, too, it would melt back for some distance and then start to grow forward again. All this took thousands of years.

Some scientists think that even now we are just in the period between the melting back of the last glacier and the start of a new one. That shouldn't worry us, however. You and I couldn't possibly live to see that new glacier come. It takes too many thousands of years. But even though we can't be around to see the next glacier, if it does form, there is a way that we can go back ten thousand years and almost see how the glacier behaved in Two Creeks, Wisconsin.

The glacier had melted back from Two Creeks (of course, it wasn't called Two Creeks!) and left some new clay soil on the ground. Plants and trees began to grow and some of the trees had gotten quite large.

Then back came the glacier again! Nature's bulldozer came slowly forward — oh so slowly — and down went the trees before it. Can you imagine this huge mass of ice sliding slowly southward, knocking down trees as it came, crushing them under its tremendous weight?

After it had knocked down the forest that we call "fossil forest," it melted back again. Once more it left several feet of clay, this time on top of the forest it had crushed.

It is this clay that saved fossil forest for us. If the clay had not covered the wood, air and fungus and plants and insects would have gotten to it and the trees would have rotted. You know how it is with trees that fall down in the woods — they get soft and crumbly and become soil again. This didn't happen to the trees at Two Creeks because of the clay that covered them.

Fossil forest is now at the edge of a lake. If you want to visit it, a good time is in the spring. But if you didn't know anything about its being there, you might go there and never see a single thing.

If you stand on the shore of the lake, the land rises up sharply beyond the beach. This is called a *bluff*. It is mostly bare reddish clay with a narrow dark strip running across it.

If you go over and examine this dark strip carefully, you will discover that this dark strip is made up of sticks, twigs and roots all squeezed together. This is the fossil forest! Above it is clay dropped by the glacier, and below it is clay dropped by the glacier.

The cliff by the lake is really like a sandwich, but instead of bread, jam, bread, it is made of clay, fossil forest, clay. If you dig into the dark band of twigs and sticks you will find that it goes far back into the cliff.

In among the sticks and twigs there are even some little cones that look like those on our spruce trees. These cones have seeds in them. Scientists who have tested the wood from this forest say it is ten thousand years old. So the seeds must be that old too. Imagine seeds ten thousand years old! I wonder whether they would grow?

Unless you knew about the fossil forest, you probably wouldn't even notice that the sticks and twigs have been flattened out. Sometimes in storms pieces of the wood are washed down on the shore of the beach. Probably some people have roasted wieners and marshmallows over ten thousand-year-old wood and have never known they were doing it!

### OTHER IDEAS

1. Has the place where you live ever been covered by a glacier? If you find out that it has, see if someone can show you some of the things glaciers did to the land there: left rock around, hollowed out valleys, made lakes, scratched rocks, etc.

### SUGGESTIONS

1. *The Story of The Ice Age,* by Rose Wyler and Gerald Ames, (New York: Harper's, 1956) is a very fine simple account, well illustrated, written for children age eight and over. It would give an adult excellent background for this conversation and the two conversations on cave men.
2. It would be helpful to have a map of the United States showing the farthest reaches of the ice sheet in North America. (See Casanova's *Fossil Collecting Guide,* p. 64.)
3. A drawing of a bluff showing a cross-section of the forest would clarify this for younger children.

*An important new discovery, made perhaps by an amateur, may be reported in your newspaper tomorrow or next week or next month. It may prove to be just the clue prehistorians have been hoping to find. Or it may upset one of their theories entirely, and send them off on a new track.* — SAM AND BERYL EPSTEIN, All About Prehistoric Cave Men\*

## 11. *The Puzzle — Finding the Pieces*

Perhaps you live in a part of the country where there are real caves; or perhaps you and your family have gone on a trip and you've had a chance to visit one.

I wonder why it is that grownups and children always seem to find caves so interesting?

When I was a little girl I lived in the city. There weren't any real caves there. But there was a large apartment house near my home with hollowed-out places all along the front of it. My brother

\* (New York: Random House, 1959), p. 130.

and I used to pretend that the hollows were caves and we'd hide in them and be cave men.

Did you ever pretend something was a cave? Sometimes piles of rocks make good make-believe caves, or you can even pretend to be in a cave under the dining-room table.

When you play at being a cave man, do you have to make up all the things you do, or are there some things you can really and truly know about cave people? Some things you can really know, can't you? Lots of books have been written about cave people, and more are being written all the time (see Suggestion 1). Museums sometimes have wonderful cave men scenes, too.

It is interesting to think that you and I can know more about the people who lived in caves than our grandfathers and grand-mothers did. Why? Because people are digging in many of these old caves and discovering more and more things left by cave people. And it's like putting together a puzzle: the more pieces of the puzzle that are found, the more pieces can be fitted together. We are beginning to get quite a good picture of what life was like long ago.

Right now, down in Alabama, there's a cave called Russell Cave, in which men are digging (see Suggestion 2). A few years ago a man named Mr. Paul Brown heard about this cave. He had always been interested in digging for Indian arrowheads and old pots and things like that. He knew that arrowheads had been found near Russell Cave. He decided that the cave itself might be a good place in which to dig.

Finally he and a friend had time to go there and do some digging. What a surprise was waiting for them! After only a little bit of digging, they began to find arrowheads, spear points, old pottery, bone needles. They knew immediately that this was much too important a discovery for them to keep to themselves. They thought men from a real museum should come and do the digging.

Mr. Brown got in touch with the Smithsonian Institute in Washington. Did you ever hear of that? They sent Mr. Carl Miller, from the *National Geographic* magazine, to look at the cave. Perhaps your family gets the *National Geographic* magazine. Mr. Miller agreed with Mr. Brown that this was an important find, and so the *National Geographic* and the Smithsonian Institute decided to organize a real expedition to study Russell Cave.

When archeologists (that is the name for those who study ancient people) dig somewhere, they don't just come in with shovels and pickaxes and start to dig. No, indeed — they plan the whole dig very, very carefully.

Do you know why? There are several reasons. For one thing,

they want to be able to keep a record of just exactly where each
thing is found, especially how deep down in the ground. That helps
tell them how old things are. Another reason for being careful is
that they don't want to break anything, and of course they don't
want to miss anything if they can help it.

Russell Cave is a very large cave. They couldn't dig up all
of it, so they had to choose just where to dig. Mr. Miller, the head
of the expedition, marked out a piece of ground inside the cave
thirty feet square. He divided the large square into thirty-six smaller
squares. Here the digging was to begin.

A crew of men had been hired to do the digging. Each man
was given a trowel, a big square sifter and a small paper bag. Then
each man was told in which square to start and to dig no deeper than
six inches down. Can you show me how much six inches is? Each
trowel full of dirt had to be examined carefully. Every stone tool,
bone object, special shell or other object that they found was put
in a small, numbered paper bag.

Then, just to make sure that nothing had been missed, all the
dirt that had been dug out was sifted once through the sifter. When
the first six inches in each square were dug up, then the digger was
allowed to start on the next six inches, putting all objects in a new
paper bag.

Mr. Miller said that many of the men who were doing the
digging were big, strong men who usually worked as coal miners.
At first they thought he was very queer to have them dig with such
tiny tools and so slowly and carefully. They told him that, if he
would let them use shovels and pickaxes, they could clear out all
the dirt in the whole cave in just a few days!

But Mr. Miller didn't just want the dirt cleared out; he wanted
what was *in* the dirt! When the workmen began finding things —
arrowheads, bone fishhooks, jawbones of bears and even human
graves — they became so excited and so interested that they were
willing to be just as slow and just as careful as Mr. Miller wanted
them to be.

I'd like to be one of the workers, wouldn't you? Even though
you couldn't keep anything that you find for yourself, it would be
exciting to be part of the expedition.

(Note: If there has been much response from the children, it
may be that you will want to stop here, using the next section and
the conversation that follows, in several related sessions.)

When an archeologist digs, where do you think the oldest
things are found — in the top layer or in the bottom? The oldest
things are on the bottom, aren't they? The things found on the top

layers may have been left there by people alive now, like you and me, who like to visit caves. The diggers cleared the top layer away quickly.

But the very next layer of dirt began to tell about Indians. Here the diggers found stone arrowheads, pottery, bones of turkeys and turtles, fishhooks made from the toe of a deer. They found layers and layers of dirt containing these things.

Mr. Miller believes, as do some other archeologists, that when the cave people felt that the floor of their caves had become too messy and dirty, they brought in "clean" dirt and spread it on the floor. In this way they covered up all the things that Mr. Miller and his workers are now uncovering. This is partly why the floor of the cave is so much higher now than it was thousands of years ago.

We can be glad that the cave people did such a strange kind of housekeeping. If they had swept everything out of the cave, the diggers wouldn't be finding such interesting things.

When the diggers had dug down seven feet — that's deeper down than any of us are tall — an interesting thing happened: they no longer found arrowheads, just spear points. An expert like Mr. Miller can tell the two apart easily. They didn't find pottery any more, but they did find woven baskets. The diggers wondered why this was. Mr. Miller thought he knew. Keep thinking and see whether *you* know.

At about the same depth, the grave of a cave man was found. He was lying on his side with his knees pulled up close to him. With his body they found two stone points and a stone tool. Quite near the body they found the bones of a dog, neatly buried. Slabs of stone had been placed around and above both of these bodies.

The second summer of the expedition (they only dig in the summer), they went down twenty-three feet. That's as deep as many houses are high. Here they found an old fireplace with some charcoal in it. Mr. Miller was very excited when they found this. Do you know what charcoal is? It is what is left after wood or other vegetable matter has been burned.

The diggers had found old fireplaces with charcoal many times before, but never as deep down. Remember, the further down they go, the farther back in time they go. They gathered the charcoal up very, very carefully with their trowels and little brushes. They put it in a jar, wrapped it up and Mr. Miller sent it off to be tested (see Suggestion 3).

Just in the last few years scientists have discovered a way to test charcoal so that they can know how long ago the fire burned in which the charcoal was made. Think of that! The tests showed that this charcoal was nine thousand years old. And still they hadn't reached the bottom of the cave floor!

From all the things that had been found, Mr. Miller felt that he was beginning to know a great deal about the cave men of Alabama.

Here are some of the "pieces" of the Russell Cave puzzle that were most important to him:

(1) Fireplaces or fire holes.

(2) Arrowheads, and then only spear points.

(3) Old pottery, and then only woven baskets.

(4) Shells with holes in them, and bear's teeth with grooves.

(5) The body of a man buried, and nearby the grave of a dog.

Think about these for a while. They told Mr. Miller a great deal about life in Alabama thousands of years ago. I wonder what they can tell us?

### SUGGESTIONS

1. An excellent simple introduction to cave people is *All About Prehistoric Cave Men*, by Sam and Beryl Epstein.
2. The account of the Russell Cave diggings is based on two articles in the *National Geographic* magazine (new articles on this dig may appear): "Life 8000 Years Ago," by Carl Miller and Brooks Honeycutt, in Vol. CX, No. 4, October 1956; "Russell Cave: New Light on Stone Age Life," by Carl F. Miller, in Vol. CXIII, No. 3, March 1958.
3. For information on the method of testing age by "Carbon 14," see the *National Geographic* article, "How Old Is It?," by Lyman Briggs and Kenneth F. Weaver, in Vol. CXIV, No. 2, August 1958.

*A culture is man's answer to the problems of survival, as a shell is the oyster's. But though the environment sets the problem, and limits the means for its solution, it never dictates the whole answer. The culture always adds something more than the problem calls for, something unpredictable, because unnecessary, a little something extra for its own sake, a surprise. If people learn to make pots for holding water, eventually they learn to make them beautiful. There is no language without its poetry.* — GENE LISITZKY, Four Ways of Being Human\*

### 12. *The Puzzle — Putting the Pieces Together*

Well, have you thought about those five pieces of the Russell Cave puzzle? Do you remember what they were?

Have you any idea what the fireplaces, especially the one with

\* (New York: Viking), p. 19; copyright © 1956 by Gene Lisitzky.

the charcoal that was nine thousand years old, showed Mr. Miller?
It showed him that there were men living in Russell Cave as long
as nine thousand years ago who knew how to make a fire, or at least
how to use one.

There was a time, you know, when men did not know how to
make a fire or how to use it. Such men had to eat their food raw
and could only live in parts of the world where they could keep
warm without fire. We don't know yet whether or not people like
*that* ever lived in Russell Cave.

Your dog never makes a fire on a cold day in order to keep
himself warm, does he? Man is the only animal who has learned
how to control fire. Almost all other animals are afraid of it.

So this is something Mr. Miller knew: the cave men of Russell
Cave were fire-users nine thousand years ago, and perhaps earlier.

Let's look at another piece of our puzzle.

Mr. Miller was particularly interested when his diggers told
him that they weren't finding arrowheads any more, just spear
points. What is the difference between an arrow and a spear?
Which one will go farther? Why? A bow-and-arrow combination
is really a way of making a spear go farther, isn't it? Which one
would be safer for you to use if you were after a wild animal? Why?

There was a time when men hadn't discovered the idea of the
bow and arrow. How do you suppose that idea was discovered?
Is there anything in nature that would give us the idea? Perhaps
bending a birch tree gave someone an idea. A bow and arrow
is quite a tricky thing.

Mr. Miller was excited when the diggers said there were no
more arrowheads, because that meant they were down so deep
that the people who lived in the cave at this time had not yet
discovered the idea of the bow and arrow. In some parts of the
world this idea was discovered much sooner than in others.

Another puzzle piece that was very interesting to Mr. Miller
was the fact that, after a while, his diggers stopped finding old
pottery. Instead of pottery they found woven baskets.

Do you know what a pottery jar is made of? Clay. Most of
us buy our clay in stores, but the stores buy it from people who dig
it out of the earth. Down in Alabama there is a lot of red clay in the
soil.

Did you ever make things out of clay? It's fun. When my
daughter was a little girl, she and I often used to play with clay.
One year I thought I would make her a little vase out of clay, for
her birthday. I made it when she was in bed one night, and then the
next night I painted it a pretty color.

The morning of her birthday, I filled it with water and put some

Johnny-jump-ups (tiny little pansy-like flowers) in it. I put it in front of her place at the breakfast table.

She liked it very much but, as we were eating, something happened. I looked at the little vase — it was sagging and melting and collapsing. Suddenly, while we were looking at it, it made a noise — like "glub, glub, glub" — and just fell in a heap on the table. The water ran out on the tablecloth and the Johnny-jump-ups lay down on the clay.

Do you know what I did *not* know about making clay pots? Clay must be glazed or painted in a special way and cooked or baked in a very hot oven in order to become watertight. Although I hadn't learned this, early men in various parts of the world learned it long ago.

But there was a time when even the cave people did not know this either. So when Mr. Miller's diggers stopped finding pottery and found only woven baskets, he believed that they had dug back to those early days before Alabama cave people had discovered the idea of pottery-making.

Mr. Miller believes that the shells with holes that the diggers found were worn as jewelry. He thinks that the bear's teeth were also worn in this way. Archeologists have found that wherever they find the remains of early man, such as fireholes, tools and pots, they always find things which show that man even then loved beautiful things. They decorated their tools, their weapons, their houses — everything. Why? Do you like shells and pretty stones? Do you like to draw pictures and paint things? I do.

One other piece of the puzzle that greatly interested Mr. Miller was the grave of the cave man and the dog. The grave of the dog showed several things. It showed first of all that these Alabama cave dwellers had dogs for pets. There was a time, no doubt, when men were afraid of all animals except themselves. Then, somehow, they learned to tame a few animals, such as the wolflike creatures that became our dogs. Probably they were not *just* pets, however; they were undoubtedly important in helping the cave men hunt.

The cave man's grave showed Mr. Miller several things, too. For instance, someone had placed the cave man's dead body in this specially dug hole. His body had been put in a certain position with heavy slabs of stone placed around and above it. Man is the only animal that buries his dead.

Most interesting of all to Mr. Miller were the stone points and stone tool that were found in the grave with the body, and the presence of the dog's grave nearby. Why do you suppose they were there? Mr. Miller and others believe that they show that the family and friends of this man thought that he might need them where he was going. Like some people in every part of the world, from the earliest times until now, these cave people seem to have believed that when a person dies, part of him does not die but goes somewhere. So they gave him his most valuable possessions to take along with him: his weapons, his tools and his dog.

Why do you suppose men have had this idea that when someone dies part of him goes somewhere? We may not know the answer to such a question, but we do know that it is a question the men of Alabama were asking and answering in their own way many thousands of years ago.

These Alabama cave dwellers were fire users, tool users, lovers of beauty and wonderers about death. Although some of them lived nine thousand years ago, they were quite a lot like us, weren't they?

Next time you play cave men, remember some of these things that you know about some real American cave men.

### OTHER IDEAS

1. When early people in various parts of the world tried to understand and explain different things about their world, they usually did it by telling a story. Nearly all peoples have stories or myths about where the first man came from, why people get sick and die, how the moon got in the sky and things like that. One story that nearly all early people had was how man first learned to make a fire. They knew this was an important discovery. One of the old myths about the discovery of fire might be read.

How *do* you suppose early men really did learn to start a fire? Do fires start by themselves in nature? Lightning can start a fire, can't it? So can a volcano. What about sparks from a piece of flint? Perhaps there were several different ways that early men first found out how to start a fire. (If someone could demonstrate starting a fire without matches and let the children try it, they might appreciate the accomplishment more.)

2. Ideas have been discovered at different times in different parts of the world. The Indians in this country never did discover the idea of a wheel. They learned it from the men who came over after Columbus. The ancestors of Columbus had discovered that idea thousands of years earlier.

It is interesting to think that there are ideas we haven't discovered yet, too. There are also ideas that we don't know as much about as earlier people did. Some ideas are being forgotten!

How best to chip stones is an example of this. Do you know how an arrowhead or a spear point looks? It isn't easy to get it that way. Once some of the scientists from the Smithsonian Institute decided that they would make some arrowheads, and discovered it was very difficult. You have to choose the right kind of stone, and then you have to hit the piece of stone in just the right way. It takes lots and lots of practice to get so that you can do it. Try it sometime.

Just as there was a time before which men had not discovered the idea of the bow and arrow, but used only spears, there was also a time when men hadn't discovered the idea of a spear. A spear is just a stick with something hard and sharp attached to the tip of it. It is really a way of making a man's arm longer. If he held the spear point in his fist, he'd have to be closer to the thing he wanted to kill.

But there was *even* a time when no one had discovered the idea of picking up a stone and using it to hit something else. Man is the only animal really to use tools or weapons.

The exceptions to this, animals that can use tools, are very interestingly discussed in *Animal Tools,* by George Mason (New York: Morrow Co., 1951).

## SUGGESTIONS

1. This subject is one that is tremendously popular with children six through ten years old and older. They may wish to stay with it for some time. For older young people, material for an experimental course, *Teaching Anthropology in Religious Education,* is available from the Department of Education, 25 Beacon Street, Boston 8, Mass.

2. A great deal of interesting and relevant material expressed quite simply may be found in *The Rainbow Book of People and Places* by Margaret Mead (New York: World, 1959).

3. *The Caves of the Great Hunters,* by Hans Baumann (New York: Pantheon, 1954), is an exciting account of the discovery of some of the caves with paintings in France. It gives an interesting interpretation of the religious meanings of the cave paintings.

4. Pictures and artifacts would add to the vividness of this material.

*. . . the riddle of age has always fascinated civilized man.*

*Think for a moment — what is your first question when you look at a mummy or a dinosaur skeleton in a museum, or find an arrowhead in a field. Inevitably you wonder, "How old is it?"*
— LYMAN BRIGGS AND KENNETH WEAVER, "How Old Is It?"*

## 13. How Old Is Old?[8]

How old is old? Do you think that fifty or sixty is old? Do you mean that *people* are old at fifty or sixty? They may be, although many people don't feel old at that age. Let's say people are old at seventy or eighty.

But how old is an old toy? Five or six years is old for a toy, unless you're thinking about one that belonged to your grandmother.

But how old is an old dog or cat? Eight or nine years is old for a dog. And a dog is very old at thirteen or fourteen.

How old is an old house? In Wisconsin an old house may be fifty to one hundred years old. In New England an old house may be two or three hundred years old. In Europe some buildings are six hundred years old. What is an old house where you live?

I imagine that now you can see that if I ask you, "How old is old?" you had better ask *me* a question before you answer. You

* *National Geographic,* CXIV, No. 2 (August 1958), p. 236.
[8] This conversation is by Mary Jane and Peter Dunwiddie.

had better ask me, "An old *what?*" — a person, a dog, a house, or what?

I am going to ask you another question. Think for a minute before you answer. What is the oldest thing you have ever touched?

Is it a 100-year-old house? I imagine you've touched something older than that. How about a big tree? An elm tree that was cut down on our street was 133 years old. How could we tell? We counted the rings on the stump, one ring for each year. Maybe you have touched older trees than that. How can you tell how old a tree is without cutting it down? You can compare its size with that of one that has been cut down, can't you? Or sometimes scientists bore into a living tree and take out a thin core of wood that shows the rings. Then they can count the rings without hurting the tree.

People used to think the giant sequoia trees in California were the oldest *living* things in the world. Some of them are about thirty-five hundred years old and very, very large. But there are even older trees than that. These are the little twisted bristlecone pines, also in California. One of them is more than forty-six hundred years old. So the oldest trees aren't necessarily the largest trees.

If you could go to Egypt and touch that big stone figure called the Sphinx, you would touch something about four thousand years old. Perhaps in a museum you have seen things from Egypt that are nearly that old. But usually you aren't allowed to touch things in a museum. Why? If everybody who came touched those old things, nothing would last very long, would it?

But there are plenty of things *much* older than things in a museum. And these you can touch all you want to. Do you know what they are? Rocks! Some rocks in northern Wisconsin and at the bottom of the Grand Canyon are among the oldest rocks on the surface of the earth. Where they lie bare with no soil on them, you can walk right up and put your hand on something more than one billion years old. Think of that!

Even if you live where rocks at the surface are quite young, they may still be millions of years old. And a lump of coal is around 250 million years old. Do you know what coal was once?

There is one other thing you can touch even more easily than rocks, and it is probably older than the rocks. Can you guess what it is? Water! Water falls as rain or snow, runs away in streams or underground. It flows into the ocean or is drunk by people or plants or animals, and then evaporates. Then it falls again. But it is always the same water, over and over again.

All the water there is was formed when our earth was formed, and do you know how old the earth is? Between 3 and 4 billion years old. Think of that the next time you are playing in the bathtub!

### OTHER IDEAS

1. A related conversation might start with the questions "How old are *you*, really? Did you begin when you were born? When did you begin?"

### SUGGESTIONS

1. Some interesting articles pertinent to this subject have appeared in recent years in *The National Geographic:* "How Old Is It?" by Lyman J. Briggs and Kenneth F. Weaver, August 1958 (on dating by the Carbon 14 method); "Bristlecone Pine, Oldest Known Living Thing," by Edmund Schulman, March 1958; "Giant Sequoias: Earth's Largest Living Things Draw Millions to California Parks," by John Michael Kauffmann and B. Anthony Stewart, August 1959.
2. Some idea of the vast ages of rocks can be obtained by examining the "Outline of Earth History" in the section on geology in the *World Book Encyclopedia.*
3. An impressive view of the role of water in the earliest stages of earth's history is given in the opening chapter of *The World We Live In,* by the editorial staff of *Life* and Lincoln Barnett (New York: Time Inc., 1955).
4. It would be effective to have a variety of old objects on hand: an old-fashioned doll, an arrowhead, a fossil, a piece of coal, a stone and a glass of water.

## Section C. The Natural World

*Such "manual" skills as birds have are wholly utilitarian and there is little doubt that they are basically instinctive. No parent bird supervises the building of its yearling chick's first nest. The bird knows how to build a nest, doesn't have to learn. But in that building, birds do demonstrate a degree of flexibility in choosing among available materials. Orioles once used many strands of horse hair in weaving their nests. When horses became less numerous, the orioles used less hair and more string and plant fiber. I examined one oriole nest a few months ago and found not one horsehair in it.* — HAL BORLAND, The Enduring Pattern*

### 14. *The Snakeskin and the Carrot Bag*

We have an apple tree in our yard with a swing hanging from one of the branches. Our baby is too little to pump himself, so I have to push him.

Early in the summer I noticed that almost always, when we

* (New York: Simon and Schuster); copyright © 1959 by Hal Borland. By permission of Simon and Schuster.

went over to the swing, a bird made a loud "queep" noise and flew away from the tree.

One day, as we were going over there, I heard the usual "queep" sound. It seemed almost cross this time, as if the bird didn't like our interrupting her at something.

And then I thought: "That bird is *always* here when we come; I think she must have a nest in this tree."

I put the baby on the swing and gave him a big push. Then I went and stood a little distance from the tree and looked up among the branches. I couldn't see any nests from there, so I started walking all around the tree, looking up into the branches.

I remembered that one year a robin had built a nest in that tree — a big mud and grass nest in a crotch near the top. But robins don't say "queep," so I wasn't surprised that I couldn't find a robin's nest.

Then I remembered that another year a little vireo of some kind had built a lovely little nest of woven grasses and goat hairs in an end fork of a branch of this tree. But I couldn't find one of these and I was sorry. If there *had* been one I could have shown the baby how, every time we pulled the branch down to peek in the nest, all the baby birds would open their mouths and squawk, thinking we were their mother arriving with food.

Then I noticed an arm of the tree that had been sawed off, up about ten feet from the ground. Certain birds often build their nests in the bottom of a hollowed-out dead limb. Perhaps there was a nest in there.

I gave the baby another big push on his swing and I climbed up the tree. I was able to climb up above the dead arm and look down in.

Yes, there in the midst of a rather messy looking pile of pine needles and dry leaves lay four small eggs. They were creamy white with blotchy, brown lines all over them. I climbed down quickly and gave the baby another big push. "So that is where Mrs. Queep lives," I said to the baby. "I wonder who she is?"

"Queep," said the baby. He liked that noise.

"Yes, queep," I said, "and we had better go see-saw, so Mrs. Queep can come back here and sit on those eggs. If she doesn't keep them warm, they won't hatch."

In a little while I heard the "queep" sound and went over where I could see the tree. I finally found the bird that was making the noise, sitting high up in the branches. The first thing I noticed was the crest, like a little cap, on the bird's head. I decided it was about the same size bird as a robin, and I could see it was mostly brown with a yellow throat.

I said to the baby, "You'll be happy to know that Mrs. Queep is the great crested flycatcher."

"Queep," the baby said. He liked that name better.

Of course, I couldn't explain to the baby how delighted I was that it was this kind of bird, and that I knew where its nest was. Do you know why I was delighted? There is something about the nest of the great crested flycatcher that is quite unusual and it is mentioned in every bird book that I have ever seen.

One of our bird books describes how the great crested flycatchers "have a queer habit of placing a piece of snakeskin in the hole in which their nest is located, for what purpose, unless to scare away intruders [anyone who might bother the nest] is not known, but it seems to be a universal [happens with these birds everywhere] practice."

Here in my yard was the nest of a great crested flycatcher, a nest that no one had ever looked into before! Would I find an old snakeskin in it when I looked?

Birds don't like to have people fuss with their nests while they are using them, so I planned to wait until the eggs had hatched and the babies had flown before I would examine the nest.

About a week later, I climbed the tree again. Mrs. Flycatcher had given her rather irritated "queep" and had flown away before I looked into the hole. Two very big, wide-opened mouths "looked" up at me. Only two of the eggs had hatched. Perhaps my baby and I had bothered the mother too much with all our swinging.

Much as I would like to have looked for the snakeskin then, I climbed down quickly so mother flycatcher could fill those big baby mouths with food.

It was almost two weeks after that, I think, that I climbed the tree again. Mrs. Flycatcher did not seem to mind my coming this time. I didn't hear her at all. I looked down into the hole.

No babies! No wonder I hadn't heard the usual "queep!" Mrs. Flycatcher and her family had flown away. A bird's nest is only a place to raise bird babies, not a place to live. Mrs. Flycatcher was through with her nest in the hollow tree limb for awhile.

Now was my chance to look for the snakeskin.

Right away I saw the two eggs that had not hatched. I could see feathers; perhaps some were from the two babies that had hatched, but some were chicken feathers, too. The nest was made of many, many kinds of things, just piled in loosely. Pine needles, dry leaves, twigs, hair (from our dog perhaps) and — yes, I reached in and pulled out a piece of snakeskin!

Have you ever found a snakeskin that a snake has shed? This isn't the skin that you would find on a dead snake, but the thin, thin layer of skin that a living snake pulls itself out of when the skin gets too tight. The snake can pull himself out of his skin just as we can pull a glove off our hand.

As I looked at the nest more carefully, I found many small pieces of snakeskin scattered through the nest. I took several of these out. Then I saw a very large piece and pulled it out. But do you know what it was? It wasn't a piece of snakeskin at all. It was a piece of man-made plastic bag, the kind carrots come in at the store. This didn't have the scaly design that a snakeskin has. Do you suppose that the bird thought it was some new kind of snake-skin?

I climbed down out of the tree, and as I pushed the baby on the swing, I wondered.

Next summer one of those baby flycatchers may come back to our yard. If she comes, her mother won't be with her. The bird books say that great crested flycatchers don't like to nest near each other.

And somehow that baby (she'll be a mother next summer), if she nests in that tree, will choose that hollow limb for her nest.

She won't choose the tip end of a branch of the big elm tree; some new oriole mother will know that she should hang her lovely woven-bag nest there.

She won't fly in the barn window and build a nest on a beam in the hayloft; some new swallow mother will know that she should do that.

The new flycatcher mother won't fly up to the wooden gutter outside the guest room window of our house; a new starling mother will choose that place.

She won't make a grass and mud nest in a high crotch of the apple tree, either. Mrs. Robin may choose that. And perhaps next year, a little vireo will choose to make a woven cup on the fork of a low branch, but the new flycatcher mother will never in the world decide on this.

No, somehow — and I wish I knew how — she'll choose that hollow limb or one just like it.

And, for reasons we don't know, she'll pick up pine needles, twigs, chicken feathers, dog hairs, *and* the cast skin of a snake, and perhaps a piece of an old plastic carrot bag, and put them in the bottom of that hollow limb for her nest.

On top of all this, she'll lay four small creamy white eggs with blotchy, brown lines all over them. Out of these eggs will come new great crested flycatchers that somehow know all this, too.

How can this be? I wish I knew.

### OTHER IDEAS

1. Of course, there are many kinds of nests that could be the subject of very interesting conversations. Whichever one is used, the conversation will be far more vivid if it (along with several other nests) is in front of the children. Then they can look carefully and see the variety of materials used. A whole cast skin of a snake would also be of interest. Children often find them. On a perfect one, the skin over the eye is visible, as is the slit where the snake pulled out.
2. The chapter "Spider Silk" in *A Cup of Sky*, by Donald Culross Peattie (Boston: Houghton Mifflin), has material that would be very interesting in a conversation. It would open the children's eyes to wonders very close at hand, but that they probably have never noticed.

### SUGGESTIONS

1. A guide, devoted solely to bird's nests and how to identify them, is *Birds' Nests*, by Richard Headstrom (New York: Ives, Washburn).
2. *A Handbook of Nature-Study*, by Anna Comstock, has material on birds' nests (p. 46). She suggests the kinds of questions to ask about a nest.
3. The poems "Carrot Seeds" (p. 60) and "Something Told the Wild Geese" (p. 85) both in *Poems to Grow On* might be used with this conversation. The song "Fly Away" (No. 26) from *Martin and Judy Songs* (Boston: Beacon Press) might be used also.

*This grand show is eternal. It is always sunrise somewhere; the dew is never all dried at once; a shower is forever falling; vapor is ever rising. Eternal sunrise, eternal sunset, eternal dawn and gloaming, on sea and continents and islands, each in its turn, as the round earth rolls.* — JOHN MUIR, The Wilderness World of John Muir*

## 15. *When Does a Year Really Begin?*

One day early in September, I heard a boy and a girl arguing. They sounded awfully cross with each other.

"It is *too* New Year's Day," said the boy.

"Of course it isn't," said the girl. "New Year's Day is in the winter. It comes after Christmas."

"It does not," said the boy. "Today's New Year's Day."

"It is not," said the girl.

"It is too," said the boy. "It's our New Year."

"Well, I don't know about *your* New Year, but the *real* New Year's Day comes after Christmas," said the girl.

* Edwin Way Teale, ed. (Boston: Houghton Mifflin, 1954), p. 312.

"This one's real," said the boy. "My father and mother said so."

"It is not," said the girl.

"It is too," said the boy.

They may still be arguing. I don't know. Who was right, the boy or the girl? When does the year *really* begin?

When I heard them arguing I wished that I could have taken them home with me to listen to a record that we have at our house. Perhaps you know it — it goes like this:

> Horace, the horse on the Merry-Go-Round
> Went up and down, round and round,
> He's been sad since the day he found
> He's the very last horse on the merry-go-round.
> The music begins and away they go
> High and low, to and fro,
> Poor old Horace would always say,
> "I'm the very last horse again today."
> How he tried and tried and tried,
> But he just never could win,
> Horace cried and cried and cried,
> 'Cause all the other horses were ahead of him.
> Then came the day on the merry-go-round
> Horace turned, looked around,
> Then said, "Gosh o gee,
> "I'm the very first horse on the merry-go-round
> " 'Cause the others are following me."[9]

Which was he really? Was he the first horse or the last horse? Every horse is the first horse *and* the last horse *and* the middle horse on a merry-go-round. And our year is like a merry-go-round of days. You can think of the year as a big circle. And where does a circle begin, really?

A year could begin on any day, and yet if you study and find out the different times that different people in the world have chosen to have the year begin, you find something very interesting. You discover that there are four times of the year that have been chosen for New Year's Day over and over again.

One of the times that has been chosen often is around March 21. The people who lived in Babylonia long ago celebrated New Year's Day then. Another popular time has been around September 21. The New Year of the Jewish Church comes in September, and

[9] Victor Record, Y–459.

the ancient Egyptians and Persians celebrated in September, too.

June 21 was a time when the Greek people of long ago had their New Year's Day, and December 21 was the date chosen by the Romans. If you draw a big circle and put the names of the months around it, you will find that the four times of the year that have been most often celebrated as New Year's Day are opposite each other: June 21 opposite December 21, and September 21 opposite March 21. Something very special happens to our world at those four times during the year. They are all four of them very good times to celebrate something new that is happening.

In order to understand what this something is, there are a few things you need to know about our world. Probably you know most of them already. You know, for instance, that our world is a big round ball and that it is moving. It's moving in several different ways. We need to talk about two of the ways it moves.

If one person will be the earth and another will be the sun, we can act it out as we talk about it. The earth is turning around like a top in front of the sun. When your face is turned toward the sun, we'll call that "day," and as you turn away it becomes "evening." When your back is toward the sun it is "night," and as you keep on turning, "morning" comes. This is what makes a day. If our earth were not turning in this way, like a top, we would not have night and day.

But the earth is also moving in another way. It is traveling around the sun. Remember, as it travels around the sun it must also turn like a top. Do you know how many times it must turn like a top as it goes around the sun once? Just about 365 times. If each one of those turns is day, that trip around the sun has taken just about 365 days. Do you know what we call that trip? One year.

Now if you have a globe at home or at school, you know that the globe is always tipped a little sideways. And this is the way our world really is inclined as it moves around the sun. This explains why some of our days are longer and some are shorter, and why we have the four seasons in some parts of the world — winter, spring, summer, fall. In the Northern Hemisphere winter starts about December 21, spring about March 21, summer about June 21 and fall about September 21. In the Southern Hemisphere the seasons are just the opposite.

The four points at which people in various periods and places have so often chosen to celebrate New Year's Day are the times when, for many parts of the world, the sun shines the longest each day (June 21), the shortest each day (December 21), or the two times a year when, for the whole world, day and night are exactly the same length (September 21 and March 21).

So, to go back to the boy and girl who were arguing about the *real* New Year's Day, who *was* right? I guess both of them were. The little boy was talking about the New Year of the Jewish Church. The little girl was talking about the January 1 New Year's Day that so many people celebrate now, instead of celebrating around December 21.

If you ever find yourself in an argument like this one, it is a good idea to try to find out why the other person thinks the way he does. If you find out enough about the other person's reasons, you may find that it is possible for both of you to be right.

### SUGGESTIONS

1. *Stars,* a Golden Nature Guide (New York: Simon and Schuster) contains information and a chart of the causes of the seasons on page 114.
2. The song "The Procession" (No. 28) in *We Sing of Life* (Boston: Beacon Press) celebrates the cycle of the seasons. If the conversation is used near Christmas time, the song "We Believe in Christmas" in the same collection, celebrates the winter solstice.
3. This conversation will be more vivid, and also clearer, if the children dramatize it as suggested. A blackboard might also be helpful.

*The earth has its own pulse and rhythms, and the wise and fortunate man leans into the wind, sows with the season, and searches for water in valleys where water flows.* — HAL BORLAND, High, Wide and Lonesome*

### 16. Nancy and the Calendar[10]

In Japan there are a great many cherry trees. When they blossom in the spring, it is a very beautiful sight. People actually stop their work and go on long trips, if necessary, just to see the cherry trees in bloom.

One year when the cherry trees were later than usual in flowering, a certain emperor [king] grew so impatient for the coming of the blossoms that he gave orders for the great bell in the temple to be struck and drums to be beaten, to bid the trees to begin to bloom:

---

* (Philadelphia: Lippincott Co., 1936), p. 39.
[10] The story about Nancy and the calendar is by Phyllis Buddenberg, copyrighted in 1958.

Strike the great bell,
That it may tell
The cherry trees to bloom!"[11]


Do you think that the cherry trees did start to bloom right then, because someone as important as an emperor told them to? No, they didn't, because it isn't people that make the world wake up in the spring, is it?

Here is a story about a little girl, a real little girl, who acted a little like the emperor.

The little girl's name was Nancy, and she was five and a half years old when this story happened. She had a little brother Bobby, who was almost three, a big brother Rich, almost seven, and a baby sister Becky, one and a half years old. They lived on a big farm in Nebraska.

The day before the story begins, this family had had a wonderful picnic outdoors. It was still early March and not yet spring, but it had felt like spring, and so they had decided to celebrate with the first picnic of the year. But the *very* next day — well, listen to the story about "Nancy and the Calendar."

The day after the picnic wasn't like spring! Oh, my, no! The air was cold! When Rich got up, he looked at the thermometer and got out his long underwear to wear to school. Daddy put on his warmest clothes when he went outside to feed the calves.

"But I thought it was spring," sighed Bobby, as he pressed his nose against the kitchen window.

"Mommy," asked Nancy, "when *will* it be spring, really truly spring?"

"Well," said Mother, wondering how she could explain the changeable weather to Nancy, "by the calendar, spring comes next week, about March 21." Mother helped Nancy find that day on the big kitchen calendar. Nancy got her red crayon and drew a fat ring around it.

Nancy liked to look at that calendar. On the top of each page was a picture of children having fun. The January page showed children building a snowman; the February page showed them making valentines. This page showed a boy flying a kite.

Nancy was beginning to understand what the calendar was all about. Each morning she put a big cross mark through the number for that day. When the days on one page were all covered

[11] *Little Pictures of Japan*, ed. Olive B. Miller (Chicago: Book House for Children). Quoted by permission.

with cross marks, Nancy knew a whole month had gone by. Then Nancy would tear off that page and throw it away.

"Mommy," said Nancy, "show me where it is summer on the calendar."

Mother started turning the pages. "Here, now it's March, next comes April, then May and June — these are the spring months. By July it should be really hot. Here, June 21 says 'first day of summer.' "

"Three more whole pages of days," sighed Nancy. She drew another red ring around June 21, the first day of summer.

Later Nancy and Bobby pulled on their snowsuits and went outside. They didn't stay long. "It's brrrrr cold," said Bobby coming in. "The wind is passing by." He knew a song about that.

"March wind brings April showers," said Mother, pulling off his snow pants.

"Well, it's really windy today," puffed Nancy. "Too windy even for kites."

Mother put Becky to bed for her morning nap. Then she and Bobby went to the basement to hang up the wet clothes.

Nancy wandered out to the kitchen. She looked at the calendar. There was the first red circle: Spring. Slowly Nancy turned the pages: one, two, three — and there was the second red circle: summer! "How I wish it was hot enough to go swimming," thought Nancy. "I wish it was summer *right now.*"

Suddenly, Nancy had an idea. Can you guess what it was? Quickly she just tore off those three calendar pages and threw them into the wastebasket. There! On the calendar was a picture of a barefoot boy wading in a brook. "Now!" thought Nancy. "It really *is* summer . . . the calendar says so!"

Soon Mother and Bobby came upstairs. "Mommy," called Nancy, "it's summer right now!"

"Why, Nancy," said Mother, surprised. "What makes you think so?" Mother had thought Nancy really understood about the calendar. "Do you see leaves on the trees, or green grass, or flowers blooming?"

"But, Mother," insisted Nancy, "it's June. That's when summer starts. You told me so."

"But Nancy," replied Mother, "do you see any June roses or any . . . ?"

"But the calendar," interrupted Nancy. "Don't you see it really *is* summer!"

And then Mother saw the calendar! "Oh Nancy," said Mother slowly. "I do see. I see how much you *wish* it were summer. I see how badly you want it to be warm outside so you can go wading like that boy on the calendar." Mother waited a moment. "But Nancy — look outside."

Nancy looked. It was still grey and cloudy. The wind was still sending leaves and dirt through the air. There were no leaves on the trees yet. "*Is* it summer out there, Nancy?" asked mother.

"I wanted it to be summer," said Nancy, "but it isn't."

"No, I'm afraid not," replied Mother. "Why not, Nancy?"

Nancy thought a minute. "Well — I guess the outside doesn't do just what the calendar says. It does what it *has* to do — and then *we* make the calendar say what it is already."

And then Mother knew Nancy really did understand about the calendar. Mother and Nancy took the crumpled calendar pages out of the wastebasket. They smoothed them out as well as they could and stapled them back onto the calendar.

"Next time," said Nancy, "I'll tear them off when it's time."

Things happen in nature, not because a great king rings a bell or a little girl tears the pages off a calendar, but because something much stronger than our wishes makes them happen.

The emperor must ring his bell as the blossoms open and Nancy must tear off the calendar pages one by one when it is time.

Did you ever try to make nature do something instead of finding out what nature *had* to do?

OTHER IDEAS

1. The children might want to talk about what does cause the seasons of the year.
2. You may have heard how some Indians do rain dances when they need rain for their crops. Some people have thought these Indians were acting like the Japanese emperor or like Nancy and trying to make it rain.

Other people have said, no, these Indians do their rain dances when their wise men, who have studied the weather over long years, have told them that rain is on the way. They dance with the forces that are bringing the rain, and their dance is a dance of welcome and rejoicing.

This might lead into a discussion of prayer. Is prayer an attempt to make nature do what we want?
3. A large calendar, such as the one Nancy had, should be used with the story. A calendar is full of fascination for primary-grade children. Many good conversations can center around one. Why are some numbers in a special color? Many calendars have pictures or symbols marking birthdays of great people or special events in history. Questions about these often lead into rewarding conversations.

SUGGESTIONS

1. Pictures of cherry trees in bloom would make a good background for this conversation.

2. The song "Who Has Seen the Wind" (No. 8 in the *Martin and Judy Song Book*) is the song Bobby knew.


*Permanence is but a word of degrees.* — RALPH WALDO EMERSON, "Circles"*

### 17. *Are Stones Still Being Made?*

One day one of my boys and I were sitting by the brook near our house. He was throwing stones into the water. Did you ever do this?

"You know," I said, "it's a wonder all the stones there are haven't been thrown into the brook already. Before you started throwing them in, your big brother did, and before he started throwing them in, your big sister did, and I threw them in when I was little. Wouldn't you think that they'd all be in the brook by now?"

"Mum," he said. I could see that he was thinking. Perhaps he was wondering whether there would be any stones for his little boys to throw in the water. "Mum, are stones still being made?"

I had to think about that question for a little while.

What would you say? Are stones still being made? Might they get all used up? How do stones get made?

Well, I figured out that stones *are* still being made. Even my little boy, when he was throwing his stone into the brook, was helping to make one kind of stone.

I'll explain.

Men called geologists, who study rocks, have figured out that there are three main types of rocks. As I explain what each of the three kinds are, you see whether or not you can answer the question: are they still being made?

One kind of rock is called "igneous," or "fire," rock. Lava that comes out of volcanoes is one kind of igneous rock; granite is another. Now, you tell me: Is this kind of rock still being made?

A second kind of rock is called "sedimentary" rock. Have you ever played out in the yard barefoot and gotten very dirty and then come into the house and taken a bath? When you let the water out, there may have been a layer of dirt left on the bottom of the tub. That is called a "sediment." Sedimentary rock is rock that is made by being laid down, just as the dirt was laid down in the bottom of the tub. Do you think this kind of rock is still being made?

* *Essays, First Series,* I (Boston: Houghton Mifflin) p. 302.

When I said that my little boy was helping to make one kind of rock when he threw his stone into the brook, I was thinking of sedimentary rock. We live in a part of the country where there is a lot of granite. The stone he threw into the brook was granite. This piece of granite may have been carried along by the brook and broken into smaller pieces. Each spring, when the brook is full and moves very quickly, the pieces of granite are ground up smaller and smaller.

Gradually — and that means very, very slowly — those small pieces of rock will be carried along by the brook and finally laid down as sand or mud. Years and years will pass and more sand or mud will be laid down on this layer. The layers that are deepest down in the earth will be hardened and cemented together and become a sedimentary rock, perhaps sandstone or shale ("mud stone").

Brooks and rivers and oceans, floods and rainstorms, as well as little boys, are making sedimentary rock all the time.

The third kind of rock that geologists talk about is "metamorphic" rock. That may seem like a big and difficult word but it is a good one to know. It just means *changed* rock. When a caterpillar becomes a butterfly, we say it has gone through "metamorphosis": it changes.

Metamorphic rock is rock that has changed from one kind to another. For example, if some sandstone is pressed very tightly and hardened even more, it becomes a different kind of rock — quartzite.

Shale, which may be formed from layers of mud and is a sedimentary rock, may be changed into the metamorphic rock — slate. You may have stepping stones in your yard made out of slate, or you may have the floor of a patio made of slate.

Do you think that this kind of rock is still being made?

Yes. Rock, like everything else in our world, is changing all the time. Sometimes we think of rock as the one thing in our world that doesn't change, but we are quite wrong about that.

If we just open our eyes, we can see rock being changed all the time by man and nature. Some of the changes take a long time and some happen quite quickly.

If you like to collect rocks and study them, as we do in our family, perhaps you have a rock hammer, an especially strong hammer for cracking rocks apart. Every time we use that hammer we are changing rocks and helping to make new ones. Men change rock when they dynamite, use bulldozers, or rock-crushing machines. Nature changes rock every minute every day, with rain, snow, ice, rivers and streams. Every time you go to the ocean and see the waves crashing against the rocks or on the sandy beach, you are watching rock being changed.

Even plants, which seem so weak and fragile beside rock, are changing rock all the time. Have you ever noticed flat, gray, rough things that seem stuck to rocks? They are called lichen, a kind of plant that can grow on rock and, by growing there, begin to turn some of that rock into soil. Lovely, soft green mosses often grow on rocks, too, and they also begin to change it into soil.

Sometimes, after the weather has made small cracks in a rock, a seed of a flower or a tree will be blown there by the wind. Then, because the seed is alive, slowly, slowly the plant or tree grows and makes the crack bigger; sometimes it even splits the rock into pieces.

Our earth is a ball of rock. The rock we see changing is mostly just the outer crust. This crust cracks, wears away, and builds up, over and over again. Some rock from below the crust pushes up and forms new crust.

So my little boy doesn't need to worry and you don't need to worry. There will be plenty of stones for his children and your children to throw into the brooks. Stones *are* still being made.

### SUGGESTIONS

1. Pages 130–147 in *Child and Universe,* by Bertha Stevens, contains an interesting discussion of rock and water cycles.
2. Try to have specimens of the three classes of rock for the children to examine. Invite the children to bring specimens. Even if you can't identify all of them, you can admire them.
3. Zim and Shaffer's *Rocks and Minerals,* a Golden Nature Guide (New York: Simon and Schuster), especially pages 109–140, will help a beginner.
4. The children might enjoy this poem, used by permission:

#### TREASURE

I'm finding pretty stones: here's one
That's black and shiny in the sun.

And one that's round and white and flat;
I'm going to make a wish on that.

This one is striped with pink and grey;
I wonder how it got that way?

And this one looks like gold to me.
It glitters in the sunshine — See?

JEAN MCKEE THOMPSON

*. . . in the middle of winter, the live, tiny seeds lying buried beneath the surface of the ground are not asleep or inactive, but . . . step by step, steadily and gradually, they are evolving toward that appearance of continued life which spring will reveal.* — BERTHA STEVENS, Child and Universe*

## 18. *Heffie the Turtle*[12]

Did you ever have a turtle for a pet? Perhaps you've had one from the woods, a painted turtle maybe, or a spotted one. Or perhaps you live in the city and you've had one of those tiny little green ones that you can buy at a pet shop or sometimes at the ten-cent store.

I think almost everyone has a turtle for a pet at least once while they are growing up. But I don't think that very many pet turtles have had the experience that Heffie, a pet box turtle I read about, has had.

A man named Colonel McMannus found Heffie in the middle of a big highway in Maryland. He didn't want a car to run over her, so he stopped his car, picked her up and took her home to his family.

He had three children, Roreen, Howdy and Kerry, and he was pretty sure that they would like to have a pet turtle. And he was right! They named her "Heffie," because she made a kind of "hffffff" sound when she pulled herself into her shell.

But being rescued from a big highway was not the special experience that made Heffie different from other pet turtles. I imagine a lot of turtles are rescued from the middle of busy streets. After all, they don't know they are in one of our streets. We wouldn't know if we were in the middle of a turtle street (if they have them), either. No, the thing that was special about Heffie was something that happened quite a bit later.

Heffie liked the McMannus family very much. They did a very smart thing, too. They didn't keep her and then just hope that they would know how to take care of a turtle. They bought a guide book about turtles and found out as much as they could about Heffie. (See Suggestions.)

They found out that she was a box turtle and that she was forty years old, because she had a design with forty boxes on her back. They read that box turtles can live to be as old as eighty! They found out also that she was a girl because she had dark eyes, not bright red ones, as do boy box turtles. They discovered in the guide that she would eat some fruits, green vegetables and raw meat. The guide book said that box turtles make very good pets.

Heffie did make a good pet. The family found out some other things about her that were not in the guide book. They found out that she liked the sound of bells, and they bought her some of her very own. They found that she liked to go for walks, so they put a piece of friction tape around her waist and attached a long piece of string to it, and then they took her walking. They discovered that her favorite food was raw meat served on a clean paper napkin.

So Heffie was very happy with the McMannus family all during the spring, summer and early fall. But then something happened. In order to understand what it was that happened, there is something you need to know about turtles.

When your mother takes your temperature to see whether or not you are sick, do you know what number she hopes to read on the thermometer? If you are well, it will be 98.6 degrees. No matter whether it is 100 degrees outside (that's very hot), or 32 degrees outside (that's freezing), your body *inside* stays at 98.6. If you are sick, it goes up higher or lower, but not much. You and I are called "warm-blooded" animals because of this.

But turtles and snakes and frogs and toads are different. If you want to take their temperatures, all you have to do is find out the temperature of the room or place they are in. They stay pretty much the same temperature as the world around them. They are called "cold-blooded" for this reason.

This means that when winter comes and the temperature goes below freezing, turtles and other cold-blooded animals have to get away from the cold or they will freeze to death. The best place to go is deep in the ground, or under rocks, in caves, or deep in the mud under ponds. Down there, where the freezing cold can't reach them, they hibernate; that means they go into a kind of long, deep sleep. They do not need to eat, and they just lie still. When the earth above them begins to get warm again in spring, they wake up and come up to the surface of the ground again.

So when fall came and Heffie went out walking on the end of her string, she felt the cold, and she did not like it. She wanted to hibernate, and she turned toward a dark corner and just stood and stood. Roreen and Howdy and Kerry McMannus were very worried. They were afraid their pet was sick.

But Colonel McMannus thought he knew what to do. He took a shovel and went out in the yard. He dug a hole three feet deep. That is about as far down as they put the pipes that bring

water into our houses, because the ground does not freeze that
deep in our part of the world. He made it muddy in the bottom of
the hole and then he had the children lower Heffie into it. Then they
filled the hole up with dirt, marked the spot carefully, and left
Heffie for the winter.

When spring came and the earth had thawed, the whole family
went out together to dig Heffie up. Although she looked like a cake
of mud, she was alive and in good health. She was ready to listen
to her bells, go for walks on the end of her string and, especially,
to eat lots and lots of raw meat on her paper napkin dish!

"Well," you may be thinking. "What's so special about that?
If all turtles hibernate, Heffie was just like the rest." No. It wasn't
just that she hibernated, but it was *where* she hibernated during the
next two winters that was special.

Perhaps you noticed that I didn't call the father of the family
Mr. McMannus. I called him Colonel McMannus. A colonel is
an officer in the army, and Colonel McMannus' regular job was
working for the army. Early in the summer Colonel McMannus was
told that he must get ready to go to France to live for a while. This
is called "being transferred." He could take his family with him.

So Mrs. McMannus, Roreen, Howdy, Kerry *and* Heffie all went
off to France with Colonel McMannus. It was certainly a good
thing that he wasn't transferred in the middle of the winter, with
Heffie three feet underground! Everyone liked living in France,
even Heffie. The McMannuses had brought along her bells and her
string and, of course, they fed her her favorite food.

But, when fall came and the cold weather began, Heffie began
to feel just the way she had felt in Maryland. She wanted to
hibernate. So, once again, Colonel McMannus got out his shovel
and dug a hole three feet deep and they lowered Heffie in for the
winter. In the spring they dug her up, and once again she was
feeling fine and hungry.

And once again Colonel McMannus found he was to be transferred, this time to Germany. Of course, the whole family came
along, including Heffie. And of course, when the cold weather
began, Heffie didn't like it any better than she had in Maryland or
in France, and the McMannuses knew just what to do. They dug
another hole, and down she went for the winter.

That is as far as I can go in the story of Heffie and her underground homes. I wonder whether any other turtle has spent three
winters in three different countries? I wonder how many more
different countries Heffie will visit? After all, she could live almost
forty more years and Colonel McMannus could be transferred quite
a few more times.

## OTHER IDEAS

1. Perhaps the children can visualize the soil that covers our earth as a kind of blanket. What other creatures have tucked themselves in for the winter? It does not matter a single bit to Heffie and the others what names people give to the countries where the earth blanket is; down underneath it is all the same to them. Some people have thought of the earth as a mother who provides a safe warm place for her animal children.

2. The poem "Waiting" in *Poems to Grow On* (p. 79) suggests some other winter sleepers. And "Mrs. Brownish Beetle" (p. 92) is a humorous poem about a beetle preparing for the coming cold.

## SUGGESTIONS

1. *Reptiles and Amphibians,* by Zim and Smith, a Golden Nature Guide (New York: Simon and Schuster), is a good inexpensive guide.

# Section D. Our Senses and Our Feelings

*Sunsets, rainbows, mountains high,*
*Stars atwinkling in the sky.*
*Little kittens' shiny eyes,*
*Lazy flitting butterflies.*
*The world is full as it can be*
*Of lovely, lovely things to see.*
*— "The Little Gray Ponies"**

## 19. Hello, World![13]

When I get up in the morning, one of the first things I like to do is to give my face and hands a good scrub.

Water is nice. I like it *hot* for washing myself, and cold, cold, cold for drinking. When there is ice in it, it *sounds* cold, doesn't it?

I have a pretty washcloth and towel. Mine are pink. What is your favorite color?

And a cake of soap fits so nicely into my hand. It feels so soft and smooth, and it always smells good, too.

Then I usually give my teeth a good brushing. My toothbrush is yellow. What color is yours? It has a long, slim handle. It is just right for my hand. It is plastic, and I can almost see through it.

Everybody likes tooth paste! It comes out in a pretty ribbon shape. It smells and tastes good, too. Then I have a drink of water.

---

* Young People's Records, 735B.
[13] Conversation adapted from material by Ardanelle Dishon.

It feels especially cold right after you brush your teeth, doesn't it? I wonder why?

I always give my hair a good combing and brushing in the morning. My comb and brush are both blue. Brushing my hair makes my head feel good and it makes my hair shiny and pretty.

Think of it! In just that short time, I have used my *eyes,* for seeing, my *ears,* for hearing, my *mouth,* for tasting, my *nose,* for smelling, and my *hands* and *face* and *skin* for feeling.

And the day has only begun. All day long I will be using these wonderful senses of mine. Isn't it amazing how the world outside of us gets into us? Can you name our five common senses? Sight, hearing, smell, taste and touch.

While I've been talking, you have been using your sense of sight and hearing, mostly. But because you have tasted toothpaste yourself, and smelled soap and held a bar of it in your hand, my talking about these things has almost given you the smell and taste and feeling of them, too. Words can almost make us feel things, if we have really felt them once.

Our senses wouldn't be able to tell us much, however, if we didn't have something else that is very wonderful in our bodies. Do you know what that is? It's our brain and the nerves that go to our brains from our senses.

Our senses experience the world outside of us, and then they send messages to our brain about what they have felt. Gradually over the years, as we have many kinds of experiences, we use our brains to learn to use our senses.

Another thing our brain does is to make it possible for our senses to work together. Did you ever have a very bad cold — so bad that you couldn't smell anything? When that happens, we find that we can hardly taste anything either. That's because our sense of smell and our sense of taste work closely together.

I never thought that the sense of smell was very important until I discovered that a friend of mine didn't have any at all. She was a mother and a wonderful cook. When I'd go into her house sometimes, I'd smell such good things! I'd say, "What smells so good?"

She'd say, "I don't know. I don't have any sense of smell, you know. I do have some cookies in the oven; perhaps that's what you smell." Then I realized how much you miss when you don't have a sense of smell. What are some of the things you think of right off that have wonderful smells?

Not to have a sense of smell could be pretty serious, too. Can you think why? If your house were burning and you couldn't smell it, it could be serious, couldn't it?

All of our senses not only give us pleasure, but they are important to our safety. Can you think of some serious things that might happen because someone couldn't hear? A person drowning and shouting for help, or the baby hurt and crying, or a train whistling near a crossing — these could all be pretty serious, especially if the only person nearby were deaf.

We really need our senses, and they certainly help us enjoy life, too. Let's make a list of some of the sounds and smells, sights and tastes and "feels" that we like best. I asked some children once to list a few for me and here they are:

The *smell* of brownies cooking.

The *feel* of the bottom of a baby's feet.

The *taste* of maple sugar.

The *sound* of rain on the roof.

The *sight* of a full moon shining on snow.

### OTHER IDEAS

1. Young children would enjoy hearing and dramatizing the whole record of "The Little Gray Ponies." It tells how the little ponies discover that the world is full of wonderful sights, sounds, smells and so forth.

2. The poem "The Great Lover," by Rupert Brooke, might be interesting to use with older children. This may be found in many collections, including *The Book of Living Verse,* Louis Untermeyer, ed. (New York: Harcourt, Brace). If some of his loves are discussed, it would be good to have examples there: freshly baked bread, smooth wood, and so on.

3. "In talking about the eye I told of a game I play, using both my regular eyes and my 'inner eyes.' Because I once read that a tree is really like a fountain, sucking up water, and then losing it in invisible mist through the leaves! I can now 'see' a tree in the summer with my outer eyes, and 'see' a fountain at the same time. There are many things we can see this way. What about an egg?" (Mrs. Roy Wensberg)

### SUGGESTIONS

1. The conversation about the senses will be very vivid if the items on the first page — water, towels, cake of soap, etc. — are right before the children. Some leaders may want to plunge in and dramatize it.

2. A blackboard or other device for listing some of the children's ideas will be needed.

3. The poems "When It's Thanksgiving" and "Christmas Coming" in *Poems to Grow On* (p. 58) both stress sights and sounds and smells of the holidays. The song "World To Know" in *Martin & Judy Songs* (No. 27) could be the core of a whole session, too; or "Such Lovely Things to Hear and See" in *We Sing of Life* (No. 22).

*One day in the south of England I was walking through a great beech wood on an old estate near Shrivenham. There was a little brook flowing through the woods, and its gurgle as it ran through a rocky dell seemed to accentuate my sense of the age of those magnificent trees. I was far from home, as far away from the wilderness of the north as I had ever been. Those great trees were comforting to me even though I knew that just beyond them was open countryside.*

*Then suddenly I heard a sound that changed everything: a soft nasal twang from high in the branches, the call of a nuthatch. Instantly that beech grove was transformed into a stand of tall, stately pines; the brown beech leaves on the ground became a smooth carpet of golden needles, and beyond this cared-for forest were rugged ridges and deep timbered valleys, roaring rivers and placid lakes, with a smell of resin and duff in the sun. The call of the nuthatch had done all that, had given me a vision of the wilderness as vivid as though for the moment I had actually been there.*
— SIGURD OLSON, The Singing Wilderness*

## 20. Remembering[14]

Do you ever lie in bed at night, before you go to sleep, and think back to something you've done that was especially nice?

I think we all like to remember things that were fun. But do you know that, although we're all alike in enjoying our memories, we don't all remember in the same way?

Let me show you what I mean.

Each of you think for a minute about something that has happened to you. Now keep that in the back of your mind while I tell you about what I'm remembering.

I'm remembering a trip to a cave. In my mind I can *see* again the lantern that one of us had to carry as we went down into the cave. I can *see* the dark rocks that rose up all around us, and I can see our shadows that the light from the lantern threw up against the rocks.

Now all the things that I've remembered so far are things that I *saw*. We call these "visual" memories.

But I could have remembered in a different way. I might have remembered how echo-y our voices *sounded* down in the cave. I might have remembered the *sound* of water dripping off the rocks in one part of the cave. Or I might have remembered how loud the silence sounded down in the cave!

All these would be memories of things heard. These are called

* (New York: Knopf, 1956), p. 201.
[14] Conversation adapted from material by Mary Jane Dunwiddie.

"auditory" memories. (An auditorium is a place where we go to *hear* speakers and concerts.)

I could have remembered in still other ways. I could have remembered how damp it *felt* in the cave and how hot the air felt as we stepped out of the cave. The air in the cave had an unusual *smell,* too, and that might have been the most important thing that I remembered.

These are all different kinds of memories. People differ in the ways they remember best. Earlier I asked you to remember something that had happened to you. Now think about it again.

Is most of what you were remembering about how things *looked,* or how they *sounded,* or *smelled,* or *tasted* or *felt?* Some of us have better visual memories, some have better auditory memories, and some of us use our other senses most in our remembering. I wonder which kind of memory you use most?

Actually, we remember something much better if we use all these different kinds of memories together. Remembering something is like having the experience all over again. When we actually have the experience it can come to us through all of our senses. When we do our remembering, therefore, if we try, we ought to be able to remember something about the sounds, smells, sights, tastes and how things felt.

But, just as we may not use all our kinds of remembering, we may not really use all of our senses. Some of us use our eyes pretty well, but don't really stop to listen very carefully. It is the same with our other senses, too. If we try to use all of our senses, it will not only make life more interesting for us right now, but we'll have much more wonderful memories, too.

Sometime, when you have grown up, a certain smell or sound may suddenly bring back a memory of something that happened to you years and years ago.

One bright spring morning, I was hanging up clothes in our city yard. A fresh breeze was blowing from the north. Suddenly — why I did not know — I thought of some western mountains, fifteen hundred miles away, where I had visited long ago. I thought of the trails through the evergreens and campsites beside mountain lakes. I could almost see a snowbank I had spotted up in those mountains — it was in July and the snow still had not melted from the winter before.

What had reminded me of all this? The wind had smelled like a mountain wind, although I couldn't say why.

Later I found out why. I learned that, although the snow had melted in our yard weeks before, on that morning there still was snow in the tall pine woods, a hundred miles north of us. The north wind had brought right into my city yard the smell of wet snow mixed with evergreens, the same smell I had smelled years before in the mountains fifteen hundred miles away.

Our memory is amazing, isn't it? We think a tape recorder is wonderful, but it can only tape sounds, although now some can tape sights too. But our minds "tape" sights, sounds, smells, tastes and how things feel.

Everything that has ever happened to us is in our memories. We don't have to carry around a big tape recorder to "play" our memories; we can just turn it on when we wish.

Someday you may have to move from where you live now, but you can just take your wonderful tape-recorder brain and all your memories with you.

To live is to make memories.

### OTHER IDEAS

1. The leader might begin by asking for memories from the children, and pointing out which are visual, which are auditory, etc.

### SUGGESTIONS

1. Such poems as "The Coin," by Sara Teasdale, and "Daffodils," by William Wordsworth, sum up the idea of this conversation very well.

> . . . *It struck me at once that here was an opportunity of assisting an unfortunate child, and, moreover, of deciding the question so often asked, whether a blind-mute could be taught to use an arbitrary language.* . . . — MAUD HOWE ELLIOTT and FLORENCE HOWE HALL, Laura Bridgman*

### 21. *A Little Girl from New Hampshire: Part I*[15]

A little girl was sitting in a rocking chair by the fireplace. She was about seven years old and, although she was rather pale and thin, she was quite pretty. Back and forth she rocked, back and

* (Boston: Little, Brown, 1903), p. 38; quoting Samuel Gridley Howe.

[15] This is a true story of something that happened almost 150 years ago. The stories in Parts I and II are based on information from Laura Richards, *Laura Bridgman, The Story of an Open Door* (New York: D. Appleton and Co., 1928), and Maud Howe Elliott and Florence Howe Hall, *op. cit.*

forth. In her arms she held something. What was it? A doll? No, it was a man's old boot! But she hugged it like a doll. A cat was curled up near her on the hearth, sleeping.

A woman, her mother, was busy cooking, but not at a stove. She had no stove. Few families in New Hampshire had cooking stoves in those days. The big kitchen fireplace was her only stove. It was a great huge one, with a long crane across it from which hung pots and kettles.

The mother stirred the dinner that was cooking in one of the kettles. She did not speak to the little girl and the little girl did not speak to her. The fire crackled, the dinner burbled in the pot, the cat purred; otherwise all was silent.

But the little girl in the rocking chair did not *see* her mother stirring the dinner, she did not *hear* the fire crackle or the cat purr, she probably did not smell the good dinner cooking. And yet, she was not asleep. She was wide awake.

The little girl was named Laura Bridgman. She was blind and deaf and mute. "Mute" means she could not talk. She also had almost no sense of smell and very little sense of taste. Yet she knew a great deal that was going on in that old farm kitchen.

She could feel the warmth of the fire on her face and body. If she placed her hand on the cat, she could feel his soft fur and she could feel his purring even though she could not hear it. She could feel the smooth leather of the old boot in her arms, the only "doll" she had. When her mother moved about the room, she could feel her pass. If someone came into the kitchen and closed the door, she knew that, too, by the way the floor shook or vibrated.

At the time our story begins, a young man named James Barrett was sitting at a table in the corner of the Bridgman kitchen. He was a student from a nearby town and was doing a few days' work for Mr. Bridgman. He was writing, but often he stopped, looked up from his work and watched Laura. He had never seen anyone like her before.

Once, as her mother went past her, Laura caught hold of the edge of her mother's dress, hopped up out of the chair and followed her over to the large kitchen table. Mrs. Bridgman was making bread, and as she kneaded the dough, Laura placed her hands on her mother's arms and followed all her motions.

Later in the day Mr. Barrett asked Laura's mother, "Was Laura always like this?"

"No," said Mrs. Bridgman, "she wasn't. When she was a very tiny baby she was sickly most of the time. She was just beginning to run about and be like other children, when, at the age of two, she became terribly sick with scarlet fever. For weeks the fever raged through her body, and for five months we did not know whether she would live or die.

"At last, very, very slowly, she began to get well. Most of the time she just lay in her cradle by the fire. And then we began to discover what the sickness had done to her. Although she would live, we found that she would be blind and deaf. And because she could not hear our voices, she has never learned to talk. She seems to be able to smell and taste very little, too."

Mr. Barrett thanked Mrs. Bridgman for telling him this sad story and he went back to his writing. Mrs. Bridgman went back to her housework — and work it was! For her three children (several other children had died), Mrs. Bridgman — as did most farm women in those days — spun wool, made all the clothes, made soap and candles, raised sheep, bees and chickens. She had very little time to spend on Laura.

Fortunately for Laura, there was someone who could spend time with her — Mr. Asa Tenney, or "Uncle Asa," as the Bridgmans called him. He had no family of his own and found in the lonely little Laura someone to love and someone who loved him in return. Most people thought he was queer, because he wore such old clothes and spent most of his time in the out-of-doors.

One day, when James Barrett was working for Mr. Bridgman, Uncle Asa came to pay one of his regular visits to Laura. It was a lovely May day, and he and Laura went off, hand in hand, to spend the whole day out-of-doors. All day they roamed the woods and fields, and Uncle Asa taught her many things. How could he teach her, you may wonder, since she could not see or hear or talk with him?

When they sat on the fresh green grass, now soft and warm in the May sun, she was learning that it was different from the cold, hard earth they had walked on in winter. When the gentle, cool breeze blew on her cheeks, she knew it was different from the biting cold wind of March. When Uncle Asa put a long stick in her hand and helped her put one end of it in the rushing water of a stream, she was learning that water moves and pushes. They could not talk about what she learned, but she felt these things and, in her own way, she thought about them.

It was probably because she had such days as these with Asa Tenney that she kept on being curious and eager to find out all she could about the world that lay outside of her. It was the eagerness and curiosity that Laura showed, as she followed her mother around the kitchen or went out with Uncle Asa, that interested James Barrett so much. And it was because of his interest that, a short time later, something very wonderful happened to Laura Bridgman.

When James Barrett finished his work for Mr. Bridgman, he went back to his studies in the nearby town. But he could not forget that little deaf-blind child, rocking by the fire, following her mother about the house, walking in the meadows with Asa Tenney. He told a man at the school, Dr. Mussey, about Laura and asked him to go and see Laura himself. Dr. Mussey went and he, too, thought that she was an extremely bright little girl. He went home and wrote an article about her for the newspaper.

Dr. Samuel Gridley Howe, head of a school for the blind in Boston, read the article. At that time people did not think that children who were deaf and blind could be taught anything, and they thought that it was foolish to try to teach them to read and write. Dr. Howe did not believe this. He believed that they could learn through the sense of touch what the rest of us learn with our eyes and ears.

Dr. Howe decided to go to New Hampshire where Laura lived and get permission to bring her to his school. He got on the train and went to the Bridgman farmhouse. He was so impressed with Laura that he urged Mr. and Mrs. Bridgman to let Laura be taught at his school in Boston. They agreed, and everyone was delighted.

That is — not quite everyone. Laura, of course, had no idea of what had been decided and Uncle Asa Tenney was very, very sad. He loved her and believed that he could teach her all that she needed to know. In spite of all the wonderful things that later happened to Laura, he was never happy about her having gone away to school.

But Laura Bridgman never forgot Uncle Asa. She knew that if he had not spent days and days with her, from the time she was four years old until she was almost eight, she would never have been able to learn what Dr. Howe taught her.

*. . . The poor child had sat in mute amazement, and patiently imitated everything her teacher did; but now the truth began to flash upon her, her intellect began to work, she perceived that here was a way by which she could herself make up a sign of anything that was in her own mind, and show it to another mind, and at once her countenance lighted up with a human expression; it was no longer a dog or parrot, — it was an immortal spirit, eagerly seizing upon a*

*new link of union with other spirits!* . . . — MAUD HOWE ELLIOTT
and FLORENCE HOWE HALL\*

## 22. *A Little Girl from New Hampshire: Part II*

How would you begin to teach someone to understand you and
talk to you, if she could not see or hear or talk?  Dr. Howe knew
that he could never make Laura Bridgman see with her eyes, or
hear with her ears or talk with her mouth.

But, from watching her, he knew that Laura was already "seeing" a great deal through her hands, and that it was through her
hands that he would have to make her hear and talk.  Dr. Howe had
been thinking for many years about ways to teach the deaf-blind
and he was eager to try these ideas out with Laura.  But he knew
that first he must give her a chance to get used to her new home.

Can you imagine how she must have felt?  No one could explain to her why she had suddenly left her mother and father and
brothers and sisters and her beloved Uncle Asa, and was now living
among strangers in a strange place.  Remember, she was only seven
years old, and even for those of us who can see and hear and talk, it
would be very upsetting and frightening to be taken away from
home to live with strangers.

How much worse it must have been for Laura!  Where was the
old farm kitchen she knew the feel of so well, the warm fireplace,
the purring cat, the feel of her mother's skirt?  Suddenly they were
no longer out there for her to touch and no one could tell her why.
No one could tell her by words, or by the looks on their faces, that
what was happening to her was being done because people cared
about her and wanted to help her.

But Dr. Howe was a wonderfully gentle and patient teacher
and in a very short time he was able to make Laura feel that she
was with friends.  Dr. Howe had her live right in his apartment with
his sister and himself and, by the end of the first week, it was clear
that Laura trusted him and was interested and curious about this
new experience of hers.  At the end of two weeks he felt that he
could begin his experiment with the help of a special teacher,
Miss Drew.

Dr. Howe wanted especially to teach Laura language, our
words for things.  She already had a kind of language of her own.
For example, for "cat" she made a motion like scratching with her
fingers, and for "scissors" she made two of her fingers cut.  But only
people in her own family knew what her language meant.  Dr. Howe

\* *Op. cit.,* p. 51.

wanted to teach her that people have words for these things and that, if she learned these words, then everyone, not just her family, could understand her.

But how to begin? Dr. Howe decided to take some things that Laura knew well, such as a key and a spoon, and to try to teach her our names for them. He took a large spoon and a large key and below these he pasted their names — SPOON, KEY — written in raised letters. Then he took Laura's hands and had her feel of the spoon and, underneath it, the word "spoon." He then had her feel of the key and the word "key."

He guided her hands over these objects and words again and again and again, until he thought she could understand that the *word* for spoon and the *word* for key were just as different from each other as a spoon and key are different from each other. Of course, Laura had no idea yet that the word at the bottom was a *word* or that the word was the *name* of the thing.

The next day he tried something a little different. He had the word "spoon" and the word "key" printed in raised letters on little slips of paper. He let Laura feel of the spoon itself and of the key. Then he let her feel the words that were separate from the objects. Very brightly, she took the one that said SPOON and laid it on the spoon and the one that said KEY she laid on the key.

Before doing anything else new, he did all these things with other familiar objects such as a book, a pencil, a knife. In a few days she was able to take, from a whole pile of names, the right name for whichever object she was given.

So far, she knew only words, not letters. Now they wanted to teach her that words, such as "spoon," are made up of letters, like S-P-O-O-N. So they cut the whole name up into separate letters, and Dr. Howe lined them up again into the word. In a very short time, Laura was able to take a mixed-up pile of letters, perhaps Y-K-E, and put them in the right order to make KEY. Soon she could do this with all the letters of the words she knew — KEY, SPOON, PENCIL, BOOK. She was really a very bright little girl and was already doing things that would not be easy for a regular first-grader.

In order to make it easier for Laura to work with these letters, Dr. Howe had some metal letters made for her and a frame into which she could fit them. She soon learned to put the letters of all the words she knew in rows in this frame.

Now Dr. Howe wanted to teach her one more difficult new thing. He wanted to teach her the manual alphabet. Manual means "hand," and the manual alphabet is an alphabet that you can make with your hand. By holding your hand and fingers in different positions, you can spell words (see Suggestions).

In order to spell words to a person who is deaf and blind, the right hand of the person "talking" spells into the left hand of the person "listening." But Dr. Howe could not say to Laura Bridgman, "Look, this is how the letter S is made in the manual alphabet." How could he tell her? This is what he did.

Dr. Howe placed Laura's fingers on the letter S of her metal letters. Then he held his hand in the position of S in the manual alphabet in her hand. Then he placed her hand on the letter P. Then he made P in the manual alphabet, and so on for all the letters in SPOON. Over and over he did this. Sometimes he changed to the word KEY, letting her feel of the letters and then spelling into her hand.

And suddenly it was clear to her! These motions of Dr. Howe's hand in hers were another way of making these letters. Dr. Howe was *talking* to her and she was *hearing* him, all through her hands. Dr. Howe later wrote that he could almost name the moment and the look on Laura's face when she really understood what he was doing. Her face seemed to shine with a new light.

For the next few days Laura Bridgman nearly wore her teachers out asking the name of everything that her hands touched. She seemed almost to be dancing with joy, and although her eyes were still blind, her ears deaf and her lips unable to form words, at last she could see and hear and talk, all through the wonderful sense of touch.

### SUGGESTIONS

1. *The Helen Keller Story*, by Catherine Owens Peare (New York: Crowell, 1959), contains illustrations of the manual alphabet that are unusually clear. They are by Jeanyee Wong. A chart showing the whole alphabet might be mounted, and then the words "spoon," "key" and "book" added as they are worked out by the children.

*If all the world were children*
*With fathers, mothers gone —*
*Who would there be to feed us*
*And help the whole day long?*
  — SOPHIA L. FAHS, "If"*

* From *Martin and Judy Songs*, No. 53.

### 23. *"What if —— "*

When one of the children in our family was about seven years old, I noticed that just about every day we would have a conversation something like this:

"Hey, Mum ——"

And I'd say, "What?"

And he'd say, "Guess what?"

And I'd say, "What?"

And he'd say, *"What if* there wasn't any gravity?"

And I'd say, "Well, what would happen?"

And he'd say, "I guess you would go flying right off into space, maybe all the way to the moon!" And then he would go away and think about it.

He could think up more "what if's" than any person I ever knew. But I know that a great many other children are great "what-ifers," too.

Here are just a few "what if's" that I have heard lately:

What if everyone had a face that looked just like everyone else's?

What if you went to sleep one night and didn't wake up in the morning?

What if the sun set and never came up again?

What if a fire started in your house when everyone was asleep and no one discovered it?

What if you were going over a bridge and it broke?

What if you were promoted into the second grade and you couldn't do second grade work?

Just listen to your family and your friends for a few days, and see if you don't hear quite a few "what if's."

Why do you suppose people make up these "what if's," especially children about six, seven or eight years old?

I have been thinking about this for several years and have some ideas about why it happens.

For one thing, I've noticed that quite a few "what if's" are worried "what if's." "What if you couldn't do second grade work? What if a fire broke out in the night? What if the bridge broke?"

Do you think perhaps these "what if's" are a way of saying "I'm worried about something," without coming right out and saying, "I'm worried"?

I think I understand a little about why six-, seven- and eight-year-olds, in particular, are such great worry "what-ifers." People this old aren't babies any more. They are doing many new things by themselves and they are finding out many things about the world beyond their own homes. It is an awfully big world really, and people six, seven or eight are still rather young to be out in that world alone. But they want to be, sometimes, and it worries them, sometimes. And that's all right, too, because being able to worry is something pretty special. It means that we are able to think back to things that have happened and ahead to things that are *going* to happen or *might* happen. Because we are able to worry, we are also able to plan ahead.

As far as I know, human beings are the only animals there are who can do this. It goes together with our being able to talk.

So, if you find yourself asking a worried "what if," first of all pat yourself on the back. It means you've grown up enough to think back and think ahead and imagine different things that might happen. But then, after you've felt really good about being able to worry, you need to do some clear thinking and acting.

For example, let's take the very common "what if" of a six-year-old, "What if I missed the school bus," or if you don't take the bus, "What if I'm late for school?"

A three-year-old who goes to nursery school couldn't even worry abut this. His mother just gets him there. She knows he couldn't plan to be ready. But by the time you are in regular school, probably your mother and father have said that it is mostly up to you to be ready on time. They are giving you a chance to be your own boss. You like that, but you may worry about it some, too.

You could *just* worry about it all the time, or you could *do* something about it. What could you do? You could ask for an alarm clock for Christmas perhaps and plan to get up the minute it rings. Or you could ask your mother to wake you up at a certain time. You could be sure to get most of the things you want to take to school the next day all together in one place the night before. What else could you do?

There are two good things to remember about worry "what if's": find out what you need to know, and do what you need to do.

There are other *what if's* that aren't worry ones. There are some just plain fun ones, and there are some that show us imagining the world just a little different from the way it is now: what if people had two heads and one arm? Probably some of the greatest inventors and discoverers have been good "what-ifers."

There's another boy in our family who is going to be seven years old pretty soon. The other day we had this conversation:

"Hey, Mum ——"

And I said, "What?"

And he said, "Guess what?"

And I said, "What?"

And he said, "What if you hadn't married Dad, would I be me?"

And I said, "Oh, oh, another 'what-ifer.' "

And he said, "Would I?"

OTHER IDEAS

1. Two well-known stories are examples of worry "what if's." They are good examples of what happens when the worrying gets in the way of thinking: "The Nervous Little Rabbit," which may be found in the collection, *From Long Ago and Many Lands,* and "The Three Sillies," found in *My Book House,* Vol. VI. Among other things, they show that "what if-ing" is an old, and a world-wide phenomenon. 2. The whole of the song "If," quoted at the beginning of this conversation, would be interesting to think about.

*. . . Use your eyes as if tomorrow you would be stricken blind.*
— HELEN KELLER, "Three Days to See"*

### 24. A Big "What if ——"[16]

Probably you have heard of Helen Keller. (See Suggestion 1.) If you have, you know that when she was born she was a healthy little baby girl. She grew, like any healthy little baby, and by the time she was almost two, she could walk and run, and say a few words. But then she became very, very sick.

When the sickness was over, it was found that she had become deaf and blind. Because she was just learning to talk, and now could not hear other people, she was soon unable to talk any more. She was mute.

For the next four years she kept on growing but no one could teach her anything because she could not hear them or see them. She lived almost like a little animal.

Fortunately, when she was six years old, her parents were able to find a wonderful teacher for her. The teacher's name was Anne Sullivan. This teacher taught her to understand language by spelling words into her hands, and she was soon able to teach her all the things you learn in school.

* *Atlantic Monthly,* January 1933.
[16] This conversation is based on the article quoted above.

Helen Keller has lived a long and wonderful life. She has helped other blind people all over the world. She has written many books and articles.

Once she wrote an article for a magazine in which she asked herself a big *"what if"*: "If I were given the use of my eyes for three days, what should I most like to see?"

Before I tell you the things she chose to see in those three days, let us think what *we* would most want to see if we had always been blind.

Let's not begin naming things right off. First, let's just think for a few minutes. Remember, there are going to be only three days in which to see.

When Helen Keller wrote this article she was a grown-up woman. But I wouldn't be a bit surprised if many of the things that she wanted to be sure to see in her three precious days will be the same as many of the things you'll mention. (A list might be made from the children's suggestions. Then the conversation might continue somewhat as follows.)

### The First Day

First of all, Helen Keller wanted to see her own family, her dearest friends, and of course her teacher, Miss Sullivan. She said that she especially wanted to see people's eyes. Aren't eyes amazing, when you think about them? With our eyes, we somehow see into each other. How do we do it?

Helen Keller also wanted to be sure to spend some time, that first day, looking at the face of a baby. She wanted to see how people look before they have lived very long and before they have any worries and problems.

She also wanted to spend quite a bit of time looking at the things in her own home. She had felt these things many times. Now she wanted to see them: the rugs she walked on, the pictures that she knew were on the walls, the books that were like old friends.

She wanted to see the printed books that other people read to her (into her hand, of course, not into her ears), and the books written in Braille that she had been feeling and reading to herself for many years.

The afternoon of the first day she would spend taking a long walk in the woods. For years Miss Sullivan took Helen Keller for walks, even climbing trees with her. All the time they were walking Miss Sullivan was spelling into Helen's hands. She was telling Helen all about everything that she, the teacher, was seeing.

Miss Sullivan wrote something interesting about those walks

to a friend: "Indeed, I feel as if I had never seen anything until now, Helen finds so much to ask about along the way."

It's interesting to think about that: a sighted person saw much more because she had a blind person with her. Can you understand why that might be?

In her article, Helen Keller wrote about a friend of hers who came home from a long walk in the woods. Helen asked her what she had seen. "Oh, nothing in particular," said the friend. Miss Keller wrote that a person would never say a thing like that if he or she knew what it was like to be blind.

The last thing that Helen Keller wanted to be sure to see on her first day of sight was a sunset. How many of us, who can see, ever bother to watch the sunset? And yet, if we had to pay to watch the sunset, we would probably form long lines to buy tickets to see it. Or if it only happened once a year, probably millions of people would be sure to go out and watch it.

*The Second Day*

On the second day there were four things in particular that Helen Keller wanted to see. Can you guess the first? Watch the sun *rise!* How many of us bother to get up very often to see that amazing and beautiful sight? I know *I* don't!

After breakfast she knew exactly where she wanted to go, and I imagine every one of us would like to go right along with her. She would go to the Natural History Museum! She had read about cave men and glaciers and dinosaurs, and she had been to museums many times. People at the museums had been very wonderful, too, and let her feel of many of the exhibits that seeing people are not allowed to touch. But she wanted to go and see with her eyes those dinosaurs whose enormous legs she had been allowed to feel. Feeling of them just couldn't give her a picture of how the whole dinosaur really looked. She planned to spend the entire morning at the museum.

In the afternoon she wanted to visit an art museum. When she wrote this article, there were no jet planes and so she couldn't possibly have chosen to take a quick whizz around the world. But by going to an art museum she felt that she could see examples of how people from all over the world in earlier times and in the present have shown their feelings about life.

The evening of the second day Helen Keller would spend at the theater. She often did go to plays. How do you suppose she "saw" a play? The person she was with had to spell as much as she could of what was happening into her hand. Really to see a play would be very different, however, wouldn't it?

## The Third Day

On her last day of seeing, after having watched the sunrise again, she would go to a big city. She wanted actually to see many of the things that had been described to her, but that she just couldn't really imagine.

She wanted to stand on a bridge, go to the top of a skyscraper, see a great boat on the water. She wanted to see all the hurry and confusion and bustle of a great city. But most of all, that last day in the city, she wanted to watch people: rich and poor, old and young, sad and happy. She wanted to see people playing and working, laughing and crying. Then, in her memory, she would take all these people and the expressions on their faces back into the darkness with her.

The last night of her last day of sight she would again go to the theater. This time she said that she would be sure to go to a funny play, a comedy. Her last glimpse of the world would be of people, on the stage and in the audience, laughing together. It makes us feel good to laugh with other people, doesn't it?

To those of us who can see *every* day Helen Keller wrote at the end of her article: "Use your eyes as if tomorrow you would be stricken blind."

SUGGESTIONS

1. The first two chapters of *The Helen Keller Story,* by Catherine Owens Peare (Crowell, 1959), tell of the early years. The whole book is excellent and, with very little adapting, can be used with children aged six to ten.
2. On a large blackboard the children's list might be made, and then Helen Keller's list.
3. The pictures on page 108 in *The Family of Man* (published for the Museum of Modern Art. New York: Maco Magazine Corp., 1955) and the lower one on page 121 in *The World is Young* (Copyright, 1958, Wayne Miller; New York: The Ridge Press, 1958) could be used with this conversation. The children might be asked to look at one of these pictures, and then to close their eyes and see how long they could hold the picture in their mind.

*"That's the most important thing about our country," the old man went on, "You can never hide your feelings. You can't fool people or pretend you are different from what you really are. Your cloud, by its color, tells the truth to everyone you meet whether you want it to do so or not."* — SOPHIA L. FAHS, "A Visit to the Land-of-Great-Men"*

* *From Long Ago and Many Lands, p. 74.*

### 25. *What Color Is Your Cloud?*

Have you ever been to a party and not had any fun at all? But, when it came time to say good-bye, you went right ahead and said, "Thank you for a very nice time"?

How would you like to live in a place where you could never hide your feelings like that? Instead, everyone would always know just exactly how you were really feeling. This is a kind of "what if," isn't it? What if everyone always knew just how you were feeling?

Here's a story about such a place. It's not a true story. You might call a story of this kind a fable. Although it couldn't happen, there is something true about it. It is a story that comes from China. (Read or tell the story referred to in the quotation above.)

Well, how would you like to live in the Land-of-Great-Men? Do you feel as the Chinese travelers did and wish we all had clouds, too? Remember, before you heard the story, I asked you whether you had ever been to a party and had a perfectly terrible time? If you had had a cloud under your feet, it would have been looking rather black when it came time to go home, wouldn't it? Would that have been bad or good?

The person who gave the party might have been a little embarrassed to find that you hadn't had a good time. Perhaps the next time she would be more careful to see that all of her guests were enjoying themselves. Whose fault is it when you don't have a good time at a party?

Why do you suppose so many of the clouds in the Land-of-Great-Men were rainbow-colored? Have you ever tried to keep *in* your real feelings for hours and hours or even for days and days? I have and it makes me feel almost sick to my stomach. When I finally let my real feelings show, I feel much better, and I think the people around me feel better, too.

The people in the Land-of-Great-Men knew that they couldn't hide their real feelings because of their clouds. Most of them had discovered how much better they felt when they said what they meant and meant what they said. So most of the time they did just that, and their clouds were rainbow-colored.

Sometimes, when the children in our family come home from school, I like to pretend that they have clouds under their feet and I try to find out what color they are. It doesn't take very long, especially with the first-grader.

If he didn't like the hot lunch, or if someone pushed him into a mud puddle, or if the teacher was cross, or if he made lots of mistakes on his papers, I can see his black cloud just as clearly as anything. He yells at me, fights with his big brother, gets cross with the baby and ends up in tears.

Sometimes, before he has a chance to do any of these things, if I can see that he's wearing a black cloud, quick as I can I make a big, fat, peanut butter sandwich and pour him a glass of cold milk. Then I start to make supper and pretty soon he begins to tell me how his day went.

In between mouthfuls of sandwich and milk, I hear about some of the worst things that happened. Then I begin to hear about a few fun things, and then he kicks off his shoes and I see that his cloud is turning blue, then green, then red, then yellow and, by the time the sandwich is all gone and the milk all drunk, the cloud is rainbow-colored — at least for a little while!

When the big girl in our family was a little girl, she liked this story about the Land-of-Great-Men. She liked to draw better than to talk sometimes and, when she came home from school one day, she was terribly mad at her best friend. She went to the playroom and she got a big piece of paper and she drew a picture of her friend with a black, black cloud under her feet.

"There," she said. "That's how Patty looked today." Then she took off her school clothes, put on her play clothes, went over to Patty's house, and they had a lovely afternoon.

Would it help if your mother or your father or your teacher had a cloud? I think it would. Don't they almost seem to, sometimes?

We can pretend, once in a while, that we have clouds, and can suddenly ask ourselves, "What color would my cloud be, right now, if I had one?"

#### OTHER IDEAS

1. Think to yourselves a minute about all the people with whom you've had much to do from the time you got up this morning until now. Pick out the one who made the biggest impression on you for some reason — your mother, or sister, or brother, or a friend, etc. Just think it to yourself. Now, if you were going to make a picture of that person with one of these clouds, what color would you paint?

Can you tell, without saying who the person was, what sort of things about the person made you decide to put a rainbow cloud there? What sort of things suggested the black or dark clouds to some of you?

When you think about yourself, what color cloud do you picture yourself wearing? (By Mildred Lester.)

*And it came to pass, when the evil spirit from God was upon Saul, that David took an harp, and played with his hand: so Saul was*

*refreshed, and was well, and the evil spirit departed from him.*
— I Samuel 16:23.

### 26. *Wrinkles*

Have you ever taken a bath and stayed in the water so long that your fingers got all puffy and wrinkly?

Here's a poem a little girl just five years old made up about that. She called her poem "Wrinkles."

> Whenever I take a long, long bath
> And stay in the tub to play,
> My fingers get puffy and wrinkled
> In the funniest sort of way.
>
> Then what I really need to have —
> If there ever could be such a thing —
> Is a just-a-little-bit, not-very-hot
> Kind of an iron for my skin.[17]

That's funny, isn't it? You know, of course, why she didn't want the iron *very* hot? So she wouldn't burn herself! I guess she wanted it tiny so it would iron down around the edges of her fingers.

I think all of us have our fingers get wrinkly that way when we stay in the water too long. It happens to all of us, because, as far as I know, we all enjoy playing in water.

Babies like to splash in water and to pour water into the sink. When they are old enough, they like to walk in puddles. Bigger children like to play in wading pools, and lakes and oceans. Even grownups like water, to swim in and especially for taking nice hot baths.

There's something interesting about hot baths, too. The little girl who made up the poem about wrinkly fingers made up another one about baths. She noticed something that I've noticed too, but I'd never written down my noticing. Poets, like this little girl, are good noticers, and they often are able to *say* what the rest of us have been feeling.

Did you ever take a bath with someone else, maybe your baby sister or your brother? And did you ever discover that the littler the person, the colder they want the water, and the bigger the person, the hotter they like it?

The little girl who made up the poem that I'm going to read

[17] Ellen Jean Thompson, *Ellen's Poems: Twelve Poems for Children* (privately printed, 1960); used by permission of Roger and Jean Thompson.

to you had a big sister and sometimes they took baths together.
This is what she said in her poem, "Our Bath."

> I think the water is tippy-toe hot,
> But Kristin says it's *cold*.
> Maybe I won't think it's quite so hot
> When I am a seven-year-old![18]

So if you want your bath at just the temperature that *you* like
it, it's better to take your bath alone. When you have the water just
the way you want it, it makes you feel good all over to stay in it for
a long time, even if your fingers do get wrinkly.

I wonder why it makes you feel good? I think that I read once
that we have little tiny nerve endings all over the outside of our
body. When we get in water, those nerve endings are covered by
the water and have a chance to rest.

There's a boy at our house who is six years old, and sometimes
when things haven't gone just right I run him a big, deep bath. He
sometimes says he doesn't want any old bath. But finally he gets
into it, and then he plays and plays and plays.

We have a whole shelf full of cups and boats and plastic toys
that we keep near the tub, and pretty soon I hear him in there,
singing and talking to himself.

Finally I have to call in to him and say, "If we are going to
have any stories before bed, you'd better get out now."

"O.K.," he says, in the happiest voice you ever heard.

When he finally gets out, of course, his fingers are very wrinkly,
but do you know something about his face? Sometimes his face is
still dirty! His face isn't a bit wrinkled! Sometimes he hasn't even
gotten it wet!

But I don't care, because even if all the dirt was not washed
off, whatever was making him feel mad got washed away.

Did you ever take a bath to wash away your mad feelings?

Of course, there are other ways to get rid of them, too. One
day at our house we made a list of all the different ways we could
think of to get rid of mad feelings.

Do you use some of these?

(1) Music:
   Listening to records or the radio
   Playing the piano or some other instrument
   Singing
(2) Talking about what's bothering us or reading stories
   about other children with the same troubles

[18] Ellen Jean Thompson, *op. cit.*

(3) Acting things out: with puppets, or in a play, or just in make-believe with our dolls or our friends, or with our blocks and trucks

(4) Playing with clay, dough, sand, water, paint, crayons

(5) A good cry: a good screech, shouting or yelling, or slamming doors

(6) Biting or kicking something

As you grow up, it's a good idea to try to discover ways of getting over your mad feelings that not only make you feel better, but that also make the people around you feel good. That screeching way isn't really very pleasant for the other people in the house; neither is door-slamming or kicking or biting.

What ways do you use and how do they make the rest of the family feel?

### SUGGESTIONS

1. The story "King Saul Finds A Harpist," in *From Long Ago and Many Lands,* tells the biblical story of how King Saul used music to calm his nerves.

*. . . This was the gladdest moving day that Laura had known. Ma and Mary were glad because this was the end of traveling; they were going to settle on the homestead and never move again. Carrie was glad because she was eager to see the homestead, Laura was glad because they were leaving town, Pa was glad because he always liked moving and Grace sang and shouted in gladness because all the others were glad.* — LAURA INGALLS WILDER, By the Shores of Silver Lake*

### 27. *Shall We Move?*

How many of you are living in the same house that your family was living in when you were born? If you are not, it means you have moved, doesn't it?

How many of you have moved twice since you were born? How many have moved three times? How many have moved more times than you can remember? Nowadays people move a lot!

How many of you have moved to a different country at some time? How many have moved to a different state? We move great distances nowadays, don't we?

* (New York: Harper's, 1939), p. 232.

Why do you suppose people move often and far nowadays? There are several reasons. Here's a hint about one. Is it easier to move by covered wagon or by moving van? Big vans and trucks can move quickly, can't they? Jet planes and great ocean liners can whisk people across oceans and around the world.

So it is easy and quick to move; that's one thing. For another thing, with telephones and mail reaching all parts of the world, businessmen and governments of countries can have people working for them in very distant places.

You may have moved often, for example, because your father works for the United States Army or some other branch of the government. Or perhaps your father works for some big business: an engineering company or an oil company or an automobile company.

What if your father were working in Boston and came home one night and said: "We're moving! I'm to start work in San Francisco next month." How would you feel? Would you want to move, or wouldn't you?

I once read in the newspaper a story written by a mother. She told about the time that the father in their family came home and said something very much like this. Only he didn't say, "We're moving." He said, "Shall we move?"

There were three children in the family, and that night at supper they talked about the idea of moving. When the meal was over, the father took a large sheet of paper and a pencil, and divided the paper down the middle. At the top of one side he wrote, *Reasons we should move,* and at the top of the other side he wrote, *Reasons we should not move.*

Then, for the next hour, they filled in the two sides of the paper and talked about their reasons. Here are some of the things they put down.

| *Reasons we should move* | *Reasons we should not move* |
|---|---|
| (1) Daddy thinks he would like this new job better. | (1) We would have to leave our house just after we've built our new porch. |
| (2) We would see a new part of the country. | (2) We would have to leave our best friends. |
| (3) We would be near the San Francisco Giants. [That's a baseball team, and the 11-year-old boy gave this reason.] | (3) We couldn't go to the Red Sox games any more. [That was the 11-year-old baseball fan again.] |

(4) Daddy would make more money.

(5) We could swim in the Pacific Ocean. [The 8-year-old girl gave this reason.]

(6) We would be lots nearer one of our grandmothers.

(7) We'd make new friends and still, in a way, have the old ones. We could write to them and they could come and visit, maybe.

(8) We'd see cowboys and Indians. [The 6-year-old boy gave this reason.]

(4) We couldn't swim in the Atlantic Ocean any more. [This was the 8-year-old girl.]

(5) I like my school and my teacher. I won't go! [That was the 6-year-old.]

(6) I like the church we go to here. [That was the mother.]

(7) We *know* we like it here, and we might not like it there.

What do you think of the reasons they gave? Are there some that they didn't put down that you would have?

The mother who wrote this story for the newspaper said that, in the end, they did decide to move and now, a year later, the whole family is glad they did.

Perhaps you and your family have done something like this list making at the time you were moving. Or maybe your father couldn't *choose* whether or not he wanted to move and you all just *had* to move if he wanted to keep that job.

In the olden days when people moved, they often had to be very brave. Can you think why? Imagine how the Pilgrims must have felt as they started across an enormous ocean in sailing boats. The trip took several months; they weren't sure they would make the journey safely, and when they landed, what was waiting for them?

Were there nice motels, new houses, or even old houses? Were there stores, doctors, hospitals, schools, all ready and waiting for them? No indeed! There was a rocky shore, deep woods, wolves, and Indians who did not understand their language or what these strange new people wanted.

And the people who helped settle our country in the years after the Pilgrims — they had to be brave, too. Have your mother or father or teacher at school read you any of the wonderful books that have been written about the men and women and children who opened up our country? Oh, there are some exciting and some sad stories — *The Little House in the Big Woods, Palace Wagon Family, On to Oregon* and loads of others. (See Suggestions.)

Yes, people often had to be brave to move in the olden days. You don't have to be brave to move now, although perhaps in some ways you do.

How many of you have moved since you started going to school? How did you like being new at school? Many children find that they don't like it one bit, especially if their family moved after school had started. The regular first day of school is always rather exciting and fun, but if you're the only one for whom it is the first day, it's mostly just scary! Everyone else has a friend, or seems to. Everyone else knows what the playground rules are. They all know just which room to go to when the bell rings. They know the way this teacher wants you to write capital G, and things like that.

If your family has ever moved in the middle of the year, I think you know what I mean!

It can be almost as bad out of school, too. When you're new in the neighborhood, it seems that everyone has a best friend already. They have different rules for playing marbles, or hopscotch or jump-rope, and sometimes they even say your rules are cheating. All they are, really, is different.

But maybe there are some good things about being new in a place that I haven't thought about. Do you know any *good* things about being new?

### SUGGESTIONS

1. The quotation at the beginning of this conversation is from one of *The Little House* Series by Laura Ingalls Wilder. These wonderful books make superb family reading and, for families who must move often, have other values beyond their intrinsic excellence. They show a family that moved again and again but, because of their rich family life, thrived on it. Reading together can give a family a unity that frequent moves cannot touch. Friends in books can go anywhere with us.

Other good books are: *Palace Wagon Family*, by Margaret Sutton (New York: Knopf, 1957), a true story of the Donner Party, for older children; *On To Oregon*, by Honoré Willsie Morrow, also a classic, for older children.

*At the same time, the displacement of the permanent homestead by the modern rented tenement — now here — now there — has cut another anchor-line of the human mind. Most people have no home that is a symbol of their childhood, not even a definite memory of one place to serve that purpose.* — SUZANNE K. LANGER, Philosophy in a New Key*

* Cambridge: Harvard, 1942), pp. 291–292.

## 28. *Pulling Up Roots*

(A large flower pot containing a plant that has been transplanted the previous day might be at the front of the room. It should look extremely droopy. A tomato plant would be excellent. Beside it should be another pot with the same kind of plant, not transplanted, and looking very healthy. If this cannot be arranged, begin with a question such as "Have you ever seen a plant the day after it was transplanted?" instead of using the beginning below.)

What do you think is the matter with this plant? (Point to the droopy one.) It looks as if it were dying, doesn't it? It isn't though. It has just been moved, that's all. When a plant is moved, we say it has been "transplanted."

This other plant hasn't been moved. In a few days this droopy one will have gotten used to its new surroundings and it will soon look like the other plant.

One big difference (and there are several) between plants and animals is — perhaps you know — plants can't move themselves around. This is because plants have roots that reach into the soil. Down in the soil the roots divide up into smaller and smaller rootlets. They help the plant grow and they help hold it in place.

When a plant is moved the little rootlets are broken and the larger roots are disturbed. That is why the plant droops for a while after it is moved. Some plants, carrots and California poppies, for example, can't be transplanted at all. Many others, like this one, are all right if you move them when they are small and if you do it carefully.

Animals (and that includes people) can move themselves around. They don't have roots. Look down at your feet. There are no little roots going down into the floor holding you in place, are there?

But in a way, animals, and most especially people, *do* have roots. The roots we have don't show. They are invisible. But when our family moves to a new town we may *feel* just as droopy as this transplanted plant *looks*. Our invisible roots have been disturbed!

Let's see whether we can see what some of the invisible roots are that people have. I'll draw a picture and we'll try to make the invisible roots visible — that means "able to be seen."

I'm going to draw a family. It may not be just exactly like your family, but that won't matter. I'll draw a father and a mother, a sister and a brother and a baby. (Draw large stick figures, very rough, on a large easel or blackboard.)

Every person in the family is separate from every other person, isn't he? But they weren't always separate. Did you know that when you were growing inside your mother's body, you really had roots? They grew out from the round sack in which you were growing, right into part of your mother's body.

When you were born you came out of this sack and from then on you were separate from your mother. But a tiny baby and even a little child almost seems to have roots still, like a plant. He wants to be near his mother most of the time.

So let's draw some roots going out from this baby here to his mother. We won't make them grow out of his feet though. Where *shall* we make the roots come from that show he loves his mother and wants to be near her? From his heart, his brain, or where?

If the whole family moves to a new town, will these roots from the baby to his mother be disturbed or broken? No, they won't, will they, because his mother comes right along, too.

Now perhaps we should draw some of these roots that feed the baby's feelings to everyone else in the family. Don't you think the baby loves his daddy? I think so. And what about that brother and sister? All the babies that I know seem to smile their biggest smiles for their brothers and sisters. You should hear our baby squeal when he sees the school bus come up to our house! He knows that his brothers and sisters are in it.

And, of course, we'll want to draw some roots from the mother and father to each other, and to all three of the children. Then we'd better draw some roots from the brother and sister to the baby and to the mother and father and to each other.

Can you remember the first night you slept away from home? Didn't you feel a little as though some part of you had been broken off, and didn't you feel rather droopy, when no one from home was there to say goodnight?

So we had better connect up all the members of the family with these roots. These are roots, however, that don't get bothered much when we move, since the whole family comes along. That's a good thing to remember when you're moving — at least you have your family! Sometimes it *is* necessary for the father to go ahead of the rest of the family, but for the most part, the family stays together.

What about the roots that go out to all the *friends* of the family? A good many of those are going to be disturbed, aren't they? There are the father's and mother's friends, the friends with whom the children play, the friends at school, in Scouts, at church. But, of course, you'll be able to write letters still to your old friends and perhaps visit them some time. One of the first things you'll want to do after you've been "transplanted" to a new neighborhood is make some new friends. It takes time, but we need friends just as much as this plant needs good new soil. I'll draw roots going out to all their friends.

One *good* thing about having people move a lot, as they do now, is that more and more of us know how droopy moving away from our old friends makes us feel. So, when a new family shows up in our neighborhood, we can remember how we felt when we were new and do something about it.

Then we ought to have roots going out to the *places* near where the family lives. Once, when one of the children in our family was eighteen months old, or a year and a half, we went on a long trip. We went six hundred miles from home and we stayed there for a week. All the time that we were gone, that poor little baby walked around the house where we were staying, saying, "Home, home, home, home." He was too little to understand words very well, and we just couldn't make him understand that home was far away and that we would be going home in a week. Perhaps, if your family has moved when someone in it was about two years old, you've seen something like this happen.

It isn't as bad when we're older, but we do all have invisible roots going out to our house, our own room in the house, the playground we like to play at, or, if we live in the country, the trees we like to climb in, the woods we walk in and the river we fish in. There are the places we like to go for picnics, for swimming, for hiking. All these roots are going to be broken when the family moves, aren't they?

Of course, just as soon as we get settled in our new home, we'll start sending out new little rootlets — to the new house, new school, new playground, new fields and new woods. In a very short time our droopy feelings should begin to leave us.

Can you think of any invisible roots that I've forgotten to draw?

> *And nothing so calls the thoughts of a man back home as a few notes fluted far away and long after. A bird travels light, but he can carry with him a whole countryside and way of life. I cannot hear the red-winged blackbird's metallic trill that I do not regain, for an instant, a lost marsh and the friend of my boyhood.* — DONALD CULROSS PEATTIE and NOEL PEATTIE, A Cup of Sky*

\* (Boston: Houghton Mifflin), pp. 84–85.

### 29. *What Shall We Take When We Move?*

A few years ago our family was going to move.

At first we all thought it was exciting and fun, but as the time came nearer and nearer, we began to feel sadder and sadder. One night, before the children went to bed, we were talking about the things we could take with us when we went, and the things we would have to leave behind.

We all thought that there were many, many things that we would have to leave behind us, and this was what made us sad. But as we talked we discovered more and more things that we really did not have to leave behind us. When the children had gone to bed, I wrote a poem about some of the things we had talked about, and called it "What Shall We Take When We Move?"

> We'll
> Take our beds
> And our sleds
> And our clothes —
> We'll need those,
> And our bikes
> And our trikes.
> All the blocks and the trains,
> All the dolls and the planes,
> And the pots and the pans
> They can go in the vans
> When we move.
>
> Now the swings on the trees
> We will surely take these,
> But the branches must stay.
> We can't take those away.
> (We could take a few shoots.)
> No — we can't take the sky.
> We don't need to, know why?
> It will be here and there,
> Like the clouds and the air.
> Like the sun up above.
> Like the stars that we love,
> And the planets and moon,
> And like April and June,
> They are with us wherever we go.

No, we can't take the birds.
But we'll find the same kind;
Sparrow and Chickadee,
Robin and Jay,
Oriole nests hung just the same way.

Oh, we'll take all the fun,
All the walks in the sun,
In the woods, by the brooks.
All the hopscotch and jump rope,
The kite-flying hours,
The smell of the flowers,
The fruit of our gardens,
We have them, forever,
They are part of ourselves.
We're bigger than the biggest van.
We hold more than it ever can.
Like a bottomless cup
That is never filled up.
We'll take all this when we move.

Did you ever think of all the things that we take with us when we move that don't go in the moving van? Some of them go with us because certain things in nature are so much the same everywhere.

Think of the sun, the sky and the clouds, for example. Did you ever lie down on the grass and look up at the sky and think that, whether you were a Chinese boy lying on his back on the grass in China, an African boy lying on his back on the grass somewhere in Africa, an Eskimo boy lying on his back on the snow in the North, the blue sky, white clouds and warm sun would look just the same? The sky, the clouds, the sun are everywhere we shall ever go on this earth.

Sometime, when you're lying on the grass, looking up at the blue sky, make believe that you are twenty years older than you are now, but that you are lying on the grass, looking up at the sky. Where do you suppose you will be living? How many children do you think you will have? Do you think man will have reached the moon?

Everything about you and your family may be different by then, but the sky will be blue, the clouds will be white and the warm sun will be shining. Make believe you are lying on your back looking up at the sky one thousand years ago; would it look different? Make believe it is one thousand years from now; will it look the same?

What about the moon?

We had a guest staying with us once from Egypt. While we were eating supper, the moon came up and our baby saw it out the window. "Moon, moon," shouted the baby, and he clapped his hands.

"He sees the moon," said our guest, smiling happily.

"Does it look the same in Egypt?" I asked.

"Just the same," said our guest. "And Egyptian babies love it too."

Of course, if we move from the northern part of the world to a place far to the south, there will be very different kinds of plants, birds, animals, colors of human skins and even different stars overhead.

But almost everywhere there will still be *some* kind of plants and birds and animals and humans and stars. There will be rocks and trees and insects. Bird nests and spider webs, ants and frogs will be waiting for us to discover them.

When we move, we do not move away from the world of nature, because the world of nature is in us and around us everywhere and always.

There are other things that we can take with us when we move, but again, we do not need a moving van for them. They are everything that has ever happened to us, and they come with us as our memories and as the kind of people we are.

Some people who have studied man's brain say that the human brain is very much like a tape recorder. They think that everything that we have ever seen, heard, touched, smelled, felt and thought has been recorded or put down on our tape-recorder brain. We may not be able to remember all of it, but they say it is all there.

Sometimes we play a game in our family. When there is something particularly beautiful or interesting, one of us says, "There's something to get down on your tape!"

One sunny day, when the snow was sparkling white and the sky was a bright, bright blue, one of us noticed how white the birch tree in our field looked against the blue sky. We all looked at it, and often on a hot summer day now, one of us will say "Remember how the birch tree looked against the blue sky and the white snow?"

But you know, I've discovered that I can *even* feel glad about some of the things that we *couldn't* take with us, such as the house, the gardens and the trees.

I read an article a few years ago by a father who had to move very often. And what he wrote gave me a whole new way to think about these things we had to leave behind.

This father liked his job very much, but to keep that job he had to be willing to move almost every two years. He said this almost broke his heart at first, because he loved to garden and to build things.

One year he planted daffodil bulbs and in the spring, when the tips of green were just coming up through the ground, he had to move. Another year he built some shelves so that everyone in his family would have a place to put their boots and rubbers. But they had to move before they had a chance to use the shelves.

Then one day he had an idea. Why should he feel sad about leaving these things. After all, even if *his* family couldn't enjoy them, some other family would.

From then on, he said, he never felt one bit sorry if he had just gotten a job done and he had to move. He just wondered what family *would* eat the strawberries from the plants he planted, or who would smell the roses on the rose bush he had put in. He said it made him feel as if he were a part of lots of families — not just his own family.

I like his idea. We live in a very old house now, and ever since I read about this father, I enjoy thinking in two directions. I enjoy thinking *back* to all the mothers who have swept this house before me. I like to wonder about the mothers who lived here and listened for the peeper frogs down in the swamp and watched the lilac bushes open in the spring.

And then I like to think ahead to the mothers who will do these things after I am dead. Will my children's children hear the peepers and see the lilacs open from this house? Even if they are not my children's children, they will be someone's children. It makes me feel that I am part of a family that began long ago and goes on forever.

### SUGGESTIONS

1. There are three poems on moving in the collection *Poems to Grow On*, pages 38, 39, 48.

## Section E. Families

*Many peoples wondered where the little human being had been before he was born. They did not think of him as having a new* *beginning with a father and a mother, but instead thought that a father and a mother simply made a place for him to come into the the world. Some peoples thought that a new baby was a grandfather or great-grandfather come back again into the world, and so they came to think of living in this world and another world as being rather like having two homes, a winter home and a summer home, for instance. —* MARGARET MEAD, The Rainbow Book of People and Places*

## 30. *Over and Over and Over*[19]

When a baby is born, what is the very first thing he does? Cry! Isn't it? Did you know that if a baby doesn't cry by himself, right off, the doctor usually makes him cry by slapping him on his bottom or on the soles of his feet? The doctor wants to be sure that the baby can breathe and that he has good strong lungs.

When the new baby is brought home from the hospital, at first everyone in the house listens for that baby's crying. Why is he crying? Is he hungry? Is he cold? Is he wet? Mother feeds him. Father makes sure that he is warm enough. Grandmother checks to see that he is dry.

Sometimes he *still* cries, even when his tummy is full and he is cozily tucked in his basket. Why *does* he keep on crying? Finally big sister thinks to pick him up and pat him gently on the back. Then she puts him down again. Now he's comfortable and goes off to sleep. He sleeps until the next time he's hungry, or cold or a little uncomfortable.

The new baby's first and only thought seems to be *"Me, me, me —* Feed *me,* keep *me* warm, hold *me,* take care of *me."* And Mother and Father and Sister and Brother and Grandmother try to do just that, over and over and over.

The baby soon learns that he can depend on this family of his. Why, they are such a smart family that pretty soon they think they can tell which cry he is crying: his hungry cry, his pain-in-the-tummy cry, his wet diaper cry, or his "pick-me-up-and-give-me-some-loving cry"!

And so the baby grows. Now he doesn't sleep as much as he did at first; he doesn't cry as much either; and pretty soon he does something very wonderful — he smiles his first smile. I don't mean that little puckered-up smile that often flits across a tiny baby's

---

* (New York and Cleveland: World), p. 50; copyright © 1959 by Margaret Mead.

[19] Adapted from a conversation written by Mary Jane Neuendorffer.

face when he's asleep and needs to get up a bubble. (I think every mother, when she sees that little gas-smile the first time, thinks she has an extra smart baby — smiling at only two weeks!)

No, I mean the first real smile. Did you ever see a baby smile the very first time? How did it make you feel? It always makes me feel just wonderful.

It usually happens when the baby is about six weeks old. It's interesting to think that, even before a baby can turn his head in the directions he wants to, or before he can make his hands do what he wants them to, he can smile at a friendly face.

A smile is really his first way of reaching out beyond himself and touching the people around him. Did you ever think of a smile or any look on your face as a way of touching someone? Can your teacher touch you this way? A smile is a way of reaching out to people that you use all through your life.

When this new baby we are talking about smiles at his mother and his father and his sister and his brother, he feels good and they feel good. He is really beginning to be a part of the family. If he's a little boy, he is beginning to be a little brother to the other brothers and sisters who were there first. If the baby is a girl, right away she is beginning to be a little sister.

Some people who study this kind of thing say that if a little new baby *gets* lots of smiles and hugs and squeezes and songs and rockings (and the word for all those together is "loving"), he'll be able to *give* lots of it back to his family as he's growing up. If he doesn't get enough loving, he won't be able to give it to his own children when he gets older. I wonder if that is true?

And so that little baby keeps on growing. He learns all the things that babies learn: to crawl and to walk and to talk and to do lots of things all by himself. Pretty soon he's a real little boy and, before we know it, he's ready to start school.

Kindergarten or the first grade is a very strange place on the first day. Do you remember your first day of school? Were there lots of things that you didn't know and that you were worried about? There were for me. I wondered what my teacher would be like and how I would know where to sit and where the bathroom would be and lots of other things.

There's one thing that this little boy *does* know though. He knows he can smile at the teacher and at the other children. It ought to work about as well at school as it does at home. So he tries it, and it does work.

After a few more days the little boy knows pretty well the things he *can* do and the things he *can't* do at school. You might call that "knowing the rules." When he knows about these, school is not quite so scary and he can begin to enjoy himself and look around a bit.

Of course there are a lot of other children in the class, and he begins to make friends. He finds out that, even though all the children in the first grade are pretty nearly the same age, in many ways they are really very different from each other.

Susy has brown hair and Jane has bright red hair. Johnnie is so short he looks like a four-year-old, but Mike is so tall he looks like a third-grade boy. Anne is so smart she seems to know everything already, and poor Tommy doesn't seem to know what is going on at all.

Do you suppose that our little boy likes everyone in his room? Do you suppose that they all like him? Probably not. I wonder why it is that we like some people and don't like others?

Then, just as all of you will, this boy keeps on growing until he goes to high school and perhaps to college. Through the years he meets all kinds of people and he keeps on using that smile of his to reach out to them. Even when people talk a different language, have a different skin color, think different thoughts, they can understand a smile and they smile back at him. He finds out that he can learn a lot from people who are very different from him, too.

While he is growing up, he often thinks about what he is going to be as a grown man. Should he be a doctor, a policeman, a teacher, a garage man, a minister, a jet pilot, a scientist, a printer, an actor or just what? Do you ever think about what you would like to be when you have grown up? Probably you will change your mind lots of times. Most people do.

Then at last this little boy, who is a man now, finds one girl whom he likes better than any other, and they get married.

Do you remember that little baby at the beginning of this story? All he seemed to care about, at first, was Me, me, me. Look at him now! Of course he still cares about himself, but he also cares about his wife, and his parents, and his friends, and the people he works with, and some people far away, *and* — if everything goes as it should — pretty soon he and his wife have a new little baby of their own. And of course they care about *him!*

What do you suppose is the first thing that this little baby does? Cry. And whom do you suppose this baby thinks of most? Me, me, me!

So this new mother and father begin right away to love him and feed him and smile at him, and very soon he smiles back at them. It's like a circle, isn't it? Being born, growing up, having children — over and over and over.

## OTHER IDEAS

1. Do you think that a person's life is like a circle? Part of a man is born again in his baby. That's like a circle, but part keeps on as the father.
2. After the salmon have laid their eggs, they go off and die. We say they have finished their life *cycle* or circle. Would this work well with people?
3. Every time you smile at someone or do something for someone that makes that person feel good, you're putting some good feelings into the circle of his family. When does that smile stop?
4. When you feel really mad about something and you give someone a mean look, or if you're very mad and give him a punch, you are putting some mean feelings into the circle of their family. How far does that punch go?
5. People have worshiped their ancestors and they have worshiped their children, because they thought their children were their ancestors starting the circle of life again.

## SUGGESTIONS

1. A series of pictures — a baby, child, young man or woman, middle-aged person and old person — might be shown at appropriate places in the conversation.

*First come the pioneers, lean, hungry, fierce, dirty.*
*They wrangle and battle with the elements.*
*They gamble on crops, chills, rheumatism.*
*They fight wars and put a nation on the map.*
*They battle with blizzards, lice, wolves.*
*They go on a fighting trail*
*To break sod for unnumbered millions to come.*
     — CARL SANDBURG, "Good Morning, America"*

## 31. *Frontiers*[20]

Do your mother and father ever tell you stories about when they were little? Stories like that are fun. Sometimes it is difficult to believe that our mothers and fathers *were* little once. Even our grandmothers and grandfathers were children once.

Here is a story one mother often tells her children:

When I was a little girl, my mother used to tell me about when *she* was a little girl. She was born in the state of Washington. It had just become a state a few years before she was born. So my mother was actually born on the frontier.

Do you know what a frontier is?

* From *Good Morning, America* (New York: Harcourt, Brace).
[20] By Mary Jane Neuendorffer.

The frontier of a country is the part of the country that is just being settled by people.

Do you suppose that a place stays a frontier very long? No. The old frontier towns grow into large settlements and cities, and the frontier keeps moving along, out *front*. Do you know where the frontier was when the Pilgrims came to America? Do you know where it was when George Washington was President, or when Abraham Lincoln was a boy? See if you can find out.

Well, by the time my mother was born, the pioneers — that is the name we give to people who settle a frontier — had pushed all the way across the United States to the Pacific Ocean. It was here, in a small town called Seattle, in the state of Washington, that my mother was born. You should see that "small town" now!

Little Eda Chrysanthea (that really *was* my mother's whole first name) had to work very hard when she lived on the frontier. Her father was away in Canada hunting for gold. He hoped he would find a lot of it and come home rich.

Eda Chrysanthea (let's just call her E.C. for short) was living with her grandmother because her mother had died. By the time E.C. was ten years old, she was no longer going to school. She was needed at home to do chores. And what chores!

Her grandmother ran a boarding house. That means that she had people other than her own family eating and sleeping at her house. Running a boarding house was a way of earning money, and a good way in a frontier town. Do you know why? There were new people coming into town all the time and no hotels or motels for them to stay in.

But these boarders weren't just ordinary boarders. They were stevedores, and there were twelve of them. Stevedores are men who work at loading and unloading ships. Remember, the state of Washington is on the Pacific Ocean. Seattle is a seaport town. Probably one reason it grew so fast was that it had such a good harbor. Grandmother's boarders were kept busy loading and unloading ships that were going all over the world.

Sometimes little E.C. helped her grandmother bake as many as seven or eight loaves of bread each *meal!* People who lived and worked on the frontier could get mighty hungry, especially stevedores.

E.C.'s grandmother not only cooked for these twelve men and her own family, but she did all their washing and ironing too. In E.C.'s time there wasn't any hot water that came out the minute you turned on the faucet. And there weren't automatic washing machines or electric irons. E.C. had to pump pails and pails of water, and she had to keep the fire going in the stove. The water had to be heated on the stove, the clothes all had to be scrubbed by hand, and the flatirons had to be heated on the top of the stove. Did you ever see a flatiron? All they are good for now are door-stops and book ends! Even on scorching hot days, E.C. had to work in the hot laundry shed with her grandmother.

E.C.'s grandmother also took in laundry from all over Seattle. A lot of men came out to the frontier without their wives and families, and, until their wives could come and join them, they needed someone to do their washing. So E.C.'s grandmother made more money doing this. It also made more work for little E.C. But, you know, she didn't seem to mind it. In fact, gathering up the washing of the men around Seattle was one of her favorite jobs. She had an old wooden cart which she pushed around the town as she picked up and delivered laundry.

One reason she liked this job was that it gave her a chance to see all the new buildings going up and to share in the other excitement that goes with living on a frontier. Sometimes, too, she found time to stop at the docks and talk to her stevedore friends from the boarding house. They would tell her whenever a ship was expected in from the Yukon, gold country to the north, where her father was. Little E.C. was always hoping that her father would be on one of these boats.

And he did finally come home, but not until he had been away five long years. E.C. was happy when she and her father were together again, even though he had not found much gold in all that time. E.C.'s father decided to go back east to New York State and do the kind of work he knew best. In this way he could earn enough money for his family. So back they went, and there E.C. grew up, married, and my brother and I were born.

When I was a little girl, lots of times on a cold winter afternoon, my brother and I would sit in our kitchen while our mother, *big* E.C. now, was cooking and ironing. As we sat there, she would tell us about when she was a little girl on the frontier of America.

We didn't have to bring any wood to her cookstove — she used gas; and we didn't have to heat flatirons for her — she had an electric iron. We could just sit and listen as she told us about those days long ago in Seattle.

"Oh, it was so exciting," she'd say. "Something new and special was always happening."

"Yes, but you had to work so hard!" we'd say.

"I know," she'd say, "but sometimes hard work is fun, especially on the frontier."

And my brother and I who had been feeling so sorry for *her* because she had to work so hard, now felt very sorry for ourselves because there was no frontier for us to go to. America was all settled from ocean to ocean.

Or were we wrong? Is there still a frontier?

I have a little girl and boy now and, sometimes on a cold winter day when I'm working in the kitchen, they sit nearby and I tell them about the little E.C. who had to push a laundry wagon through the streets of Seattle when she was a little girl.

My little girl gets all excited when I tell her about the frontier that her grandmother went to — because my little girl is thinking about another frontier that maybe she, or her little girl, will go to. Do you know what that frontier is? The moon, or one of the planets — these are the new frontiers that men hope someday to settle. I wonder whether they will?

Why do you suppose people, especially young people, like to open up frontiers? Do you suppose there will ever be a time when there really and truly are no more frontiers, anywhere? Some of the men who study the skies and the stars (we call them "astronomers") think that the sky, with stars in it, goes on forever and ever and ever in space. How could it?

*There is a time in every man's education when he arrives at the conviction that envy is ignorance; that imitation is suicide; that he must take himself for better or for worse as his portion; that though the wide universe is full of good, no kernel of nourishing corn can come to him but through his toil bestowed on that plot of ground which is given to him to till. The power which resides in him is new in nature, and none but he knows what that is which he can do, nor does he know until he has tried.* — RALPH WALDO EMERSON, "Self-Reliance"*

## 32. *Which Is It Best to Be?*

Which are you in your family? The youngest, the oldest or somewhere in between?

I was the baby in my family. Sometimes I hated being the baby. But sometimes it was rather nice. I hated it when my big sister and brother could stay up late to do something special, and I couldn't because I was too little! I liked being the littlest when I didn't have as many or as difficult chores as they did.

* *Essays,* First Series, I (Boston: Houghton Mifflin, 1904), 46.

Which do you think it is best to be, the oldest, the middle, the youngest or one of the in-between ones, if there are more than three in your family?

One day we had a funny conversation in our family about this. It didn't start out to be about this at all. I had just brought our new baby home from the hospital and the three older children and I were having a nice visit with him on my big bed.

"Aren't his hands tiny," said one of the children. "How come they are both the same size?"

"Oh, but look at his ears," said the big sister. "They are like little rosebuds all folded up."

"I've been thinking," said the third one of the children. "He's the first baby not to have been born in the same hospital as the rest of us. Do you think he'll mind, when he's big enough to know?"

You should have seen the faces of those three children! You would have thought that something really terrible had been discovered about that poor little new baby: that he had three heads or seven feet, or something like that.

I just had to cheer them up somehow. So I said, "Well, I know one good thing about where he was born. He is the only one to have been born in New Hampshire. That's special!"

Everyone began to look much happier, and you could see, too, that they were beginning to search their minds for things that made them special and different from all the rest.

In just a minute the oldest one said, "I'm the only one to have lived in Alabama." We moved away from there before any of the other children were born, so no one else could be in on that.

Now the two older boys were beginning to look all sad again. Wasn't there anything extra special and different about them?

"One of you was the first baby in our family to have a big sister," I said, and the oldest boy began to cheer up.

The next boy was thinking fast. "I was the first one to have a big sister *and* a big brother."

"And the baby will be the first one to have a big sister and two big brothers," said the big sister.

Well, that conversation went on and on and on. The new baby fell fast asleep long before we had finished.

And we never really finished! We couldn't begin to name all the things that were different about each one of the children. But the thing that was really interesting was that, as we went on talking, we discovered that none of the things we named made any one of them better than anyone else; it just made them different.

You might think that all of the children in one family would be pretty much alike, but what we found out was that there were dozens and dozens of things about each one of them that made them different from each other.

You might say: "Oh well, they all have the same mother and father." Am I the same mother for the fourth child as I was for the first? I'm fourteen years older than I was when the first one was born. Do you think you will be the same as you are now in fourteen years? I hope not. I hope I'm not the same, either.

No, there are dozens and dozens of things about me and about the children's father that are different for child number one, child number two, child number three and child number four. When one of the children was little, my husband was away from home a lot. Now he has a different job, and he is home all the time. Doesn't it make a person different if their father is at home instead of being away?

We have moved several times so that there have been different yards to play in, different playmates, different schools. And the world is changing all the time so that, even aside from the changes in our family, there are many other changes. There was no TV when our oldest child was little; there were lots more trains to watch when our first boy was born; there are many, many more airplanes going over our house now than there used to be.

All of these differences mean that there never have been and never could be two people in the world exactly alike, not even twins. It would be fun to hear a pair of twins name the differences that have gone into the making of themselves. The first one that I think of is the fact that one of them was born first!

Which is it best to be? That is about the silliest question I have ever asked. What you are, you are — first, second, third, fourth, fifth and so on. The really smart question is: What are you going to do with what you are, and all the different things that have happened and will happen just to you.

Once, when one of the children in our family had been reading a whole series of books about the lives of famous people, she said to me: "Well, I guess I'll never be famous."

"Why?" I asked her.

"Because almost every single one of these famous people had their mother die when they were younger than I am. You are still alive."

Of course, having their mothers die when they were little didn't *make* them famous. Many people have had that happen who aren't famous. But it was one thing that was part of them and they had to do something with it.

Some people are born blind; some have to use crutches all of their lives. Some people have a father and mother who have been divorced and so they live with only one parent. Some children are born into very rich homes and some into very poor homes. No one of these things completely *makes* any person be one kind of person.

I like to think that each person in the world is something that has never happened before and will never happen again.

### OTHER IDEAS

1. Many interesting ideas on the physical uniqueness of every individual born can be found in "You and Heredity," by Amram Scheinfeld, in *A Treasury of Science,* ed. Shapley, Rapport and Wright (New York: Harper's). One or two of these ideas might be shared with the children.

### SUGGESTIONS

1. The poem "Everybody Says," in *Poems to Grow On* (p. 59), could be used with this conversation.
2. The song "Each Is Needed," in *We Sing of Life* (No. 62), expresses a relevant thought.

*Imagination is usually regarded as a synonym for the unreal. Yet is true imagination healthful and real. . . . Indeed, the power of imagination makes us infinite.* — JOHN MUIR, The Wilderness World of John Muir\*

## 33. *A Kind of Magic*[21]

When I was a little girl, I hated to have our family plan something, like a picnic or a trip, and then not be able to do it. Did that ever happen in your family?

Here's a story about a family in which this happened, and what they did about it. Do you think that what they did was "a kind of magic"?

It's funny what a difference half an hour can make. Half an hour ago, all the family was bustling and bubbling and telling each other over and over what they were going to do, starting tomorrow.

Tomorrow would be the first day of their vacation and they were going to spend the week at a lake. First, they were going on a long drive into another state, to reach the cottage that they had rented.

\* *Op. cit.,* p. 321.
[21] Adapted from a story by Patricia Shuttee.

Then, for seven days, they would play in the sand, swim, hike, read, collect things. Each one in the family knew just what he especially wanted to do.

In this family there were three children. There was two-year-old Keith. Of course, he didn't really understand that the whole family was going away for a week. But he *did* know that his pail and shovel had been put in the car and that meant *beach*. Most of the time he would just want to play in the sand and the water when they were there.

Big sister Jill was seven years old, and big brother Marcus was nine. They really knew what was about to happen and they could hardly wait. Jill could swim well now and, of course, Marcus could swim *and* dive.

Jill planned to get some garnets for her rock collection, and Marcus wanted to add to his collection too. He had a funny collection — he collected mountains that he had climbed. He hoped to add one mountain, at least, during the week.

Dad and Mother were looking forward to the vacation, too. Mother collected ferns and made prints of them, and she hoped that she and the children would discover some new ones on some of their walks. Daddy *always* went fishing and bird watching. Sometimes he brought back fish for breakfast, but mostly he brought back names of birds he had seen. Marcus went along sometimes, if Daddy didn't get up *too* early.

Well, there was just the rest of this afternoon, supper, early to bed and their vacation week would be here!

But — something happened! Keith was having his nap and Jill was the first one to hear him crying. He sometimes cried when he woke up from his nap now. Mother said children his age often did and, if you just moved slowly enough with him, he was all over it in a minute.

"I'll get him," said Jill. She had loved having a baby brother and she loved him just as much now that he was a little boy. She ran upstairs. But in just a minute she was back.

"Golly," said Jill. "Guess what?"

"Quiet!" said Daddy, "I'm adding." He had road maps spread out all over the floor.

"But Daddy ——"

"One hundred ninety-two miles, plus 176 miles, plus . . . oh, bother!" said Daddy.

"Well, let me *tell* you," Jill insisted.

"Tell us what?" asked Mother. She was finishing the ironing in the kitchen.

"Keith's just covered with red spots. He doesn't look right, and he's really crying."

Just half an hour later everyone was back in the living room again. Mother had called the doctor and they were pretty certain already that Keith had the measles.

Daddy was slowly folding up all the road maps. Marcus was folding up his map that showed what mountains were near the lake. Jill was crying, very loudly. Mother *felt* like crying. Keith had gone back to sleep after having mother rock him.

"Mom," said Marcus, coming up with his fifth bright idea in the last seven minutes. "Couldn't we leave Keith here, and have Grandma take care of him?"

"No," said Mother wearily. "He's too young to understand about our vacation. If we go away and leave him when he's sick, he'll just feel worse. He doesn't know we'll be back in a week."

"Even if Grandma stayed with him?"

"No, not even with Grandma," said Mother. "He's not used to her, and when babies are sick they especially want their mothers and daddies."

"So what are we going to do, just *sit* here all week?" grumbled Marcus.

"Well, we could sit here and cry for the whole week," suggested Daddy, who was getting a little tired of listening to Jill.

But right then Mother brightened up. I don't know whether Jill's tears reminded her of a homemade lake or what. "I know," she said. "Suppose we have our vacation right here?"

"That wouldn't be any vacation, staying home," wailed Jill.

"We're going to have to be here anyway," said Daddy. "Let's see what Mother's idea is."

"First," said Mother, "let's make a list of what we were *going* to do at the lake."

"Swim," sobbed Jill.

"Climb my mountain," said Marcus. He had a pencil and a paper and he was already writing things down.

"Eat supper out of doors every night," said Mother.

"Go bird watching," said Daddy.

The rest of the day was even busier than it would have been if they had been leaving for the lake in the morning.

Dad and Marcus went over to their uncle and aunt's house and borrowed the huge plastic pool that they had. Their children were all away for the summer. It really was big enough to swim in and jump in, but Dad said no diving. It took a long time to fill it. Marcus and Jill decided that they couldn't swim in it until the next day, because if they had been going to the real lake, they couldn't have gone swimming until then.

While the pool was filling, Marcus and Dad took down the bed in Marcus' room and put up an old army cot from the attic.

"Jill can have some turns on the cot, too," said Marcus. "I'm sleeping out in my sleeping bag some nights."

Jill and Mother were as busy as Dad and Marcus. Mother had to spend quite a bit of time with Keith, he was so fussy and hot. But Mother was able to tell Jill how to hard-boil the eggs, and then Jill peeled them and wrapped them in wax paper.

Mother and Jill decided that they would go ahead and stop the paper boy from delivering the papers, just as if they had gone away. They unplugged the television set, because they wouldn't have had one at the lake.

All week everyone tried as hard as they could to do things differently from usual. Mother pretended that she had to find a grocery store and found one she had never been to before. She went there during the week when she needed things, instead of to the big supermarket where she usually went.

Jill and Marcus and Daddy and Mother all told their friends that they weren't at home. Everyone thought it was a wonderful idea and pretended that they weren't there right along with them.

One day it rained. They decided that, if they had been at a cottage in the rain, they would have sat on the floor and made up stories and games. So that is what they did. They didn't even look at the shelves of books, or the drawer full of games that they usually used on rainy days at home.

Grandma came to spend the last three days at their "lake" with them. On the first of these three days, Dad and Marcus took the car, just as they would have at the real lake, and drove to a mountain that Marcus wanted to add to his collection. It wasn't as high as his others, but it was better than none. They had to get up very early, and Dad saw three new birds to add to his collection.

On the second day that Grandmother was there, Jill and Mother took the car and drove to a copper mine. Jill had never known there was a mine so near home. Mother found two kinds of fern that she had been hoping to find up at the lake. Dad and Marcus had stayed with Keith and Grandma at the "home lake."

Keith was feeling much better now and was really getting to know Grandma. So, on the last day of their vacation, Grandma and Keith stayed home alone, and the rest of the family went on an all-day trip to a real lake.

Dad rented a rowboat and they took their picnic lunch out onto a small island. Marcus was able to do some diving off the end of the boat, and Dad was able to do a little fishing. He didn't catch anything, but he saw a heron.

Rowing back to the shore they didn't go very fast, because Dad had one oar and Marcus had the other. Dad could pull much harder than Marcus and so they mostly went in circles.

"Look at that cloud!" said Jill. She pointed up to where she was looking. "It looks like an elephant. See his long trunk and his tail."

"No," said Marcus, leaning on his oar, "it's a map of the United States. There's Florida down there, and Mexico, and there's even Alaska!"

"Well," said Dad, trying to make the boat go straight, with only one oar, "I guess our vacation week is about over. We haven't been to Mexico, or Florida, or Alaska, but I've had a good time."

Marcus began rowing again. "We had a vacation, but we didn't have one, in a way."

"We were home," said Jill, "but it wasn't like being home. Everything was special."

"That's because we made it special," said Mother, "It *looked* as if we were at home."

"It's a little like that cloud up there," said Daddy. "Jill sees it as an elephant, Marcus sees it as a map, but some people would just see a big white cloud. We *could* have just spent a week at home but, with our imaginations working, we made it a special week."

"I guess we're magic," said Jill. "We can just make everything be the way we want."

"I wouldn't say that, Jill," said Mother. "Remember, we didn't want Keith to have the measles, we couldn't 'magic' them away. But by using our imaginations we certainly made it into a different kind of week, didn't we?"

What do you think of what this family did?

### SUGGESTIONS

1. The poem "Summer Sky," in *Poems to Grow On,* would be nice to use with this story; also the song "Today the Sky Is Very Far Away," in *We Sing of Life* (No. 15).

*Everybody makes wishes,*
*Everybody likes to play.*

*Everybody needs some loving,*
*Everybody — every day.*
— SOPHIA L. FAHS, "Everybody"*

## 34. *Are Birthday Parties Always Fun?*[22]

How many of you like birthday parties? They are usually lots of fun, aren't they? I want to tell you the story of one and then I want you to tell me whether or not you think it was fun.

Jimmy was almost seven years old, and there was going to be a birthday party right in his house! It wasn't going to be Jimmy's party, though. His sister, Janie, who was going to be nine years old, was the one who was going to have the party.

Mother had helped Janie make a list of her friends in the neighborhood and some of her friends at school. Janie had invited all of them to come and, of course, she had to invite Jimmy, too, because he was her brother.

When the day of the party came, Jimmy and Janie raced home from school as fast as they could. They were laughing very hard, and by the time they reached their house they were puffing and out of breath.

They found Mother in the dining room, and *she* looked red in the face and out of breath, too. She hadn't been running and laughing, though; she had just finished blowing up about twenty balloons! She should have had one of those balloon pumps, but she didn't.

Janie and Jimmy helped pick up all the balloons by their strings and mother tied them in a great big bunch and fastened them to the light over the table in the dining room.

"Mother! What are these?" shouted Janie suddenly. She had just noticed three packages sitting on the hall table. The mailman must have brought them that day and Janie could see that they were all addressed to her.

Jimmy saw the packages, too, and he wished that *he* could open up just one of them. But he knew that they were all for Janie. It was her birthday. He opened all the packages on *his* birthday. Still, he wished . . .

Jimmy watched as Janie opened the first package.

"Look, Mother — a beautiful, blue ski parka from Grandmother. You must have told her I wanted one." Janie held it up in front of her to see if it would fit. It looked just right.

Then Janie started to open the second package. Jimmy

* From *Martin and Judy Songs*, No. 48.
[22] Story by Dorothy Brandt.

watched. This one was from Aunt Ruth and it was a bright green umbrella! "This is just what I need for school on rainy days," said Janie.

The third package, from cousin Sally, was a big box. Janie tore off the paper and on the cover of the box it said in big letters, A RAINY DAY BOX. Janie took off the cover and saw puzzles and games, the kind you can play with on a rainy day, or when you are sick in bed, or on any other day, for that matter.

Jimmy knew that he could work one of the puzzles. It was just like one his friend Timmy had.

"Let me try that one, Janie," said Jimmy, reaching into the box. "I can show you how to do that one."

"No. Not now," said Janie, pulling the box out of Jimmie's reach. "We'll have to get ready for the party pretty soon and we don't want to make a mess in here, now." Janie put the cover back on the Rainy Day Box, picked up all her new things and carried them upstairs.

When she had put them away in her room, Janie ran downstairs to the basement. She wanted to take a quick look at the shiny new bicycle that her mother and father had given her at breakfast time.

It was a big bicycle, a 26-inch two-wheeler, and it had a light on it and a bell and a basket for carrying things. Jimmy knew why Janie was going down cellar and he followed her. He watched as she took a piece of soft cloth and dusted off all the shiny parts. Janie was proud of her new bicycle and she planned to take very good care of it.

"Will you let me try to ride your bike?" asked Jimmy. He could ride his own two-wheeler, but it was smaller. He was pretty sure that he could ride a girl's big two-wheeler because a girl's bike doesn't have that bar across.

"No, Jimmy, you might scratch it. You have your own bike. This one's too big for you."

Even before Jimmy had a chance to explain how he was sure he could ride a girl's big bike, their mother called down the cellar stairs.

"Janie, it's time for you to get dressed and then I want you to help me do a few last things for the party."

So Janie ran upstairs and put on her best pink nylon dress with the two starchy petticoats underneath. Then she came down and got out the "Pin the Tail on the Donkey" game and the Scotch Tape. She started to put the big picture of the donkey on one of the walls.

Jimmy went into the kitchen. Mother was putting the frosting on the birthday cake. There were two bowls of frosting on the table, one of pink and one of green. They were Janie's favorite colors. Mother was making little roses around the edge of the cake, and then she began to write "Happy Birthday Janie" across the top with pink frosting. It looked awfully good, and Jimmy began to feel very, very hungry.

"Mother, may I lick the bowls?" he asked.

Mother usually let Jimmy lick the bowls and spoons when she had finished making frosting, but today she glanced up at the kitchen clock and said, "It's awfully late, Jimmy. I had to wait until the cake was cool before I could frost it, and I want to clean the kitchen up quickly. Couldn't you go find something to do and let me finish decorating this alone? Please run along."

"Aw, jeepers," said Jimmy, very loudly and he stamped out of the kitchen. He was feeling rather mean inside now. Do you know why? He wanted his mother to know it!

"Jeepers," he said again. "I can't play with one little puzzle. I can't ride her *old* bike. I can't even lick the frosting bowls!" Jimmy gave the side of the door a good kick as he went out.

The living room was empty. Nothing to do in there. And then Jimmy had an idea. "I think I'll get out my trucks and cars and play with *them,* since everyone around here is so *busy."*

So Jimmy brought his trucks and cars downstairs. He lined them all up in front of the sofa. He would have them go under the sofa and around the TV and under the coffee table, and . . .

But just then his mother came into the living room. She took one look at Jimmy. *"Please* take those trucks and cars right back upstairs to your room. I cleaned this room today and I don't want *any*body to get it all dirty again before the party."

"AW, JEEPERS," shouted Jimmy. "I can't do *anything* around here!"

Mother looked at Jimmy. He was really mad. Mother was hot and tired. "Jimmy," she said, "you can do *anything* you want up in your own room, but not in here."

Mother could see now that Jimmy couldn't decide whether to yell or cry. She didn't want to spoil Janie's party. "I'm sorry you feel the way you do, dear, but we *are* trying to get everything ready for Janie's party. You do want her to have a nice party, don't you? We're going to have a nice party on *your* birthday!"

Jimmy didn't say anything. He was thinking. He was thinking about the packages that were just for Janie. There would be even more of them at the party! He was thinking about the new bike that he couldn't ride. He was thinking about the frosting bowls

he couldn't lick. He was thinking about having to keep the house
so doggone neat. He wasn't so sure he really wanted Janie to have
a nice party!

He could stay mad. Should he?

## THINGS TO THINK ABOUT

1. Do you think you know why Jimmy felt the way he did. Are other people's
birthdays as much fun as your own? Why may your sister's and brother's
especially not be so much fun?
2. Can you think of anything Jimmy might think about that would make him
decide not to stay mad?
   Remember that he'll have his turn for a party.
   He wouldn't want his sister to get mad on *his* birthday.
   The games and the cake and ice cream will be fun, if he doesn't stay mad.
      He'll spoil them for himself if he stays mad.
   Probably Janie will give him a turn on the bike and with the games and
      puzzles in a few days.
3. Can you think of anything Jimmy's mother could have done so that all this
wouldn't have happened?
   Let Jimmy blow up the balloons, and help in other ways.
   Invited a friend of his to the party, if Janie agreed.
   Had a small present for Jimmy.
   Not had everything so fancy.
   Suggest he take the trucks and things outside.
4. Could she do anything now to help him decide not to stay mad?
   Think about the kind of party he wants, maybe a cook-out.
   Put him in charge of some of the games.
   Let him be the one to bring the lighted cake in.
5. Can you think of anything Janie could have done to have made him feel better?
   Let him have one ride on the bike, or promise him one soon.
   Let him try that one puzzle while she was dressing.
   Let him put the pins in the donkey tails.

## SUGGESTIONS

1. The song "Everybody," quoted at the beginning of the conversation, perhaps
suggests part of what Jimmy needed.

*Ralph, suppose you dress that big fat Buff Orpington hen that didn't
lay last winter. Philip, you get Grace two or three armfuls of
wood and some shavings, so she can start a fire in the cookstove.
And Muriel, do you think you could get the new tablecloth out of
the dresser drawer, and set us a table right here by my bed? When
you get the fire going, Grace, put on the big iron pot with some fat
in it so it will be good and hot when the hen is ready. And, Hal,
would you get Mother a drink of water? I can't think of a thing*

*that would taste so good as a nice cool dipper of water, right from
our own well.* — RALPH MOODY, Little Britches*

## 35. *Family Fun . . . ?*

Do you ever make Christmas cookies or Easter cookies at
your house? We do, but not very well. I don't mean the cookies
aren't good, but I mean it is sometimes rather wild while we're
making them. There is usually a baby who wakes up just when we
don't want him to; or one of the children is just the age to put
cookie dough on the piano keys; or someone bigger than that is
mad because he didn't get the cookie cutter with the green handle;
or the person who has the kitchen stool this time had it last time
and it isn't her turn; or the dough won't stick together — or it
sticks too well!

I am usually glad when it is all over. But a few years ago I
read a story about a family making cookies and, whenever we are
getting ready to make cookies for a holiday, I remember that story.
It's called "Making Bunny Cookies."[23] After you've heard it, I'll
tell you why I liked it.

> Hop, hop — hop, hop
>     Goes the Easter bunny.
> Hop, hop — hop, hop
>     Goes the Easter bunny
> Eating Easter eggs.

Bobby was singing as he cut out bunny cookies. Bobby was
not quite three years old, but he cut the cookies out very well.

"There's a bunny," he said, as he lifted the cookie onto the
cookie sheet with the spatula. "And there's a bunny —

> Hop, hop
>     Goes the widdle bunny
> Hop, hop
>     Goes the widdle bunny."

"Want to give them raisin eyes?" asked Mother.

"Yes," said Bobby. "Make eyes for the bunny. I want to shake
on the sugar myself." Bobby put a raisin on each bunny. He shook
the sugar shaker hard. "I want to put them in the oven myself."

* (New York: Norton, 1950), pp. 259–260.
[23] Story by Phyllis Buddenberg, copyright, 1958.

Mother opened the oven door. Slowly Bobby carried the big cookie sheet across the kitchen and pushed it into the oven. "I want to take 'em off myself."

"I'll call you."

"Yes," said Bobby. "Now it's my turn to play with Becky."

"Nancy," called Mother. "Your turn to cut out cookies."

They had planned to make the rabbit cookies while Becky was asleep, but during the exciting preparations someone had dropped a cookie sheet. The crash had awakened Becky right in the middle of her morning nap.

Now, these days Becky wanted to be in the midst of everything. And she knew how to get into the midst of everything. Becky was one and a half years old. She could climb up onto the table in a wink. Everyone understood how she would really mess up the cookie making.

And so it had been decided that the children would take turns playing with Becky in her crib in the playroom to keep her happy. In this way each child could have a turn with Mother making rabbit cookies for the Easter Baskets they were going to take to their friends.

This plan had worked very well *so far*. Nancy had been the first one to play with Becky. Nancy, who was five and a half, was an expert baby sitter; she could always think of something to keep Becky happy. Sometimes she sang to her or played Peek or just talked. This morning Mother heard Nancy saying "Nose, Becky. Nose. Becky's nose."

"Noh, noh," Becky would say.

"That's right. Nose! Nose — push!" Mommie could hear them both laugh as they touched noses.

While Nancy had played with Becky, Mother had rolled out a big sheet of cookie dough. Rich had cut his cookies out first. He was almost seven and he was getting pretty handy at making cookies. It was his idea to use raisins for eyes when they found all the red hots were gone. When Rich's cookies were in the oven, he went in to play with Nancy and Becky. Then Mother helped Bobby finish his.

"Happy Easter to you, Happy Easter. . . ." Mother could hear Rich trying to pick out the notes on the piano. That was one of Rich's ways of entertaining Becky. Sometimes he moved Becky's crib over close to the piano, and they both played.

"Ding!" went the timer bell. Time for Rich to take his cookies off the cookie sheet. Time for Nancy to cut hers out. And time for Bobby to play with Becky.

Bobby had his way of playing with Becky, too. Sometimes he just put a few toys for her in the crib, and he played beside her on the floor with the blocks. This morning he tumbled right into her crib. Becky squealed with delight.

"Hop, hop," said Bobby. "Hop, hop. I'm a bunny, Becky. See my ears." He hopped over and sniffed Becky's toes. "My nose goes 'wiggo,' wiggo,' wiggo,' Becky."

Mother could hear them both giggling. She thought how well Bobby had learned to play with Becky. Sometimes Bobby forgot he was much bigger and stronger than Becky and played too roughly; but many times he remembered to play gently.

"Ding," went the timer bell. Time for Bobby's cookies to come out of the oven — Rich had just finished taking his off his cookie sheet. Bobbie took his cookies off the cookie sheet all by himself. Everything was working out just fine when — CRASH!

"Oh, Rich," groaned Mother. For Rich had bumped the raisin jar off onto the floor. There were raisins and sparkling splinters of glass everywhere.

"Can we pick up the raisins?" asked Nancy.

"I'm afraid not, Nancy," answered Mother. "They might have glass in them; we wouldn't want to cut ourselves."

"I'll get the broom," offered Rich. He did quite a good job of getting everything into the dustpan. Of course, some of the raisins stuck to the floor and some stuck to the broom!

"Here," said Mother, "I'll give one more sweep. This damp cloth should get the last of the slivers."

"We can't give them to the pigs," said Rich. "They could get cut too."

"No," agreed Mother. "Better put the whole mess in the incinerator. Then the ashes will go to the dump."

"That's all the raisins there are," cried Nancy. "How will the rest of the bunnies see?" Then she answered her own question. "I know, we can poke a little hole with a toothpick where the eye should be."

"The kitchen sure smells good," said Rich, coming back in. "I'll bet all our friends will be glad to get Easter baskets with Easter eggs and bunny cookies in them."

With all the excitement, Becky had been left alone. She had started to fuss. "Becky knows there is something exciting going on out here," said Mother. "Maybe she'd sit in her high chair while we finish." Mother put Becky into the high chair and gave her some cookie dough to play with. That kept her busy until Nancy's cookies were done, and the kitchen straightened up.

How good it made everyone feel to see that big pan full of bunny cookies!

One thing I liked was that the mother didn't say: well, the baby is awake so we can't make the cookies. Another thing I liked was that she didn't yell at Rich for smashing the jar of raisins. When something is broken like that, it really doesn't help any to yell at the person who did it, especially when they weren't fooling around. But it is one way of letting the mother get her mad feelings out.

But the thing that I liked best, and that gave me the most to think about, was how the mother and children went about keeping the baby happy while they made the cookies. She didn't *tell* them that they had to play with Becky. They decided together that if they did that, they could still have the fun of making cookies.

And each one of them did what he was good at doing with the baby when it was his turn. So the whole family was working together, not by all being exactly the same, but by doing what they were good at and by being themselves.

Many times things that we think are going to be lots of fun, which the family is going to do together, don't turn out to be fun at all.

There can be many reasons for this. The grownups may not have planned very well, or they may be mad at each other, or just grouchy. The children may have gotten so excited that they are all tired out, or one of them may be coming down with the measles. There can be dozens of reasons.

But there is one really big reason for family projects not always being fun, and that is that, when a group of people all different ages are going to do something together, they are going to bump into each others' feelings.

I once read that probably a person could live without ever having any fights with other people *if* he lived all alone in a hotel room, or on a desert island. *But* it would be awfully lonely. Living in families isn't a bit lonely, but it can be awfully "fighty."

I think this bothers people more than it should sometimes. Families are really a kind of school for learning how to get along with people. It's a place to experiment with ways of behaving. Sometimes we think that other families don't fight, just ours. Probably most families fight some, but many families have awfully good times together too.

One idea to experiment with is the one I learned from the bunny cookie family. Don't try to be a family by all being just the same and doing just the same things; try being you in your family.

SUGGESTIONS

1. *Little Britches,* from which the quotation at the beginning of this conversation is taken, is the first in a series of several books about the Moody family. These are wonderful books for family reading.
2. Sometimes younger children try to do just what the older children do. They need to be encouraged to be original, even if less expert.

*When I heard you were coming, I thought maybe you would take care of her [a kitten] for me. If you want to, enough to bother to feed her and all, you can have her for your own.* — DOROTHY CANFIELD FISHER, Understood Betsy*

## 36. *What Is Your Job?*[24]

Do you have any jobs that you *must* do at your house? Most families develop some kind of system, so that everyone helps with the work.

Why do you suppose most families do this? I know that in our family there are two main reasons why we divide up the work. One of the reasons is that we think that it is part of growing up, gradually to take on a certain amount of the work. For example, by the time one of our children starts the first grade, we expect him to make his own bed and keep his room a little bit neat. We think he needs to learn to do these things just as he needs to learn how to read and write.

Another reason we divide up the work is that, if everyone shares in the work, then mother and dad can have some time to do things with the children, with each other and by themselves. It seems fairer to us this way and more fun, too.

I don't mean that the jobs are always fun. Sometimes they are and sometimes they aren't. Did you ever have a pet rabbit? In our family, if you have a pet — and you aren't still a baby — you have to help take care of it. When we first got a rabbit, our first-grade boy thought it was going to be fun. And it was for a while. But then, when it began to get cold in the morning and he had to scurry to

---

\* (New York: Grosset), p. 41.
[24] Conversation developed and adapted from ideas contributed by the Dunwiddie family.

make his bed, fix his room, get everything ready for school, *and* feed his rabbit, it began to be not so much fun. Then he had to decide whether he wanted to sell his rabbit and not have to hurry so in the morning, or keep his rabbit and get up a little bit earlier.

There is nothing wrong in deciding that you are too busy to take care of a pet. Part of growing up is learning what you have time to do and what you are too busy to do. Some children think they would like to have a horse for a pet, and horses are nice, especially if you live in the country. But horses cost quite a lot of money, and you have to spend a lot of time taking care of them and riding them.

Of course, jobs that have to do with pets are really just extra jobs. Most children have several regular jobs or "chores," as some families call them. What the jobs are, and how many you have, depends upon how large your family is, how old you are, where you live and lots of other things.

I heard about one family that has what they called a job wheel. There are four children in that family and the job wheel looks like this: The circle in the center, with the children's names on it, is a separate piece of cardboard. It is fastened to the square by a paper fastener through the center, so it can be turned. Each week they give the wheel a quarter turn so everybody has a new job.

Outside the center cardboard, on each of the four sides, they have written different jobs, such as "washing dishes," "drying dishes," "clearing the table" and "filling the woodbin." This system works very well for them, but for many families it wouldn't work well at all. In that family the children are all over six years old, so that they can really do the various jobs.

But in our family, although we have four children, our baby couldn't do any of those jobs yet. There can be a great many reasons why this job wheel idea wouldn't work well in some families. Would it work well in your family?

Probably the best thing is for each family to work out a way of dividing up the jobs that is best for them. Do you have any special way that works well in your family? During the summer everyone is at home in our family, so there are more jobs to be done. One summer we had a system that was a lot of fun. I made a list of all the jobs there were and then wrote each job down on a little card. We called it the "chance" pile. At breakfast each person chose a card and did the job on that card. Scattered through the pile were cards that said: "Take the day off." "Do whatever job Mum says." "Have a free popsicle."

No matter what system a family works out, some jobs are fun

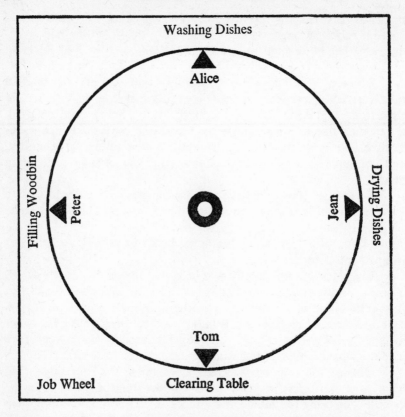

and some aren't. What jobs do you like? On Saturday mornings our first-grade boy likes to have the job of collecting the family wash. He takes a big empty laundry bag and goes from room to room shouting: "Dirty clothes, any dirty clothes?"

But he *hates* to be asked to take the garbage over to the pigs! Are there any jobs you hate?

One day he was telling me that he didn't think it was one bit fair that he had to do so many jobs and the baby didn't have to do anything. The baby is almost two now. I said that there were many jobs that the baby had to do.

"What are they?" he asked.

Here are some of the jobs that our two-year-old does. They are jobs for *him*.

Walks by himself. I used to have to carry him.

Feeds himself. I used to feed him.

Picks out his own books for me to read to him.

Puts the records on the record player by himself.

Takes off his own shoes and socks.

Dries the spoons. (Not very well.)

Gets potatoes out of the vegetable bin for me to peel.

Passes the butter at the table when someone asks him to.

Gets his father's slippers in the morning.

Perhaps you think that those should hardly be called jobs, they are so easy. But for him they aren't.

What jobs do you do? Probably your list is much, much longer than his. Do the older children in your family think your jobs are too easy?

### SUGGESTIONS

1. A delightful book relevant to the ideas in this conversation is *Understood Betsy*, by Dorothy Canfield Fisher. It is especially enjoyed by little girls eight years old and older.

## Section F.  Ethics

*Any acquaintance with anthropology is therefore bound to awaken a feeling of pride in the human race, in the inexhaustible fertility of its power to create cultures. With that comes tolerance. We may not care to adopt the customs of another culture for ourselves, but they are never again so likely to strike us as "wrong" or "ugly" or "immoral." We see that they were come by precisely as we came by ours, that it is only a matter of how one is brought up. What may possibly seem wrong is the act of needlessly imposing by force the customs of one culture on another.* — GENE LISITZKY, Four Ways of Being Human\*

### 37.  Which Is the Right Way?

One day a little girl and her mother were walking along the sidewalk in a big city. They passed a little Chinese girl and her mother.

A few minutes later the first little girl said to her mother, "That little girl's eyes go the wrong way. Why do they?"

Her mother thought for a few minutes and then she said, "I wonder whether that little Chinese girl is saying to her mother: 'Mommy, that little girl's eyes go the wrong way. Why do they?' "

Is there really a right way and a wrong way for eyes to look?

One day at school a teacher was showing her class a filmstrip

\* *Op. cit.*, p. 20.

about Japan. She showed a picture of two Japanese men bowing very low to each other, with their hands together in front of them.

One of the children in the class raised his hand. "Why are they doing that?" he asked.

"That is how Japanese gentlemen say 'How do you do' to each other," said the teacher.

"Why don't they do it the right way and shake hands the way we do?" asked the little boy.

Is there really a right way to say "how do you do?"

The little boy and the little girl in these two stories both had an idea that almost all of us have at times; that is, that if someone looks different from us or does something in a different way, they are wrong and we are right.

I can remember thinking, when I was a little girl, that my best friend's family had a great many wrong ideas and wrong ways of doing things. For example, we got our milk from one milk company and they got theirs from a different one. I was absolutely certain that we had the right milk company and they had the wrong one.

They drove one kind of car and we drove a different kind. Which family do you think I thought drove the right kind of car? There were so many things like that; they went to the wrong church, they voted for the wrong man for President of the United States. I really wonder now how their little girl and I managed to stay best friends! I remember that I even thought that going camping as a family was wrong, because her family went camping every summer and we had a house at the beach!

Did you ever have ideas like this about other people, the way they look and the way they do things? Probably almost everyone thinks this way about some things. Why do you suppose it is so easy for us to think that what is *different* is *wrong*, and that our way is right?

For one thing, it gives us a kind of safe and comfortable feeling when everyone looks the same as we do and does things in much the same way. And there seem to be some times in particular, as we are growing up, when we most want the safe and comfortable feeling that sameness gives us.

One of these times is when we first start going to school. We usually have a teacher who is a stranger to us and we have loads and loads of new friends. These friends and the teacher have many ways of doing things that are quite different from the ways our mothers and fathers say things should be done. We wonder which ways are the right ways and which are the best ways. This is just the age

I was when I was so sure that we had the right milkman and my friend's family had the wrong one.

And, although we mostly think our own family's ways are right, sometimes we suddenly decide that the ways of our friends or the teacher are absolutely right and our family is absolutely wrong about everything.

Thank goodness we do some more growing up and find out that things can be different without one of them always being right and the other one wrong! Pretty soon we like the exciting feeling that difference gives us almost as much as, and sometimes more than, the comfortable feeling that sameness give us.

Which people in the world have the right color skin: the Japanese, the Eskimo, the African, or the English? Which is the right way to eat: with a knife and fork, with chopsticks, or with your hands?

Differences in how people look and how they act have grown up all over the world, as people have fitted themselves or adapted themselves to where they live. When I was little I really could not understand why Eskimo people made houses out of snow. Why didn't they make them out of wood? They wouldn't melt every summer if they were made out of wood. I thought wooden houses were the right kind of houses.

Do you know one very good reason why the Eskimos don't make their houses out of wood? There is almost *no* wood where they live. In fact, there is so little wood where the polar Eskimos live (they are the Eskimos that live farthest north) that in 1818, when Captain John Ross, an English explorer, arrived in wooden sailing boats, the Eskimos were astonished. They asked the interpreter (a person who speaks several different languages and can help people who do not know each other's languages to talk to each other) what those big birds (the wooden sailing boats) were.

The interpreter said that they were houses made of wood. The polar Eskimos knew that the interpreter was just joking, because they *knew* that there was not that much wood in the whole world (their world)!

Today we live in very exciting times because people from every part of the world can go to every part of the world. This means that people who are very different from one another have an opportunity to meet each other. People say we live in one world now.

Some people are frightened by this. They want to feel safe and comfortable. They want just sameness. So they try not to know people who are different from them.

Some people decide that the best thing to do is to make all

the people who are different from them just like them. They think
their ways are right and all other ways are wrong.

And some people, and we need lots and lots of these, think:
"People are different. I'd like to get to know many kinds of people.
I wonder whether I could use any of their ways of doing things? I
wonder whether they could use any of mine?"


## OTHER IDEAS

1. Is there a right kind of writing? (See endpapers in *From Long Ago and Many
Lands*, by Sophia L. Fahs (Boston: Beacon Press).
2. The story "The Blind Men and The Elephant," in *From Long Ago and Many
Lands*, might be used in a related session. Each of the men thought their particular
grasp on the elephant was the whole elephant. We can never escape "particular-
ism," but by sharing insights we can cancel out the partial vision that it necessitates.
3. When a man and woman marry, to some extent (more in some cases than
others) two cultures meet. The children might be able to trace certain physical
and behavioral patterns to each "culture" in their family.
4. The story "The First Animals Make Man," in *Beginnings: Earth, Sky, Life,
Death*, by Fahs and Spoerl (Boston: Beacon Press), might be used with an older
group. What does this story demonstrate?
5. Many, many early peoples called themselves "the people," thinking that they
were the only people in the world. We call ourselves "the world." Had we better
start calling ourselves "a" world?
6. What will happen if and when two worlds meet? Which of the three attitudes
described on the last page of this conversation shall we adopt?
7. In the eastern part of the United States, children play a game called "Giant
Steps"; in the West, the game is called "Mother, May I?" Which is the right name?


## SUGGESTIONS

1. Pictures of various facial types might be posted for this conversation. Pictures
of houses from around the world, modes of travel, etc., would also be effective.
Various kinds of eating utensils, types of shoes, hats might be brought in by the
children or teacher.
2. The children might know and sing "Carefully Taught," from *South Pacific;*
also, "Children of Different Ways," in *We Sing of Life* (No. 76).
3. The poem "Birdtalk," in *Poems to Grow On* (p. 100), is a fanciful consideration of the problem.
4. Many fruitful ideas in this area can be found by leaders in *Four Ways of Being
Human*, by Gene Lisitzky, and in *The Rainbow Book of People and Places*, by
Margaret Mead.


*Money buys food, clothes, houses, land,*
*guns, jewels, men, women, time to be*
*lazy and listen to music.*

*Money buys everything except love,*
  *personality, freedom, immortality,*
  *silence, peace.*
    — CARL SANDBURG, The People, Yes*

## 38. *Christmas Lists*

We have a great big bulletin board in our house. It goes all the way across one wall in the kitchen. We use it for all kinds of things. I keep my shopping list there, Dad keeps his list of jobs that need to be done around the house on it, and the older children put up such things as the times of their school games, or meetings they must remember. When our first-grade boy brings home a P.T.A. notice, he tacks that up there.

We keep it decorated with pictures or other things that fit various months of the year. For example, in February we put up hearts and valentines; in July we put up red-white-and-blue flags; and in October we put up bright orange pumpkin pictures and black cats and witches.

Each year, as soon as Thanksgiving is over, I take down the pictures of turkeys and Pilgrims and harvest scenes and put up a great big cardboard picture of Santa Claus. Then, right underneath it, I put a fairly large piece of white paper. On top of this I write,

"Dear Santa Claus,
　　　For Christmas this year I would like:"
and then I leave the rest of the paper empty, except for the very bottom. Down there I write,
　　"Thank you very much,

　　　　　　　　　　　　　　　Mum"

Then for the next month, when I'm doing chores around the house and I suddenly think of something I want for Christmas, I go over and write it down in that blank space on my paper.

We have a father and a mother and four children in our family, and each one of us puts up this kind of letter to Santa Claus. Of course, the baby is too little to put up his own or to write his own list of things he wants, so the older children do his for him.

During the next few weeks, as each of us does our Christmas planning, we read all the lists on the bulletin board. When we see something on someone's list that we would like to give them, we put a check-mark beside that item. We do it when no one is watching, so that, even though they know they are going to get that present,

* *Op. cit.,* p. 99.

they don't know until Christmas day who will give it to them.

We like playing Santa Claus to each other this way, because we know that we are giving people something they really want or need. We know that all the presents from people outside the family will be real surprises.

Here are some of the things that I had on my Christmas list this year:

*Pencil erasers.* You know the kind of eraser you put on the end of a pencil? I do a lot of erasing and I needed new erasers for most of my pencils. I was glad to see that had a check by it and I did get them for Christmas. Our first-grade boy gave them to me.

*A large roll of Scotch Tape.* We have a baby in our house and he got hold of my Scotch Tape one day. ZIP —— That was the end of that! Someone checked this and when I opened it Christmas morning it said, "from the baby"! Probably Dad really gave it to me.

*A new coffee table.* The eldest boy in our family takes woodworking at school. I *hoped* he would check that, and he did. He made a perfectly beautiful table for the living room.

*Some ski binders.* I like to ski and I needed some new binders. They are the part that holds the boot on the ski. They cost quite a bit of money. For things like that, sometimes two of us go in on the present together. I was glad to see two checks by that and I did get them. The big boy in our family even put the binders right on my skis as one of his presents.

*A mushroom guide with good colored pictures.* I like to pick wild mushrooms in the woods and feed them to the family. But you have to be awfully careful not to pick poisonous ones. I know a few of the nonpoisonous ones and I'd like to learn some more, so I wanted a good book to help me learn them. But this present was too expensive. I didn't get it. No one checked it.

I also wanted a *good moth guide.* We raise moths and butterflies, and I want to learn more about some of the moths. But no one checked this either, so I didn't get that.

But you know, besides the mushroom guide and moth guide that no one checked, there were some other things on my list that no one checked. Some of them I got, though, and some of them I didn't get:

*Snow on the ground at Christmas.* I put that down on my list. I didn't get it, and no one could give it to me.

*A sunny day on Christmas.* Our aunts were going to drive to our house on Christmas day and I wanted them to have a nice day. This was a present I did get, but no one checked it.

*To be pleasant and nice and not shout once at any of the children the whole week before Christmas.* This was a present I wanted very much to give to myself and the family, but I wasn't able to.

*Our friend to get well.* We had a friend who was very, very sick. I wanted him to get well. I did not get this present. Our friend died.

When the children saw some of the queer things I had put up on my list, they began thinking about some of the things that money *won't* buy.

"You know," one of the children said, "when all the catalogues come in the mail before Christmas, you see all the toys and clothes and beautiful things, and you think that if you just had all the money in the world, you could buy everything you wanted. But there are a lot of things people really want that money can't buy."

So we made a list.

*Things money can't buy:*
A sunny day
Brains or good marks in school
A new baby
A healthy body
A snowy winter
A pretty face
A good husband or wife or children
Happiness
Time
Not to die
To draw a good picture or write a good story or to sing well or
    play an instrument well
To be a good athlete
An aunt or a sister
Mail

They are, some of them, just about the most important things, too, aren't they? Can you think of some we missed?

### SUGGESTIONS

1. A blackboard or other device for listing suggestions from the children would be helpful. You may want to gather their ideas before using the above list.

*If he needs a million acres to make him feel rich, seems to me he needs it 'cause he feels awful poor inside hisself, and if he's poor in*

*hisself, there ain't no million acres gonna make him feel rich.* —
JOHN STEINBECK, The Grapes of Wrath*

### 39. *Who Is Rich?*

Do you know anyone who is very rich? We aren't rich and we
aren't poor. We're about in the middle, at least for people in our
country. Don't you wish sometimes that your family were really
rich?

What would you buy if you were rich? Can you think of one
thing? A fancy automobile, a boat, a backyard swimming pool, a
color TV, a special doll, a model kit, or — oh golly, you could buy
just about anything, if you had money enough — or could you?

I'm going to tell you a story about a king; he was called the
richest king in the world. His name was Croesus, and he lived a
long time ago. We still have an expression we use when we want to
say that someone is very rich. We say, "He's as rich as Croesus."

He thought money would buy everything, until he met —
well, let's hear the story. (Read or tell the story, "The Richest
King in the World," which may be found in *From Long Ago and
Many Lands,* by Sophia L. Fahs.)

It was lucky for Croesus that he remembered what Solon had
said, and was saying his name just then! Solon's ideas had really
given him something to think about, hadn't they ?

Croesus *had* thought that his money could buy him the most
*beautiful* things in the world. But there are some beautiful things
we can have without spending money.

Can you think of some of them? Solon thought of peacock
and pheasant feathers. Bird feathers are beautiful. Lots of times
we find them when we are out walking. I always save them.

Money won't buy a baby's smile, and I think that is about the
most beautiful thing in the world. How about a shell, a stone, a
butterfly or a flower? What about a snowflake or a drop of dew
sparkling in the sun? You don't need money to have any of those.

The other thing that Croesus thought money would buy was
happiness. If you don't have enough money to buy food and clothing for your family, you can't feel *very* happy. Solon knew a man
who was quite poor, and yet he was happy, but it isn't easy.

But do you know something very strange? There are many
people who are rich, but they are not happy! Happiness is something that we all want, and yet not very many people really are
very happy. I wonder why?

Do you suppose it is partly because the people who don't have

* New York: Viking, 1939), p. 282.

lots of money think that if they just had more money then they would be happy; and the ones who have a lot of money have found out that having lots of money doesn't bring happiness with it?

Can you think of anyone you know who *is* happy? Are they rich or poor or in the middle? Can you figure out why they are happy? What is being happy? Can you think of one time you were really happy? What made you happy then? Was it something money had bought that made you happy?

### SUGGESTIONS

1. The poem "Rune of Riches," in *Poems to Grow On* (p. 53), is an expression of an idea in this conversation.
2. It may be desirable to tell only part of the story of Croesus, stopping at the end of the last paragraph on page 87 of *From Long Ago and Many Lands*. The main thought, then, is whether or not money can buy the most beautiful things in the world, or happiness.

> *Give me your tired, your poor,*
> *Your huddled masses yearning to*
> *  breathe free,*
> *The wretched refuse of your teeming*
> *  shore.*
> *Send these, the homeless, tempest-*
> *  tossed, to me:*
> *I lift my lamp beside the golden door.*
> — EMMA LAZARUS*

## 40. *An Enormous Birthday Present*

One day I was watching a group of children who were out for a walk. As they passed a very large rock, I saw one of the children climb up on the rock, hold one hand high in the air and shout something. In just a moment all the other children found rocks or tree stumps, climbed up on them, held one hand high in the air, and shouted.

What do you suppose they were doing? Do you know what they were pretending to be? I asked one of the children. He said they were shouting "Statue of Liberty!" He said that this was a game they played when they went on walks. Whenever they came to tree stumps or large rocks, they climbed up on them and pretended to be the Statue of Liberty.

* "The New Colossus," inscribed on the base of the Statue of Liberty.

Have you ever visited the real Statue of Liberty? Have you ever noticed the picture of it on stamps and postcards?

Do you know where the real Statue of Liberty is? It is in the harbor of New York City on an island — Bedloe's Island, now called Liberty Island. To get to it you have to take quite a long ride on a very large ferry boat. It's fun. If you're lucky, you may see some real ocean liners in the harbor as you go out to the island.

As you come closer and closer to the island, you see this huge, huge statue towering above you. The distance from the ground to the top of the torch she is holding is over three hundred feet. The statue stands on a tall building, the pedestal, and this stands on another building that was once an old army fort.

After you get off the boat, you can go into the lowest building and take an elevator up ten stories to the top of the pedestal. You can look out through the windows there and see the harbor and New York City.

Then if you want to — and you probably *would* want to, we did when we went — you can walk up twelve more stories. You will be walking up inside the statue until you reach the top of her head. You follow the spiral staircase and go up and up and around and around. There are little places to sit down and rest every once in a while. At the top of the statue's head there are windows and you can look all around from there, too.

If you have never been to New York City, perhaps someday you will go there. When you do, you'll probably want to take the ferry out to the Statue of Liberty. Almost everyone who visits New York City tries to go there.

Why do you suppose a great big statue of a lady is standing there in New York Harbor? How did it get there? Who is she?

The Statue of Liberty is really an enormous birthday present. It was a present from the people of France for the one hundredth birthday of our country. Do you know what day of the year we celebrate the birthday of our country? The Fourth of July.

Our birthday is the day our country became a separate country from England. It happened on July 4, 1776. Up until that time, for more than one hundred years, the king of England had been the king of America, or of the colonies, as they were called then.

Why do you suppose the people in France decided on this particular present, in this particular spot — a huge woman, holding a torch in one hand and something like a book in the other, in the harbor of New York City?

This woman is really a symbol. A symbol is something that stands for something else. Do you know what a red flying horse is a symbol for? A kind of gasoline. When you see the horse, you think of that gasoline.

The Statue of Liberty is a symbol for something. It is a statue of the Roman goddess of liberty. When we see her, we should think of freedom. The people of France said: "When we think of America, we think of freedom. Miss Liberty is the best symbol for America."

Do you know why the Pilgrims came to America? They came because they wanted to be free to think of God in the way that seemed right to them. In England they had to go to the kind of church that the king said was right.

From that time on, boatload after boatload of people have sailed across the Atlantic Ocean because they wanted to be free. They have come from many, many different countries. Some wanted to be free to own land of their own, some wanted to be free from kings, some wanted to be free to say and write what they believed. Many of the countries they left now have these freedoms, but once they did not.

You can see, then, why, when the people of France wanted a symbol for America, they thought of a statue of liberty or freedom. And perhaps now you can understand why they put it up in the harbor in New York. That is where the boats that brought these people most often landed. Now, when people come to America, they see this great statue standing there and they know what it means.

In one hand, the one that she holds over her head, the Statue of Liberty has a great torch, or light. At night the torch is lit by electricity. It is lit by very strong bulbs. The light it gives off is twenty-five hundred times as bright as the full moon.

I like to think of that great statue standing in the harbor there, a symbol of freedom to the whole world. But I like to think of those children, playing "Statue of Liberty" on the rocks and tree stumps, too. Do you know why? Because there isn't any such thing as "freedom" apart from people who will let each other be free. Do you let other people say and think a little differently from you?

If you ever go for a walk and climb up on a stone or a tree stump and pretend that you are the Statue of Liberty, ask yourself: "What kind of symbol of freedom am I?"

### OTHER IDEAS

1. Further discussion might center around several facts about the statue and American history that are too complex for the younger children or, at least, for

one discussion. The other hand of the statue holds a tablet on which is written "July 4, 1776" and "ALL MEN ARE CREATED EQUAL," from the Declaration of Independence. Are all men created equal, and how does this idea relate to the idea of freedom?

2. The boats that brought slaves to America are an example of boats that brought people here against their will and with no hope for freedom. Was freedom an idea that the slaves thought of when they thought of America? Are all Negroes free now?

*Whoso would be a man, must be a nonconformist. He who would gather immortal palms must not be hindered by the name of goodness, but must explore if it be goodness. Nothing is at last sacred but the integrity of your own mind.* — RALPH WALDO EMERSON, "Self Reliance"*

## 41. *Changing Your Mind*

Have you ever changed your mind about something? That's a funny expression, isn't it? Change your mind! It sounds as if you took your old mind out and put a new one in. You know how you can take an old battery out of your flashlight and put in a new one; it sounds as if that's what you can do with your mind. But of course you can't do that.

But you *can* change your mind. I have a million times. How do you do it? What is your mind? Your mind is what you think with. Your brain, inside your head, is where your thinking gets done. Your five senses send pictures and sounds and smells and tastes and feelings up to your brain, and somehow, I don't really know how, your brain puts them together into ideas.

To change your mind is to get some different ideas about something. Perhaps you don't like tomatoes. Lots of children don't. But most children, as they grow older, come to like tomatoes. They change their mind.

You'll be changing your mind about lots of things as you grow up. You'll change your ideas about what is pretty and what tastes good, and who your best friend is and how much you like your brothers and sisters and what you think is most fun to do.

Lots of boys and girls find they change their minds about many things when they first start school. I suppose that's partly because, when you leave home and go to school, you discover new ideas from your friends and your teachers and from the books you read.

Sometimes when you go home with one of these new ideas,

* *Essays*, p. 50.

your mother says, "My goodness, where did you ever get that idea!" She knows you didn't get it from her, or your father. Of course, before you went to school, that's where you did get most of your ideas — from your parents. Do you think it is all right to have different ideas from those of your mother and father?

I'm going to tell a story about "The King Who Changed His Mind." (Read or tell this story from Sophia L. Fahs's *From Long Ago and Many Lands*.) His name was King Asoka and he was a real king. He lived long ago in India. He didn't change his mind about little things, such as whether he liked tomatoes or what his favorite color was. He changed his mind about such big things that it almost seemed that he *had* taken his old mind out and put a new one in.

I wonder what King Asoka's mother thought of his new ideas? She had taught him that his grandfather was a very great man because he was a great fighter. Did Asoka think that a fighting king was a great king after he changed his mind?

His mother had taught him that if he conquered everyone he would be safe. Did his new friend think this was the best way to become safe and to feel afraid of no one?

Do you think most people agree with King Asoka's *old* ideas or his *new* ones? Would our country be safe if we didn't have soldiers and bombs and fighting planes?

Do you think that a person who steals should be put in jail? What do most people think?

What do you think of King Asoka's new idea that he shouldn't eat meat? Don't you like meat? Is it all right to eat vegetables (you have to kill plants to eat them)?

If you are kind to someone, are they always nice back?

Perhaps you have never wondered about these things before. King Asoka never had either, until he met the beggar. They are questions that you will be wondering about almost all your life. You may change your mind about them several times. Grownups don't agree at all about the answers to them.

OTHER IDEAS

1. This might lead into quite a discussion of war. Discussing some of the real and complex causes of war with young children is, of course, not easy. I feel that it is better to give them a glimpse of the complexity of the issue than to oversimplify to such an extent that they can't understand why "the grownups" just don't decide not to fight any more.
2. Material about the United Nations might naturally be introduced in a subsequent conversation, the attempt being made to be realistic about it and, again, not to oversimplify.

## Section G.  Universals

*In a bus where there is nothing to do for forty minutes except*
*stare into one another's faces, a baby has the great chance of his*
*life, and this baby was made to seize it. . . . So he took us in hand*
*one by one, till he had reduced us all to a state of delighted sub-*
*jection, to the pretended scandal and secret pride of his mother.*
— IAN MACLAREN, His Majesty Baby*

### 42. Babies

We have a baby at our house.

He's not the tiny, stay-in-bed-all-the-time kind. He's the just-can-walk-around, but can't-really-talk-yet kind. He's at the age when he likes to tip his head on one side and smile at you or put his face down and love the picture of the kitty in his picture book. Do you have a baby like that at your house? Did you ever have one like that, besides yourself, of course? They're fun.

Our baby — his name is Charles — can sit himself down in a chair, if he is careful. Sometimes, when he tries to back up into one of his little chairs, he misses it! Then he gets up and tries again.

He can feed himself, but he spills quite a bit. We have a dog and, whenever it is time for the baby to eat, the dog goes under the table and puts her head on the edge of Charles' high chair. Anything the baby drops, the dog catches and eats even before it lands on the floor. It saves me a lot of sweeping!

We live out in the country, but sometimes the baby and I have to drive to town and do some shopping. He likes that. We park the car and walk along the sidewalk until I find the right store: the supermarket, or the hardware store, or the drug store.

But the baby isn't looking for stores. Oh no! Charles walks along until he finds a baby carriage. Then he toddles up and looks in. You should see him grin when he sees a baby in the carriage. Once he found a carriage with twin babies in it. He was really surprised! Sometimes the baby in the carriage is asleep and I say, "Sh-sh," and I put my finger in front of my lips, and he does too, only he says "S-s," instead.

Sometimes he looks into the carriage and finds that it is empty. Then he looks very sad and I say, "Oh dear, no baby, baby all gone," and he shakes his head back and forth. He has just learned that means "no." "No baby," I say, and we look for another carriage.

* (London: Hodder & Stoughton, 1902), pp. 1–2.

Sometimes we find a carriage with a big sitting-up baby in it. Then Charles smiles and puts out one finger and touches the big sitting-up baby. After they have had a little visit, I say, "Bye, bye, baby," and we go into the store.

Our baby really loves babies!

The other day, as he was walking along the sidewalk in town, looking for baby carriages, an old man came walking along.

"Hi, Butch," said the old man. "Where are you going?"

Charles stopped walking. He looked up at the man and smiled. The old man smiled, too. Then Charles started to walk along again.

"Bye, bye," said the old man, and he walked away smiling.

I suppose our baby reminded him of one of his grandchildren.

Pretty soon an old woman came walking toward Charles. She looked awfully tired and worried and I was afraid Charles was going to go crashing into her. But she saw him coming toward her. She looked at him with his bright red boots and his big blue scarf tied around his neck and his wool hat pulled down over his ears. The tired worried look went right away from her face and she leaned down and said, "Hi, dearie, aren't you bundled up nice and warm!"

Charles stopped and looked up at her. He almost tips over when he looks up at a grownup. He smiled at her and then he started out again to look for baby carriages.

I thought to myself, "Well, I guess all old people love babies."

Then it was time for Charles and me to drive to the school where our first-grade boy goes. His name is William. We parked the car and walked into the school yard. School wasn't out yet, but Charles saw the merry-go-round in the school yard and he hurried right over. He likes to ride on it.

"Up! Up!" he said. That's one of the few words he can say. In fact, I think it was his first word. Ask your mother sometime what your first word was.

I set Charlie on the merry-go-round. He held on tightly to the iron bar in front of him and I gave him a little push.

Just then the first children began to come out of school. A boy about as big as our first-grade boy came over.

"I'll push the baby," he said.

Then a girl, about the same age, came over. "I'll sit beside your baby so he won't fall off," she said. She climbed up beside him and put her arm around him.

Soon more and more children came out and just about every one of them came over. Some of them said, "Oh, look at the baby." Or, "I have a baby at my house." Or, "Isn't *she* cute." (That person thought Charles was a girl!) Or, "Don't push it so fast; the baby might fall off."

I was standing there thinking, "Well, I guess all first-graders like babies."

Then our brother, William, came out of school and we went over to another school where the twelve-year-old brother in our family goes. His name is Graham. When he came out of his school, Charles and William and Graham and I started to walk over to the gym. We were going to see our big sister play basketball.

"I'll carry Charles," said Graham.

"Oh, he can walk," I said.

"But I *want* to carry him," said Graham; so he did.

When we got to the gym, Charles and I sat down on a bench and Graham and William went over to another part of the gym to sit with Graham's friend, George.

In just a minute Graham came back. "George wants the baby."

"Well," I thought to myself, "even twelve-year-old boys like babies!"

When the basketball game was half over and everyone was resting, all of a sudden a little girl about two years old came running across the gym floor.

"Baby. See the baby. Hello, baby," said the little girl.

Charles looked at the little girl and she patted his head.

Just about everyone in that gym was looking at the two babies and laughing and smiling.

At supper that night our big sister, whose name is Elizabeth, said, "Did you see everyone in the gym watching Charles and that little girl? Why, even some of the oldest boys in school were watching them and smiling. I didn't think *they* would be interested in babies!"

"Yes," I said. "I did notice them. I guess everybody loves babies. Babies love babies. Old people love babies. First-graders love babies. Twelve-year-old boys love babies and great big high schoolers love babies."

I wonder why?

I asked some children once why they liked babies. Here are some of the answers they gave me. "Because they are cute." "Because they grow and change all the time." "Because they are so little." One boy said, "Sometimes I *don't* like babies; that's when they get in my things!"

Do you like babies? Why?

*. . . a style so old that the hieroglyphs of Egypt, the cylinders of Nippur, and the drawings of the cave men are as things of today in*

*comparison; a writing indeed that is older than mankind, the one
universal script. I mean the tracks in the dust, the mud, or the
snow.* — ERNEST THOMPSON SETON, Animal Tracks and Hunter
Signs*

### 43. *An Old, Old Language*

How many languages do you know? Just your own? Would
you like to learn another one, at least a few words of it?

The language we have in mind is just about the oldest language
in the world. Perhaps you know some words in it already. I'll tell
you some more about it and you see whether or not you can guess
what language it is.

How many letters are there in the alphabet that you know?
Twenty-six, aren't there? We make up our *words* by putting the
letters of this alphabet together in different ways. If we put the
letter N in front of O, we have the word NO. If we put the O in
front of the N, we have the word ON.

But this language that we are talking about is different. The
alphabet of this language is really made up of words. And there
are thousands of words in the language. That makes it sound very
difficult to learn, doesn't it? Well, cheer up — there are some words
that aren't used any more, so at least you won't have to learn those.

You might think that a person would need to go to school for
years and years to learn this language, but actually some of the
people who have known this language best (Indians of the past, for
example) never went to school at all, at least not to our kind of
school.

The best place to learn this language is outdoors and the
wilder the out-of-doors, the more interesting the lesson is likely to
be. But you *can* learn a few words of it in a city, if you have sharp
eyes. You might find some words written on a sidewalk, or in the
mud, or in a dusty yard, or even on the floor of your bathroom after
you've taken a bath. But the very best place of all to learn this
language is in a snowy field, or deep in a snowy woods. Do you
know what language it is yet?

I won't keep you guessing any longer. This language is the
language of animal tracks and signs. You can understand now why
I said it is an old, old language. It began to be written when the
first creature crawled up out of the water and moved along the
muddy shore. This was millions of years ago.

This language is a *universal* language. That means it is a language that is found all over the world. If a cat walks through the

* (New York: Doubleday, 1958), pp. 17–18.

snow in China, the United States, Russia or France, he signs his
name in the same way. But if people in these different countries
*talk* about the cat, in America they say or write *cat*, in France *chat*,
in Russia *kot*, in Germany *Katze*, in China — I don't know what!

Let's see how many words you know already in this language.
Look at the page of vocabulary (that means words) in this old,
old language.

Do you know the first one? Perhaps you've seen a smaller
one like it on your bird-feeding shelf on a snowy morning. And of
course you know the second one! That is one you might find on
the bathroom floor, after your bath. The third one is difficult to
guess, but, when you know what it is, you can almost see that big
old turtle waddling through the mud. The last one is interesting. It
isn't a footprint; it's a nose print or a bill print of a sapsucker or
woodpecker. The bird makes rows and rows of these holes. This
brings the sap up into the holes. Insects come to drink the sap and
the bird comes back and eats the sap *and* the insects.

Are there any words in this language that you already know
besides the ones on our vocabulary sheet? Do you know the word
for dog and the word for cat? Do you know how to tell them apart?
Keep your eyes open in the next few days and see whether or not
you can find some more words to add to your vocabulary. When
you know a good many words, you can read a story in the old, old
language.

### SUGGESTIONS

1. Several large blackboards or pieces of tag board will be needed. The vocabulary should be written out, as well as the two stories in the following conversation.

*Man has lost his power of tracking by scent but has developed
greater intellectual refinement. He can read a more complex story
in footprints than mere identification and direction of travel.* —
CLAUS J. MURIE, A Field Guide to Animal Tracks*

### 44. *A Tragedy and a Comedy*

I think that we are about ready to read two stories in our old,
old language (see Suggestion 1). One wonderful thing about these
stories is that they were "written" when no human eye was there and

* (Boston: Houghton Mifflin, 1954), p. 1.

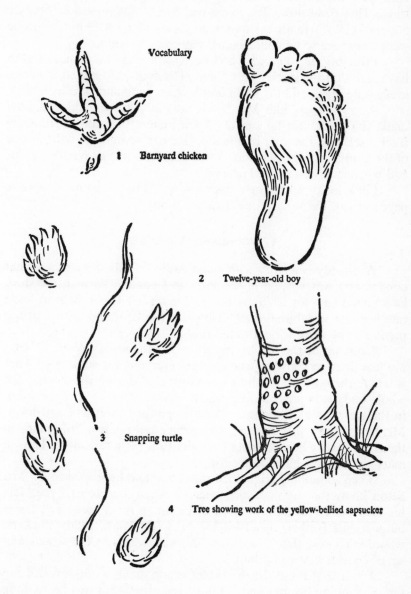

Vocabulary

1  Barnyard chicken

2  Twelve-year-old boy

3  Snapping turtle

4  Tree showing work of the yellow-bellied sapsucker

yet, if you know this language, you can almost see what happened.

The man who discovered the two stories that we are going to read spent his whole life learning the language of animal tracks and signs. He's dead now. His name was Ernest Thompson Seton (see Suggestion 2). He always took a notebook along with him when he went anywhere so he could sketch any story he found.

Probably, if you and I had been with him, we wouldn't even have *seen* that the stories were there. His eyes had learned to notice every little mark and his brain had learned to understand it.

A real expert like Mr. Seton not only knows which animal made the track, but he can often tell many other things from the track itself and the way it is made. He can sometimes tell the size of the animal, its age, whether it was a male (boy) or female (girl), and whether it was excited or calm.

Let's look at the two stories now. The first one (opposite page) is sad; the second one is rather funny.

## A WOODLAND TRAGEDY

A tragedy is a story with a sad ending. This story (somewhat condensed) was written in the snow in Canada. At first, the story looks just like a lot of funny blobs, doesn't it? It will help to learn one word of vocabulary first. Down in the left-hand corner of the picture is the word for cottontail rabbit.

Now, up at the top by the letter A (the letters A, B, C, etc., are just there to show us where to go), there is a round spot. That is where the cottontail rabbit was crouching during the storm. His whole body was pushed down in the snow. That is why the mark in the snow looks like that. Then he jumped to B and sat down. Mr. Seton knew this because the rabbit's tail made a little mark in the snow, and when cottontail rabbits run, their tails don't leave a mark, so he must have been sitting.

Then something frightened the rabbit and he leaped to C. Mr. Seton knew the rabbit leaped because when a cottontail goes fast his long back feet land in front of his small front feet. The faster he goes, the farther ahead his big hind feet land. Many trackers, who don't know this, follow a rabbit backwards in the woods and so, of course, never find him.

From C through F, the rabbit made many wildly excited big jumps, running around and behind trees. But what was he running from? There were no other tracks.

At G and H Mr. Seton found drops of blood in the snow. He knew now that the rabbit was in serious danger. But what from?

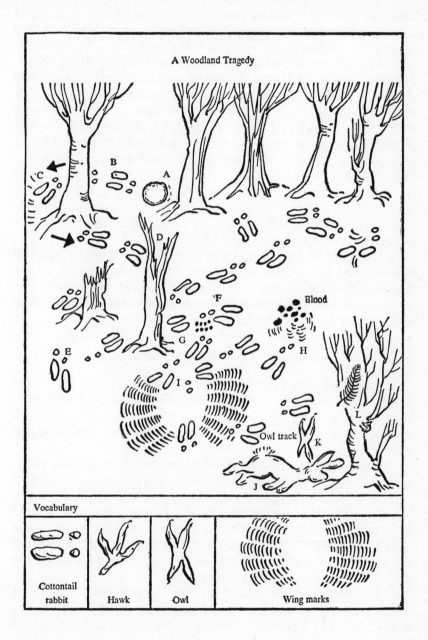

A Woodland Tragedy

Blood

Owl track

Vocabulary

Cottontail rabbit | Hawk | Owl | Wing marks

At I he found a new word written in the snow. Down in the right-hand corner is a picture of this new word: wings. It was a bird that was after the cottontail rabbit — a large, strong bird. At I the bird had reached down and clutched at the rabbit, injured it, and let go. The bird's wings left a print in the snow.

At J Mr. Seton found what was left of the body of the rabbit. He knew that if the bird had been an eagle, it would have carried the whole rabbit off and eaten it somewhere else. The bird had not done this. Therefore, he knew this bird must be smaller than an eagle, either an owl or a hawk. In the left-hand corner, at the bottom of the page, are the words for owl and hawk. Mr. Seton found a track in the snow by the body of the rabbit and saw that it was the track of an owl (K).

He knew that there were three kinds of owls in the neighborhood and he wondered which one might have done it, until he found a tiny feather at L, caught on a small tree. By this feather he knew a barred owl had killed the rabbit.

Just after he found the feather and was studying it, the owl himself came flying through the air and landed on a tree near Mr. Seton. No doubt he had come to finish eating the rabbit. Mr. Seton made him wait until he had drawn the owl's picture. That is the end of the woodland tragedy.

## THE SKUNK AND THE UNWISE BOBCAT

This story was written in dust rather than snow. Mr. Seton was living in New Mexico at this time and every night, before he went to bed, he carefully swept the dust smooth around his cabin so that any night visitors would leave a clear story for him to read in the morning.

I should have said earlier that anyone with a good sense of smell will find this language simpler to read than anyone without a good one. That's one reason animals read this language so well.

To read *this* story, however, Mr. Seton didn't need a *good* sense of smell. Any sense of smell would have been enough. Just after sunrise Mr. Seton noticed a strong smell of skunk outside his cabin. He went outside and saw, in the dust around his cabin, the story you see here. (See opposite page.)

The vocabulary you need for reading this story is down at the bottom of the page, but the footprints do not show up sharply in the dust. The larger ones belong to the bobcat and the smaller ones to the skunk. This is the story that Mr. Seton read.

A skunk had come along, at A, and was wandering about, at

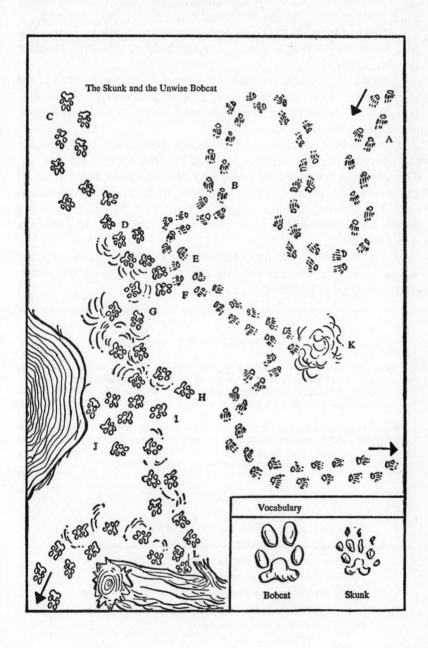

The Skunk and the Unwise Bobcat

Vocabulary

Bobcat          Skunk

B. Over at C, a bobcat or wildcat entered from another direction. At D he came toward the skunk, thinking that here might be something good to eat. The skunk turned away and started toward E.

Most older animals know enough to leave a skunk alone, but Mr. Seton thinks that this was a *young* bobcat. He kept on after the skunk, at G.

"All right," said the skunk, "if you won't leave me alone, here goes," and at F he turned himself around and sprayed the unwise bobcat with the perfume he carries in his body. This is his way of protecting himself.

The bobcat was hit at G and rushed wildly away. But because the spray hit him in the eyes, he was blinded, for the time being. Therefore, he bumped into a rock at J and into a log at L. Then he ran away. We can be sure that from then on he knew about skunks!

The skunk went on quietly exploring in Mr. Seton's dusty yard. He found the remains of a dead chicken at K and then wandered away.

The next time you have a chance to read this oldest language in the world, see whether you can find a story as interesting as one of these. (See Suggestion 3.)

### SUGGESTIONS

1. The session might start by asking whether anyone has a new word to add to the vocabulary. If someone has, he might draw it on the blackboard.
2. An interesting biography of Seton, suitable for age ten and older, is *Ernest Thompson Seton: Naturalist,* by Garst, Shannon and Warren (New York: Messner, 1959).
3. Some books on tracking are: *Nature Detectives,* by Millicent Selsam (New York: Scott, 1958); *Animal Tracks,* by George F. Mason (New York: Morrow, 1943), a very helpful track guide and quite easy; *A Field Guide to Animal Tracks,* by Claus J. Murie, an exhaustive and excellent resource book.

*When shall we all speak the same language?*
*And do we want to have all the same language?*
*Are we learning a few great signs and passwords?*
*Why should Everyman be lost for words?*
*The questions are put every day in every tongue:*
　　*"Where you from, Stranger?*
　　*Where were you born?*
　　*Got any money?*
　　*What do you work at?*

*Where's your passport?*
*Who are your people?"*
— CARL SANDBURG, The People, Yes*

## 45. *Languages without Words*

I have found another universal language besides animal tracks.
A universal language, remember, is one "spoken" and understood
all over the world. Probably there are many, many others that I
just haven't thought of yet.

I thought of this one because a woman wrote to the newspaper
that I read and asked a question: "How are animal sounds that *we*
write — 'oink, oink,' 'bow-wow,' 'moo,' and so forth — written in
various other languages?"

Here are the answers that the newspaper gave her. (See Suggestion 1.)

|          | Dog     | Cat   | Cock            | Pig         | Cow           |
|----------|---------|-------|-----------------|-------------|---------------|
| *English* | bow-wow | meow  | cock-a-doodle-doo | oink        | moo           |
| *Spanish* | uau-uau | miau  | quiquiriqui     | oink        | mu            |
| *French*  | oua-oua | miaule | coquirico      | groin-groin | beugle-beugle |
| *German*  | wau-wau | miau  | kikeriki        | oink-oink   | muh           |
| *Russian* | gaf-gaf | meow  | kookerikoo      | khro-khro   | moo-moo       |

They are all really pretty much the same, aren't they? Some
*look* quite different but, if you think about them a little bit, you'll
see that they aren't very different, really.

The Russian sound for dog, "gaf-gaf," for example, is really
like the "ruff-ruff" sound that we sometimes use for dogs. And
sometimes cowboys talk about the "bawling" of cattle, which is the
sound the French are probably thinking of when they write "beugle-
beugle" for cows.

Really, then, we could call these animal sounds such as "bow-
wow," "moo," "oink," and so forth, a universal language. No matter
what country we were visiting, we would hear these familiar sounds
and know exactly what animals made them.

Why do you suppose cows always make a cow sound, dogs
their sound, cats theirs? Do you suppose that it is because of the
way their bodies are made and the shape of their voice boxes?

There are some other things I wonder about, too. I wonder
whether animals, like dogs, talk to each other? They seem to enjoy
being together. Our dog has a special dog friend who comes up

* *Op. cit.,* p. 92.

every morning to play with her. They run around and growl a lot, but they don't seem to *me* to be talking to each other.

Perhaps you have the same record that we have at our house. One of the songs on it goes like this:

> Do animals talk to one another
> Just like me and you?
> I'm sure, I'm sure, I'm sure, I'm sure,
> In their own way they do.
> What do animals talk about,
> Moo, bow-wow and squawk about?
> As they run and walk about?
> I'm sure, I'm sure, I'm sure, I'm sure,
> I'm sure I wish I knew.[25]

Have you ever listened to a mother dog busy with a litter of puppies? She makes all sorts of little noises and the babies seem to pay attention. I wonder if they are talking?

Do you suppose that if animals *can* talk to each other, a dog from Russia would be able to talk to a dog from America? If they both say "bow-wow" and "ruff-ruff," it would seem that they should be able to. Sometimes it seems that dogs are talking to each other by smelling each other, rather than making noises at each other. Do you suppose there could be a language of smells rather than sounds?

Do you think dogs can understand cats? Our dog and cat play with each other a great deal. Are they talking to each other in some way? And then I wonder whether people will ever be able to understand what animal sounds mean?

There is another animal that the woman who wrote to the newspaper didn't ask about. I mean the human animal — us. I'm thinking about a brand-new baby. What does he say in all these different languages — English, Spanish, French, German, Russian?

"Waa-waa-waa-waa." It's the same all over the world. No matter what color the baby's skin or what shape his eyes, the first cry of a baby is the same word in this universal language — *waaaaa!*

But then something happens at about the end of the baby's first year. This something makes us different from all the other animals.

If you have a baby brother or a little sister, perhaps you know the different kinds of sounds a baby makes during the first year. At first he just cries, then he begins to make little "ah-ah-ah" sounds, and then little cooing sounds, and then, when he's about half a year

[25] From the Columbia record, *Now We Know*, CL–670.

old, he begins to make babbling noises. By the time he is just about one year old, these sounds begin to be quite clear — ba-ba-ba, ma-ma-ma, da-da-da.

And that is when, all over the world, in Eskimo igloos, in thatched houses in Africa, in apartment houses in America, the mommies and the daddies prick up their ears and say, "Oh, did you hear him? He's talking!"

And the mother in America says, "Yes, dear, ma-ma-ma — Mother, Mother, Mother."

And the mother in France says, "Oui, mon cher, ma-ma-ma — Mère, Mère, Mère."

And the mother in Germany says, "Ja, Liebling, ma-ma-ma — Mutter, Mutter, Mutter."

So it is that all the mothers and fathers and grandmothers all over the world take the little baby sounds, which are the same everywhere, and begin to shape them into the language of their particular country. And so, very soon, the babies of the world take on the language of their mothers and fathers.

In this way we seem to be different from all the other animals. Are we better? Are we happier?

### OTHER IDEAS

1. Do you suppose chickadees say "chickadee-dee-dee" in all the different countries? And crows, "caw-caw"? I have a friend who took his little boy out to listen to a whippoorwill. He let the little boy listen and then he asked him what he thought the bird said. The little boy thought it sounded like "com-for-rent, com-for-rent." Do you suppose people in different countries hear the sounds we hear, but think they say something different?
2. Do crickets and frogs make the same sounds all over the world? Do you know what a peeper frog sounds like? I like to think that I could hear peeper frogs making their same sound when spring first comes, wherever they are in the world. I wonder if they do, and I wonder in how many parts of the world there are peeper frogs.
3. Which one of the words for mother is the *right* word — *Mother, Mère* or *Mutter?*
4. Why do you suppose there are different languages? Would it be better if there were just one?
5. Would it be a good idea for all the mothers of the world to decide one day to teach all the new babies, from that day on, one language? Which language would they choose? How would the mothers learn it? How would the babies, as they grew older, talk to their older brothers and sisters?
6. Do you suppose there *are* other universal languages that I haven't thought of? How about pictures? Music? Sculpture?

### SUGGESTIONS

1. For this conversation a large chart or blackboard with the pictures of the various animals mentioned might be at the front of the room. Under the pictures, the

animal sounds in the various languages should be listed. Space might be left for a picture of a human baby, to be added when that point in the conversation is reached or, even better, a variety of human babies — Chinese, African, American.

> . . . *The testimony of great poets is of such importance. Their survival is evidence that they express deep intuitions of mankind penetrating into what is universal in concrete fact.* — A. N. WHITEHEAD, Science and the Modern World*

## 46. *Poetry*[26]

Do you think that you could draw a picture of a little boy who was awfully cross? How would you do it? Would you show him standing up stamping his foot? Perhaps you would have him shaking his fist and shouting. Or maybe you'd show him sitting down, kicking his feet.

I wonder whether you would use crayons or paint? And what colors would you use? Probably a lot of black. Or red might be good for some kinds of mad feelings. I guess you would want to use a very large piece of paper, so that the little boy's face would show clearly.

But perhaps you can't draw very well, and you think you couldn't show how someone feels. I know another way that you could make a picture of someone feeling awfully cross. You could write it. Do you know one of the best ways to write a picture?

Well, listen to this. Close your eyes while I read and see if you don't see a picture of an awfully mad little boy.

### A DREADFUL SIGHT

> We saw him so naughty and scratching and hitting
> And when he sat down, then he wouldn't stop sitting,
> Right on the sidewalk with everyone staring,
> But *he* didn't care — oh, he LIKED it not caring![27]

Can't you just see him! I wonder what had happened?

A poem is really a way of drawing a picture. A poet does with words what an artist does with colors and lines. Perhaps you

---

* (New York: Macmillan, 1925), p. 126.
26 Adapted from the conversation by Beth Scherer.
27 Dorothy Aldis, "A Dreadful Sight," from *All Together* (copyright by Dorothy Aldis, 1952; New York: Putnam, 1952), p. 83.

think that only a few people can be poets. It's too bad we get that idea. Some people say that all children are poets, at first. A little boy three years old told this poem to his mother early one morning as he looked out of his bedroom window.

> The sky is out now.
> See!
> Dark sleeps in a bedroom.
> Dark lives in a white house in the sky.[28]

You see, the words don't have to rhyme. One of my children's favorite poems, by a very famous poet, Carl Sandburg, doesn't rhyme a bit.

> Why did the children
> put beans in their ears
> when the one thing we told the children
> they must not do
> was put beans in their ears?[29]

There are many kinds of poetry, some with rhymes, some with certain numbers of lines and even some with a certain number of syllables. Do you know what a syllable is?

Japan is one country where many people keep on being poets even after they have stopped being children. So many people there love poetry and love to write it, that each January there is a national poetry contest. The emperor, their king, chooses a subject — maybe rain or a cherry tree or a baby — almost anything can be the subject. Then everyone in the whole country — young, old, rich or poor — if they want to, may send in a poem that they have written. Usually the emperor writes one too. The best ones are carefully chosen to be read in public on a special day and then printed in newspapers and magazines.

These poems are not just any kind of poems. These are poems that must be just seventeen syllables long. They are called *hokkus* — little, little, little poems. They make a picture, but oh, such a quick picture — as if a window opened for just a moment, and then closed again. Carl Sandburg says all poetry is like that, the opening and closing of a window or a door, leaving those who look through to guess what was seen in that moment.

I'm going to open a couple of windows and then close them;

[28] By Tom Dunwiddie.
[29] Carl Sandburg, from *The People, Yes.*

I wonder what you'll see! This poem and the following one are Japanese *hokkus*.[30]

### BABY'S HANDS

One chestnut, only one,
Is all his tiny hands can hold,
My little baby son.

I saw a big, round, shiny horse chestnut. You know how smooth they feel when they first come out of their case! And you know how soft and smooth a baby's fat little hand feels. A baby's hand really would hold just about one horse chestnut.

Here's another window going up:

Lo!
Fresh and green amid the snow,
A pine tree.

I've seen that many times: a pine tree, looking so green against the white snow. It's an interesting thing that after you've read a poem about something, you usually notice that something more, the next time you see it.

I wonder why it is that a poem, whether it is a tiny Japanese hokku or a longer poem of the kind we are used to, why it can make us see something so much better than just sentences about the same thing?

Did you ever see a shooting star? They are fun, aren't they? I'll open another window and we'll have a shooting star in here.

### THE FALLING STAR

I saw a star slide down the sky,
Blinding the north as it went by,
Too burning and too quick to hold,
Too lovely to be bought or sold,
Good only to make wishes on
And then forever to be gone.[31]

Now instead of reading a poem about it, I could have just told you about the shooting star I saw. I might have said something like this:

---

[30] Poems and information in the preceding paragraphs are from *Little Pictures of Japan* (Chicago: The Book House for Children).

[31] Sara Teasdale, "The Falling Star," *Stars Tonight* (New York-Macmillan).

I saw a star when it went through the sky. It went by in the north, and made the sky very bright. You couldn't hold on to it because it was much too hot and because it moved too quickly. It was too beautiful to buy in a store. You couldn't do anything with it except make wishes on it. Then it was all gone.

It doesn't sound like much that way, does it? It doesn't make you see anything or feel anything or wonder about anything. I'll read you the poem again and see how much better it is than just those sentences.

Yes, if you know a poem about something that you've seen or done, hearing the poem is like having a chance to do it over again. Probably all of us have played in the mud, sometimes. It felt good, didn't it? I'm going to give you a chance to do it again, in a poem.

### MUD

Mud is very nice to feel
    All squishy-squash between the toes!
I'd rather wade in wiggly mud
    Than smell a yellow rose.
Nobody else but the rosebush knows
How nice mud feels
    Between the toes.[32]

That feels so good, I think I'll read it again.

Poetry does something else, besides giving us an experience over again. Did you ever see a pretty shell when you were walking along the beach? Didn't you want to pick it up? I always do. Why do we want to pick it up? So we can save it, I guess, and take it home with us, and look at it once in a while, and think about it, and maybe have a collection of shells. Poetry helps us do that with our experiences and with our feelings and with our ideas.

The next time something happens to you that you want to remember or think about some more, why don't you make a poem about it? Pretty soon you might have a whole collection of them. Remember, they don't have to rhyme, and they don't have to be long. They just have to be words that make a picture. Just make believe you are opening a window for some one, for just a minute. What would you like to let them see?

[32] Polly Chase Boyden, "Mud," from *Child Life Magazine,* copyright 1930 by Rand McNally & Company.

OTHER IDEAS

1. The Japanese *hokkus* were written of course in the Japanese language and had to be translated into English. Some of the Japanese poets say that you really can't translate them and have them as beautiful as they were before. One man said that translating them was like taking down a beautiful cobweb and trying to set it up again in another place.

*In those far-off days, the great big bells that hung high in the church steeples were really needed. For how could people without clocks or watches know when to come to church unless the bells in the steeples called them to come?* — SOPHIA L. FAHS, "The Bell of Atri"*

## 47. *Two Pieces of Metal*[33]

Do you think that you could say anything by striking two pieces of metal together? Here are a few things people have been able to say that way.

> Listen
> Nine o'clock
> Come here
> Come to church
> Get up
> Time for school

Now do you know what the two pieces of metal are? They are the two parts of a bell: the bell itself and the clapper, or whatever is hit against the bell to make the sound.

Bells don't actually have to be made out of metal. There are bells of bamboo. Bells have also been made from hollowed out living trees and, possibly, out of ivory. But most of the bells in the world have been made of metal.

Bells are something people in all parts of the world have discovered as a means of telling people to LISTEN! That is the first and most important thing that all bells say.

They may be great huge bells, weighing thousands and thou-

* In *From Long Ago and Many Lands* (Boston: Beacon Press, 1948).
[33] The chief sources for ideas in this conversation were: *Encyclopaedia Britannica*, 11th ed.; *The First Book of Bells*, Helen Jill Fletcher (New York: Watts, 1959); Mrs. Berna Derby, Leominster, Mass.

sands of pounds. Or they may be tiny little bells, the kind Chinese
mothers used to sew on their babies' clothing.

But whether the bells are huge or tiny, they all say, "LISTEN!"

But each bell says something more, too. You may wonder
how a bell, which most often makes just one clear sound at a time,
can say many different things. Don't they all just say "clang-clang"
or "tinkle-tinkle" or "ding-a-ling" or "bong-bong-bong," and things
like that?

Yes. That is about all the *bells* themselves say. But when they
make these sounds, the sounds mean many, many different things
to the people who hear them. Then we say that the bell has told us
to "come here," "go to school," and so forth.

How do people know what it is that the bell is saying?

One way of knowing what a bell is saying, or what it means,
is by counting the number of times it rings. In many towns, the
number of times the fire bell rings tells the firemen just where the
fire is. Two clangs and then three clangs may mean that the fire
is at the corner of Main Street and Elm Street.

In some towns, before there were such things as newspapers,
or radio and television, the church bell rang whenever a person
died. The number of times it rang told the townspeople whether
a man, a woman or a child had died.

Of course the best example of knowing what the ringing of a
bell means by counting the number of peals (or times rung) is a
clock. If the clock strikes once, we know it is one o'clock; if it
strikes three times, we know it is three o'clock, and so on.

People don't have to see the bell to know which bell is ringing.
Very quickly even little children learn to recognize the special
sound that various bells have. Long ago, in some countries, it was
the custom for each village to ring the town bell as soon as it became
dark. This was to guide home anyone from that village who was
trying to find his way in the dark. What was that bell saying?

Because we learn to recognize the sounds of various bells, we
do not get mixed up about which bell is ringing. We don't go
looking for a fire when the church bell rings, or start off to school
when the ice-cream man rings his bell.

Speaking of ice-cream men, there is an example of knowing
what a bell means by knowing whose bell it is. This was more
important in the olden days, at least in this country, when many
different people used to come through the streets ringing a bell.

The town crier rang a bell before he shouted the news. The
scissors grinder had a bell that women used to recognize. Then
they would hurry to find all their scissors that needed sharpening.

In England the muffin man used to ring his bell to let people know that he was outside with hot muffins.

Except for the ice-cream man, most of these bell ringers are gone from our country. But in India, for example, there are still good examples of this. There are the bells of the cotton beater. When the people hear them they scurry in to bring out their mattresses for the cotton beater to make clean and fluffy. He beats all the dirt out of the mattresses, and all the time he beats, his bells are ringing. We clean with noisy vacuum cleaners. Bells would be much nicer to listen to, but the beating would be harder work.

In India you might also hear the bells of the seed crusher. Many people use the oil of crushed seeds to cook with. When they hear the bells of the seed crusher, they know that the man who does this is outside with his machine. They bring their seeds to him, and he crushes them.

Another important clue that helps us know what a certain bell means is *when* the bell rings. When the church bell rings on Sunday morning, it usually means, "time for church." But, if that same bell rings in the middle of the night, and a war has been going on, it may be saying: "The war is over!"

If the king of a country, or the president, dies, all the church bells may be rung, over and over. When Abraham Lincoln died, the church bells in many cities were rung. Or, if you lived in a place where a volcano might suddenly erupt, or a flood sweep down, or a tornado form, all the bells in the town might be rung together to try to warn you to "run."

It is pretty safe to say, all over the world, that when bells suddenly begin to ring, over and over, some unusual thing has happened, or is about to happen. Nowadays, since we have radios and television and telephones and newspapers, we don't use bells as much as people used to.

One other interesting thing about bells that I might point out is that they are a way that people all over the world have discovered to make it possible for animals to "talk." Do you know how that can be?

People put bells on animals. In the mountains of Switzerland, the tinkling bell may be saying: "Here I am, the little goat you are looking for." In a desert in Egypt, the tinkling sound during a blinding sandstorm may say to the camel driver: "Don't worry. Even though you can't see me, your camel, I'm right here."

A sled going over the snow in Russia makes hardly a sound, but the bells on the horse say "Here we come." A worker in India lets his elephant go down to the river to cool off. He hears the elephant's bell and knows "I'm right here, in the water." Even babies in some countries wear bells, so that, although they are too young to talk, they can tell their mothers or sisters, "I'm here. I'm not lost."

And of course, all over the world people have put bells on cats. If you were a mouse or a bird you would be very glad that people had ever thought of bells — talking with two pieces of metal.

### OTHER IDEAS

1. Some Eskimos, when they are fishing for sea otters, put bells on the tops of poles. The poles are stuck in the water and, when the sea otters bump the poles, they make the bells say: "Catch us, if you can."
2. Of course modern devices, such as radio and television, can "shout out" the news over much greater distances than bells can, but there are times of very sudden danger when old-fashioned bells are better. Because you have to have your radio or television turned on or you don't hear the news or warning of danger. Also, if the electricity goes off, some of the modern devices won't work. A bell will work just about any time, if there is someone around to ring it.
3. A list might be made of what different bells can say. Here is a sample list:

| | |
|---|---|
| a. Listen! | All bells. Also the town crier. |
| b. Nine o'clock. | Clocks. |
| c. Come here! | Mother with a bell at lunch or bedtime. |
| d. Come to church. | Church bells. |
| e. Get up! | Alarm clock bell. |
| f. Time for school. | School bell. |
| g. Fire! | On the fire engine. |
| h. The war is over! | Town or church bells. |
| i. It's a boy! | Church bells at time of birth of a king's son. |
| j. He is dead. | Death of a king or important person. |
| k. Run! | Time of flood, tidal wave, volcano or other disaster. |
| l. Here I am. | When an animal or person wearing a bell is lost. |
| m. Come this way. | Town bell after dark to direct people home. |
| n. Hide! | During a bombing, all the bells in town. |
| o. Catch me. | Bells on poles as sea otters swim against them. |
| p. The cake is done. | Timer on the stove. |
| q. Stay away! | Bells on rocks at sea. |

r. Go away!

Men shaking hand bells at a funeral to frighten away evil spirits or spirits of the dead.

s. Bring out your mattresses.

Cotton beater in India.

t. Is anyone at home?

Telephone or door bell. (This bell asks a question)

4. Several other sessions might follow this conversation:
   a. In two sessions, the story *The Big Wave*, by Pearl Buck (New York: Day, 1948), might be read. This is the story about an earthquake and a tidal wave in Japan. It gives a vivid picture of a bell functioning as a danger warning. This would be best with third grade and above.
   b. Robert Southey's poem, "The Inchcape Rock," about the bell on Inchcape Rock, could be read and discussed. A conversation about pirates is very interesting to these children. Was Robin Hood a kind of pirate? The poem can be found in most standard collections, for example, *The Home Book of Verse*, ed. Burton Stevenson (New York: Holt, 1927).
   c. Reading and discussion of "The Bell of Atri," as retold in *From Long Ago and Many Lands*, by Sophia Fahs, would make another interesting session. This bell said something not on the list: "Someone has done a wrong."
   d. The story "A Bell for Baby Brother," from the collection of the same name by Jessie Eleanor Moore (New York: Friendship, 1944), is the story of a bell being used to keep track of the baby.
5. Of course, anyone having a session on bells would want to bring as many bells as possible. Collecting bells is almost as universal as using bells. All the children having bells might be asked to bring them and, if possible, to know the kinds of bells they are. Pictures of some of the enormous bells in Japan might be posted.
6. Some scientific father or mother might be able to show why bells are the shape they are: what determines the sound of a bell, and how the sound can be varied.
7. If there are any expert bell ringers in the locality, they might come to demonstrate the art. If the church has a bell tower or carillon, that might be visited and explained.
8. Of course the whole subject of drums would make an interesting conversation: another universal answer to the problem of how to get word around.

*Yet not to thine eternal resting-place*
*Shalt thou retire alone, nor couldst thou wish*
*Couch more magnificent. Thou shalt lie down*
*With patriarchs of the infant world — with kings,*
*The powerful of the earth — the wise, the good,*
*Fair forms, and hoary seers of ages past,*
*All in one mighty sepulcher.* — WILLIAM CULLEN BRYANT, "Thanatopsis"

## 48. The Mustard-Seed Medicine

Did you ever go for a walk in an old cemetery? Perhaps you don't live in a part of the country where there are old cemeteries, but if you do, have you ever stopped and tried to read some of the gravestones? Sometimes the writing is difficult to read because the stone has been worn so smooth.

Many of the graves in the old cemeteries are those of little children. "Sarah, aged two years and two months." "John, seven days old." "Daniel, six years and three months." "Patience, eight years and nine months."

Why do you suppose so many little children used to die in the olden days? Now doctors know a great deal more about our bodies and germs and medicines so that fewer little children die.

Of course, there are some diseases that we still can't cure and there are accidents that happen to children, but more often, now, it is older people who die.

Why do you think it seems sadder for a little child to die than for an old, old person? A little child is just starting out, isn't he? It seems that each person should have a chance to live a good long life and to have children of his own to leave behind him. When a child dies, this doesn't happen, and it doesn't seem fair.

I'm going to tell you a story about a young mother whose only child died. She just wouldn't believe it until a famous teacher helped her. I wonder what you'll think of the way he helped her? This is a very old story, from India.

(Read or tell the story, *"The Mustard-Seed Medicine,"* in *From Long Ago and Many Lands,* by Sophia L. Fahs. In doing so, it is a good idea to change it so that Buddha asks Kisa Gotami to get the seed from a *family* "where no one has ever died" rather than a *house* "where no one has ever died." Some children are likely to be such literalists that they will suggest that their *house* is brand new and no one has died there.)

Why did Buddha ask Kisa Gotami to get the mustard seed? Why didn't he just *tell* her that people die in every family? Do you think that he really thought she could find the mustard seed? Do you think that you could ever find anyone in the whole world who wasn't related to someone who had died?

Would it have made any difference if Buddha had asked Kisa Gotami to get a cup of water or a loaf of bread from a home in which no one had ever died, instead of getting mustard seed?

Can you think of anything else that happens to every one of us besides dying? I can think of some things: being born (of course we don't remember this), growing, losing our first tooth and getting our second ones, growing old. Can you think of others?

Does it make you feel better about something to know that other people have had the same thing happen to them? Did you ever have something happen to you and then have your father say,

"Oh, that happened to me when I was little"? Doesn't it make you feel that your father understands your feelings better? It makes you understand your father a little better, too, doesn't it?

In a way, it makes you forget your own little troubles and you feel as if you were part of one great big family, the family of man.

### SUGGESTIONS

1. One teacher used this conversation and had a dead log at the front of the room with young day lilies growing out of it.

*The smallest sprout shows there is really no death,*
*And if ever there was it led forward life, and*
*   does not wait at the end to arrest it,*
*And ceas'd the moment life appear'd.*
*All goes onward and outward, nothing collapses,*
*And to die is different from what any one supposed,*
*   and luckier.* — WALT WHITMAN, "Song of Myself"*

## 49. After Ellen Died[34]

One day a group of kindergarten children were looking out of the window at a family of squirrels. The squirrels were high up in the tree, and it was difficult for the children to see them.

One of the children said, "I bet Ellen can see them better than anyone," and some of the other children agreed. Ellen was a classmate who had died not long before, and they still liked to think of her often.

The kindergarten teacher told Ellen's mother what the children had said. Ellen's mother could understand why one of the children had said this. Many people believe that when a person dies, that person goes to a place called "Heaven." Heaven is usually thought to be up in the sky. So it was natural that the children who had been taught this idea, thought of Ellen as being up high, where she could see better than they could.

Ellen's mother did not believe that there was a place where people go after they die and where they are still alive in some mysterious way. But because many people do believe this, she wanted to try to understand how people might have gotten such an

* *Op. cit.*, pp. 28–29.
[34] Adaptation of a conversation by Jean Thompson.

idea. When we find an idea that is different from one of our own, it is interesting to try to understand how this different idea might have grown in people's minds. She thought about it as she tried to get used to living without the little girl she missed so much.

Sometimes when she thought about Ellen, it seemed as if she could still see her and hear her. Sometimes it would almost seem as if Ellen came up to her and threw her arms around her, hard, the way she used to. She could almost hear her say, "Mummy, darling!" just as if she were right there. It was so real that it was hard to believe that she wasn't really hearing and feeling Ellen.

Ellen's mother thought: "It is difficult for me to realize that this is just a memory of Ellen, and not the real little girl. How much more difficult it must have been for people of long ago. Perhaps they could not think of anything as real as this as only a memory. I wonder if this is partly how they came to believe that people somehow are still alive after they are dead."

Easter came only a few weeks after Ellen died. Hearing the many stories about Jesus on the radio made Ellen's mother wonder about the story of people seeing Jesus after he had died. She knew that the people who told about seeing Jesus were his closest friends — people who loved him very much. Could it be that they had such loving memories that, when they thought about Jesus, it seemed as if he were really with them?

There were other ways in which Ellen still seemed to be with her family. For example, they still said certain things the way she had said them when she was little. Do you have any words or expressions in your family that you all say in a funny way because your baby — or even you — said it that way when first learning to talk? We all say "tomonrow," instead of tomorrow, and "mazagine," instead of magazine, because that is what our baby says.

That's how it was in Ellen's family too. When Ellen first learned to talk, if she had hurt herself or if her feelings had been hurt, she would say, "Poor wittle tid, I hoffa doe ta bed." Then she would go climb into her bed and rest until she felt better. Before long everyone in the family would say the same thing whenever something happened to one of them. And they were still saying it just the way she had, even though she was gone.

And without even thinking about it, they all said "buddon me" instead of "pardon me," the way Ellen had. Only now when they said it, it reminded them of her. And they still sometimes called a peanut butter sandwich a "Peter Yummich" the way she did when she could scarcely talk. And her sister Kristin, whom everyone else called "Krissy," had been "Frissy" to Ellen and so the family still sometimes called her that.

Another thing that made it seem as if Ellen were still part of the family was some of her possessions that were still around the house. Her library card reminded them of how proud she had been to be big enough to sign her own name, so she could get a card of her own. That was a rule at their library. Her scrapbook was full of pictures she had drawn or painted. And there was a very special little book of poem ideas that Ellen's mother had written down and her father had printed.

There was her baby book, telling all about how she grew, and her first report card, reminding them of how well she liked kindergarten. Best of all, there was her photograph album, so that they could always see how she had looked.

So, even though Ellen's family knew that she could never talk to them again, or hear them, she still seemed to be very much a part of the family. And it made them feel good when they looked at her picture or thought of the funny way she used to talk, although at the same time it made them sad to think that they would never see her again.

When Ellen's mother thought of these many ways Ellen still seemed to be with them, she felt that she understood better how some people might have the idea of people living on after they have died. But she did not think of Ellen's being off in a place called Heaven. She thought of Ellen right at home in her pictures, in her funny ways of talking, in her poems and in the warm feeling the family had as they remembered her.

> *After the two boys reached home and their chores were done for the day, the little boy ran to a cave not far from the hogan. Here it was that he kept his treasures. Not that he had many, but they were very precious.* — LAURA ADAMS ARMER, Waterless Mountain*

### 50. A Shoe Box

There are two reasons we like to buy new shoes in our family. One reason is the new shoes and the other reason is the shoe box.

Shoe boxes are very useful for storing things. We have shoe boxes of post cards, shoe boxes of rocks, shoe boxes of baseball cards, shoe boxes of stamps, shoe boxes of shells, shoe boxes of bottle tops, and — well — I think we have just about as many shoe box collections as any family could have. We never throw away a shoe box!

* (New York and Toronto: Longmans, 1959), p. 16.

And the other day, *another* shoe box came in the mail. This one did not have new shoes in it. Instead, it was just full of all kinds of interesting things for the museum at our house.

You see, we have a museum. We just had to start it, because we had so many collections in shoe boxes that they were bursting out of our rooms. So one of the children got the idea of taking many of the things out of the shoe boxes, and putting them all in one room on shelves where we could see them.

I wouldn't be surprised if a good many of you have this kind of museum in your house, perhaps in your own room, or in the attic, or the cellar or the playroom. I even heard of one little boy who had a museum in his bed! I wonder how he made the bed.

A family out in Wisconsin heard about our museum and all the children in the family (there were four children, Pete, Tom, Jean and Alice) put things from their own collections into a shoe box and sent it to us. That was the shoe box that came in the mail. We had never even seen these children and yet everything that they sent to us was something that we wanted to add to the collections in our museum.

Do you suppose that children all over the world like to collect things? Do you suppose that most children like to collect the same kinds of things?

To help you answer those two questions, let's make believe that this shoe box I have here has just come in the mail. I'll open it and we'll take a look at what is inside of it. Each specimen (that is the word that is often used for things in a museum) is wrapped in a piece of paper that tells what the specimen is, where it came from and who sent it. We call that a label. I'll read each label after I have unwrapped the specimen. I wonder how many of these things you might have picked up and sent to us in a shoe box?

(1) "The tooth of a moose, worn down by years of chewing. Isle Royale National Park, from Tom."

Is it big! A real moose tooth! The moose must have been enormous. Did you ever find any animal teeth? The teeth of different animals are very, very different from each other. We already had some teeth in our museum. We have an old cow's skull with teeth in it, and a very small jaw bone of an animal with teeth in it. We thought it might be from a rat.

We even have some of the children's teeth in our museum. Do you save your teeth?

(2) "Crystals found in a limestone quarry in Wisconsin, from Pete."

Do you know what crystals are? They are the shapes that the minerals in the crust of the earth form, as they cool or as they separate from solutions. The crystal of each mineral always cools in the same shape. Usually they are very, very beautiful. I think the ones that Pete sent are calcite crystals. Perhaps you have some of these.

When you hold a crystal in your hand, do you ever wonder how many millions of years ago it may have been when that crystal was formed?

(3) "An aluminum float used by fishermen in the Great Lakes, from the whole family."

Do you know what a float is? It is something very light, often made out of cork, that floats on water and holds up a net or a fish line. You may have a float on your fish pole if you are a fisherman.

We never saw one like this before, made out of aluminum. We were very glad to have it for the museum.

Do you suppose that perhaps the family was walking along a beach on Lake Michigan (that's near where they live) and maybe the sun shone on the float and someone in the family noticed it? I always like to collect things from beaches.

(4) "A piece of driftwood, from Jean."

The label doesn't say where she found it, but it probably was either Lake Michigan or Lake Superior. See what an interesting shape it has, and how soft it feels. I like to rub it against my cheek.

It's interesting to think that its pretty shape and smoothness were made by water and sand rubbing it over and over again. I suppose you might say it is wood, sandpapered by nature. People think driftwood is so beautiful that they use pieces of it for lampstands, candleholders and other things.

(5) "Stones from the shore of Lake Michigan, with one decorated just for fun; from Alice."

See, she has painted a design on one of the stones. We do that sometimes, and use them for paperweights or doorstops. They make nice Christmas presents, too.

These other stones are so smooth! They've been sanded too. Which do you think are prettier, the stones painted like this by people, or the ones just smoothed by nature? Both? That's what I think, too.

Here's a pretty one, with rows of black running through it. And this one has a line running all the way around it. I wonder how that line got there? Nature seems to decorate stones, too.

(6) "A chip of wood chewed off by a beaver, cutting down a birch tree for food, from Alice."

This is a very large chip isn't it? It would be interesting to have a beaver's tooth for the museum. They are very large and strong. They would have to be, to take bites like this.

It's strange to think of eating wood. I've read that some Indians ate tree bark in the winter when there was nothing else to eat. I wonder how it tastes? I imagine it wouldn't hurt any one to try it.

(7) "Bones from a bird's leg, Isle Royale, from Tom."

I wonder what kind of bird it was? I wonder where that leg has been? Birds fly very long distances when they migrate. Perhaps it has been far to the south. Now it is sitting in my hand!

Well! That was quite a shoe box. And there are still more things we haven't looked at. There are enough things right there to *start* a museum.

What would you wrap up and put in a shoe box to send to someone else?

### SUGGESTIONS

1. It would be well to have a shoe box full of specimens wrapped in labels to use with this conversation. The conversation should be altered to fit the available specimens.

2. *Waterless Mountain,* from which the quotation at the beginning of this conversation is taken, is a fine book for family reading, and can give children, eight and above, a vivid introduction to the thought world and feeling world of a very different and beautiful culture, the Navajo. The story is told through the experience of a young Navajo boy as he matures.

3. Many sessions might be spent subsequently on the children's own collections.

*Conversation is our account of ourselves.* — RALPH WALDO
EMERSON, "Woman"*

## IV. Some Suggestions for Using the Conversations

I would like to think that these conversations might find a
place in homes, church schools, public schools and in club groups,
such as the Brownies and Cub Scouts. Wherever adults meet with
children, with the growth of the whole child as their primary
interest, these conversations should be relevant.

The conversations have been grouped in several categories
which represent more the angle of vision from which the conversations have been written than a topical index. For example, a
conversation about rocks might have as its main focus the fact that
in our world everything changes, even rocks. Such a conversation I
would have placed in the category "Universals." But if the great *age*
of certain rocks were the point of emphasis, the conversation would
be found in the section, "Long Ago." If, however, the main
consideration is how rocks are *made*, then the conversation on rocks
will be found in the section, "The Natural World."

Therefore, it will be best perhaps to read through all of the
conversations before using any of them to discover just what
material there is, and how it is handled. With one or two exceptions
each of the conversations is complete in itself so that they can be
used in any order and grouped in a variety of ways.

For the most part, the conversations have been written in a
personal and informal style. Many of them describe the particular
experiences of particular people in particular settings. They have
been written in this style because this is one good way in which to
present ideas to children so that they have meaning for them. The
informal style may also make it easier for the adults using them to
get in a conversational mood.

But, in order that children in other settings and with rather
different experiences can gain the most from them, a great deal of
the material should be translated into the particular setting in which
it is to be used. Because the conversations are concerned with
universals that permeate life, this translating should be possible.

Therefore, you will want to read each conversation several

* *Miscellanies*, XI (Boston: Houghton Mifflin, 1906), 408.

times before using it. As you read it, think about the main ideas in terms of your own interests and experience and goals. How do the ideas in the conversation relate to your locale and the known interests and experiences of the children with whom you will be talking?

For example, the important point in the conversation, "The Snakeskin and the Carrot Bag," is the wonder of animal instincts. But if the eastern flycatcher, with its interesting nesting material, is not a part of your environment, you may want to do some research to discover a bird or animal in your area with some equally unusual instinctive behavior. Your conversation would then center around your local example.

There is nothing sacred about either the form or content of any one of these conversations. What is sacred are the children and our world. Although the conversations are concerned with universals, they reflect the limits of my experience and sensitivity. Perhaps you have found other ideas children enjoy dwelling on as much as the "used-to-thinks" or the "what if's." Plan your conversations around these, since what matters most is that you share known delights. The conversation on poetry may give you an idea of how to create one of your own on music or painting or some other artistic medium in which you feel at home.

Some of the conversations have more ideas in them than it would be wise to attempt to use at one time. This has been done for several reasons. Some ideas may not strike fire, either with certain children or with some adults, while others may. If a person wishes to use the material with older children, extra ideas may prove useful. Also, in a few cases, it seemed important to present a coherent conversation with many of its ramifications, and then let the adult either pick and choose among ideas according to his own insight, or present the material over a period of several sessions.

As you familiarize yourself with the material, you will find yourself thinking of many other ideas or other ways of treating some of these. Therefore it will be useful to keep a file of ideas, pictures, stories, poetry, songs, and anything else to enrich the conversations. Then when you decide to use one of the conversations you will have a mass of material from which to work.

A daily newspaper, such as the *Christian Science Monitor* or *New York Times,* or whatever newspaper is outstanding in your area, often contains material that can make some topic more vivid and contemporary. Magazines, such as the *National Geographic, Natural History, Scientific American, Arizona Highways, Life* and numerous others, contain excellent articles and pictures.

Pictures from such collections as *The Family of Man* and *The World Is Young* relate naturally to many of the conversations.

The gradual acquisition of artifacts, such as fossils, nests, rocks and items from other countries, is also recommended. The use of actual objects adds a great deal to the vividness of the conversations. Of course, if you have children of your own, you will be acquiring such items anyway. The children with whom you will be talking should be frequent contributors also and will probably loan exhibits gladly.

If you are going to use a conversation in an area in which you are not familiar with the subject matter, you will want to do some thorough preparation. If we really care about children, and if we really care about truth, we often find ourselves spending many hours tracking down information and organizing it as clearly and as simply as possible, especially for the youngest of these children. It is easy and mutually unsatisfactory to talk carelessly with children; it is challenging and rewarding to talk with them accurately and with respect for the limitations of their development. Anyone who thinks that talking with children is an activity in which adult minds grow rusty hasn't really allowed himself to get deeply involved with the children.

As for the mechanics of using one of the conversations: after you have become thoroughly familiar with the material, you'll want to go ahead with little or no reference to my printed version. Even those conversations that are largely stories, such as the two about Laura Bridgman, or the one about Louis Braille, will be better told than read.

On the matter of group participation: just how you will proceed will depend in part on the makeup of your group. If you are talking with your own children or with a very small group, you will probably want to respond to their comments and questions all along the way. But if you are using the material with a larger group, a public school class, a large church school class or assembly, there will be a question about just how much participation to encourage. It takes real skill and experience to handle participation from a large group, and probably each of us must feel his way in determining just how much of it he can handle.

Some leaders, even skillful and experienced ones, find that it works best for them to encourage responses from the children only at the beginning, to establish rapport, and again at the end, as a kind of group summary. Such a procedure at the end serves as a good check on how successful we have been in really involving the hearts and minds of the children.

Other skillful people are able to have free participation all during one of these conversations, from groups as large as sixty. Sometimes we are afraid to encourage comments lest we get off "the point." We should remember that "the point," meaning our point, may not be "the point" to each of the children. Each child listens and hears from where he is standing at this moment in his development. Of course, this is also true, although less obviously so, of listening adults.

This means that an "irrelevant" comment made from the floor may be irrelevant to us, but is very likely extremely relevant to the child who made it. If we were talking to that child alone he would be able to make the logic of his remark clear to us. If, however, we want to proceed with the point that we think has relevance for the larger group, we should feel free to do so, after thanking him for his contribution.

An "irrelevant" comment, however, if it seems to find response from the group, may help bring us back into communication with the children. There is no doubt that it takes sensitivity and art to know when to follow and when to lead in these conversations.

One might legitimately ask how a conversation differs from a discussion? Theoretically, I would say that a successful conversation is a form of art in which ideas are expressed largely in pictorial language. A story can very naturally be included in a conversation since it also is a form of presentational thinking.

A successful discussion is a process of analysis, a taking apart of ideas and then perhaps a reconstruction. Some of these conversations might serve as the basis for discussion, but in general their aim is to show or point at something, rather than to take it apart.

For this reason, it would be quite possible to use some of them in what are traditionally thought of as worship services or opening exercises in church school or day school. When using them in such a context, it would be appropriate to use songs and poetry with them, before or after or both. These may help reinforce the feelings associated with the ideas — feelings of wonder, appreciation, enjoyment, thoughtfulness or even sadness.

One of the most valid insights of modern educational theory is that if a learning experience is to be really effective it must involve the whole child, his mind and feelings. Songs and poetry and other art forms can be significant media for celebrating our feelings, if they are related to things we really care about and use language that we understand.

It is not enough just to choose a song or poem or picture that "goes with" the material used. Unfamiliar words and difficult metaphorical expressions should be explained so that the children will recognize their own thoughts and feelings mirrored in the material. With groups that meet infrequently there is good reason to use a few songs and a few poems that they like and know, so that they can sing and listen with real feeling. Selections might be drawn from a variety of sources: public school song books, family singing collections, long playing records, as well as religious song books. There are many fine collections of poetry for children now from which selections can be made.

In addition to being used in group gatherings in church schools, some of the conversations might be used in classes where a short unit or supplementary material is needed. The conversations on cave men, Laura Bridgman or animal tracks, for example, might be used in such a way.

As for their use in public schools, I think that there is an especially pressing need for material that can be used in what have been known as "opening exercises." What a daring experiment the public education of children is! We mix in the melting pot of one classroom the child of a professor, the child of a father who has shot his infant son in a drunken family brawl, the child of a bank president, the child of a plumber, and the child of a migrant worker.

We put in one classroom the child of a Catholic, the child of an atheist, the child of a Fundamentalist Protestant, the child of an agnostic, the child of a Jew, the child of a Humanist, the child of a Secularist, the child of a liberal Protestant.

Time has shown that the differences do not all melt away in the melting pot. But the public school can afford an opportunity for those who come from "different" backgrounds (and that is every one of us) to share a core of common experiences. This is important to our democracy, especially since we are so various in our constituency.

A system of public education is not only a medium for teaching the children of its citizens the essential skills of reading, writing and arithmetic, but it should also play an important role in helping these children from such different backgrounds to use their new skills to discover the wonderful world in which we live.

Our public schools can not legally deal with our religious differences, but they can deal with the great universals and basic realities that are the subsoil of all particular religions. For some reason these are often derisively referred to as the "watered-down least common denominator" of all the great world religions. The wonder of birth, growth and death; the miracle of an orderly macrocosm and microcosm; the natural world with its intricate patterning and marvelously varied forms — are all these really something watered down?

Let those churches which see it as their function to tell their members and the children of their members how these great facts should be interpreted do so, but let it be a high purpose of our public schools to bring the realities into the awareness of all children.

Many public school teachers are doing this already, and doing it exceedingly well. But they dare not call this religious. Instead, all too often, the only teaching that is allowed to bear the label "religious" is of a type that is actually divisive and often disregards the developmental limitations of the children. In many states it is legal, even obligatory, to start each day in public school with the Lord's Prayer, but it is illegal to explain it.

One of my boys came home from the first grade and announced that they said the Lord's Prayer every day. He said that he knew it and would recite it for me. He began at breakneck speed. There were the usual number of first grade inaccuracies and obvious indications that, although he might almost have it "by heart," he did not by any means almost have it "by head."

But the line that really drew me up short was the one that comes just where the second breath is usually taken.

"Give us this day," he said, rushing along, "our day-old bread."

"Our what?" I asked.

"Our day-old bread," he said, impatient to go on before he lost momentum. "You know, the cheap kind that we get for the freezer. Now let me see . . . I'll have to start that part again. You've mixed me up. Give us this day our day-old bread . . ." He hurried on, triumphantly, to the end, "the real end," he assured me, with the dogmatism of a first grader.

But I was still back in an earlier section of the prayer, thinking how appropriate a symbol of our confused approach to the teaching of moral and spiritual values in the public schools was this misunderstanding. Children's misunderstandings of adult theological material are often quoted with amusement. In reality they are tragic. "Day-old bread . . . the cheap kind" — is that the best we can give our children when we make our formal nod in the direction of teaching religious values in the great public school system of America?

No, actually we are doing much better than this. This same little boy was having some wonderful religious experiences in that same first-grade classroom, reading stories about babies, discovering many new things in the world of nature, and getting to know many kinds of boys and girls. The word "religious" should be identified, for the children, with these nonsectarian experiences. These religious experiences strengthen character, show the children the kind of world in which we live, and help them appreciate the unities that thread our differences.

The use of a sectarian prayer is divisive, separating those who go to the "real end" from those who stop the prayer earlier, separating those for whom it is the *Lord's* prayer from those for whom it is not, separating those who pray from those who do not. It is a prayer that is not easily explained to children, even if it were legal to do so. Why not let what is universal and uniting be the religious teaching of our public schools?

A group of Brownies came to visit our home museum one day. There were children of every class and every religious denomination. Yet all were fascinated by the chimney swift's nest, the dinosaur tracks, the peacock feather, the fossil fern, the quartz crystals. Is the contemplation of such wonders as these really "just watered-down religion in general," or are they not rather "every one, miracle enough to stagger sextillions of infidels?"

I hope that these conversations may be useful in some homes, as well as in church and day schools. Some of the most deeply religious experiences I have ever had have occurred while talking with my children. If parents read through the whole collection of conversations, they may find a variety of ways in which some of the ideas contained in them may be shared with their children.

A mother who experimented with several of the conversations asked herself, and answered for herself, what the goal of the conversations might be.

In a sense, these conversations are nothing new. Any good teacher or parent has always done things like this. In a classroom, some of the most important learning goes on when the teacher is "off the subject," and she and the class are pursuing something that appealed to them at the moment. What may be new is collecting them into a book for the use of people who don't feel that they are good teachers, or for parents who don't know how to talk with children.

But why these particular subjects, and what can they do for children? For one thing, they are subjects that we know matter to children, but that we have not traditionally thought of as religious. In a broad sense they certainly are, however. Presented in the form of conversations they may, and some of them certainly did for us, stimulate children to think and wonder and appreciate, and to weigh values and look at some ideas freshly. In a society that all too often hands everything to us wrapped, bottled, even pre-digested and ready to swallow, these conversations may give children something they have to chew before swallowing. They require more than a mere sponge-like soaking up of ideas, they give children something worth thinking about.*

Let us take time, lots of time, the best time we will ever spend, talking with children — our own and any others we are fortunate enough to be with. Let's be sure to listen to them, too. Perhaps, together, we may catch glimpses of realities more enduring than our short lives, and truths wider than our partial insights.

* From a letter by Mary Jane Dunwiddie.

| | | | | |
|---|---|---|---|---|
| | | | | |
| | | | | |
| | | | | |
| | | | | |
| | | | | |
| | | | | |
| | | | | |
| | | | | |
| | | | | |
| | | | | |
| | | | | |
| | | | | |